The

Making

of

Economic

Society

Other books by the author:

THE WORLDLY PHILOSOPHERS
THE QUEST FOR WEALTH
THE FUTURE AS HISTORY

ROBERT L. HEILBRONER

The

Making

of

Economic

Society

PRENTICE-HALL, INC.
Englewood Cliffs, N.J.

Library of Congress Catalog Card No.: 62-16453

Printed in the United States of America
54555–C 54556–T

PRENTICE-HALL INTERNATIONAL, INC.
London • Tokyo • Sydney • Paris
PRENTICE-HALL OF CANADA, LTD.
PRENTICE-HALL DE MEXICO, S.A.

First printing............June, 1962
Second printing.........August, 1962

for

Peter L. Bernstein

Contents

6

The Evolution of Guided Capitalism, 140

7

The Drift of Modern Economic History, 180

8

The Making of Economic Society, 222

Index, 237

Introduction

It is a little hard for us to imagine, but in the third decade of nineteenth century England, a knowledge of economics was part of a proper young lady's accomplishments. It was not a very profound knowledge (mainly it was gained from reading Miss Harriet Martineau's tracts), and it was not always very good economics—but that is not the point. In those days, economics was not only esteemed as important, but it was actually a *popular* study.

Today, alas, no such happy reputation precedes our subject. Not that the public estimation of economics has diminished; on the contrary, everyone admits that it was never more important, etc. But the very word has come to shed a pall. The student approaches his first economics course with apprehension; the layman is convinced that the whole thing is hopelessly beyond him.

In a way, both student and layman are quite right in thinking of economics as a difficult subject. When Auguste Comte classified the sciences of mankind in his general scheme of philosophy, he placed mathematics and the natural sciences at a lower stage of complexity than sociology or economics. This was not because Comte considered the logical structures of physics or chemistry to be simpler than those of the social sciences. It was because, despite their impressive architecture, these structures were founded on the solid ground of nature's dependable regularity and were thus blessedly free of human nature's undependable irregularity. Along the same line of reasoning, what made the social sciences appear so much more difficult to Comte was not their inner structure, their vocabulary, or their techniques. It was the fact that they had to form their intellectual architecture out of the stuff of human behavior itself.

Yet it is not this intrinsic and legitimate difficulty that frightens people away from economics. In fact, once its inner precincts have been invaded, these very difficulties—this challenging task of creating a "science" out of human behavior—lend fascination to the study. The problem, rather, is to crash the gates, to come to grips with this engrossing core of economics, in the first place. And here the trouble lies not within the discipline so much as in the routes by which it is usually approached.

One of the routes—that which the college student usually travels—is the road of economic theory. This is the traditional avenue into economics, but it is a very demanding and austere initiation. By dint of much hard work, the student learns about supply and demand and equilibrium and marginal cost curves; but when the textbook is closed and put away, somehow very little seems to stick. Despite the valiant efforts of his instructors, the formal apparatus of economics does not readily impart deep and unforgettable meanings to the average student, or root itself naturally into the "real world." The regrettable result is that the facts and formulae soon fade, leaving only a memory of economics as a very hard course.

But the other route to economics is equally unsatisfactory. This is the route of general events, past or present. Here is where the ordinary person comes into contact with economic matters, whether in newspaper headlines or as part of the background to a biography or a book on general history. And here the difficulty is the obverse of the first. To come into touch with economics as an immediate issue of past or present is to see it only as a series of isolated problems and, more bewildering yet, to face those problems without the larger framework of knowledge needed to understand what they are all about.

of the world, where the human being with his twenty calories of energy scratches out for himself a bare subsistence, we find the economic insecurity of the individual many times multiplied. The solitary Eskimo, Bushman, Indonesian, Nigerian, left to his own devices, will survive a considerable time. Living close to the soil or to their animal prey, the peoples with the lowest standards of living in the world can sustain their own lives, at least for a while, almost single-handed. With a community numbering only a few hundred, they can live indefinitely. Indeed, a very large percentage of the human race today lives in precisely such fashion—in small, virtually self-contained peasant communities which provide for their own survival with a minimum of contact with the outside world. This large majority of mankind suffers great poverty, but it also knows a certain economic independence. If it did not, it would have been wiped out centuries ago.

When we turn to the New Yorker or the Chicagoan, on the other hand, we are struck by exactly the opposite condition, by a prevailing ease of material life, coupled at the same time by an extreme *dependence* of the individual in his search for the means of existence. In the great metropolitan areas where most Americans live, we can no longer envisage the solitary individual or the small community surviving, short of looting warehouses or stores for food and necessities. The overwhelming majority of Americans have never grown food, caught game, raised meat, ground grain into flour, or even fashioned flour into bread. Faced with the challenge of clothing themselves or building their own homes, they would be hopelessly untrained and unprepared. Even to make minor repairs in the machines which surround them, they must call on other members of the community whose business it is to fix cars, or repair plumbing, or whatever. Paradoxically, perhaps, the richer the nation, the more apparent is this inability of its average inhabitant to survive unaided and alone.

We survive in rich nations because the tasks we cannot do ourselves are done for us by an army of others on whom we can call for help. If we cannot grow food, we can buy it; if we cannot provide for our needs ourselves, we can hire the services of someone who can. This enormous *division of labor* enhances our capacity a thousandfold, for it enables us to benefit from other men's skills as well as our own.

Along with this invaluable gain comes a certain risk. It is a sobering thought, for example, that we depend on the services of only 180,000 men—fewer than one out of every three hundred people working in the nation—to provide us with that basic commodity, coal. An even smaller number of workers—less than 75,000 —are responsible for running the locomotives which haul all the nation's rail freight and passenger service. A still smaller number— under 15,000—comprises our total commercial aircraft pilot and navigator crew. A failure of any one of these very small groups to perform its functions would cripple us: in the case of airplane pilots, slightly; in the case of locomotive engineers, badly; in the case of coal miners, perhaps disastrously. As we know, when from time to time we face a bad strike, our entire economic machine may falter because a strategic group ceases to perform its accustomed tasks.

Along with the abundance of material existence as we know it goes a hidden vulnerability: our abundance is assured only insofar as the organized cooperation of huge armies of people is to be counted upon. Indeed, our continuing existence as a rich nation hinges on the tacit precondition that the mechanism of social organization will continue to function effectively. *We are rich, not as individuals, but as members of a rich society, and our easy assumption of material sufficiency is actually only as reliable as the bonds which forge us into a social whole.*

Economics, Scarcity, and Social Organization

The problem of how societies forge and maintain the bonds which guarantee their material survival is the basic problem of economics.

It is a curious fact that unlike many forms of animal and insect life which also support themselves in "societies," men do not spontaneously cooperate to assure a successful solution to their joint economic problems. Neither instinct nor a strong sense of individual obligation automatically welds the human community together. Instead, more or less elaborate forms of social organization, operating through institutions backed by the force of law or tradition, must bear the responsibility for the task of economic survival.

Strangely enough, then, we find that man, not nature, is the source of most of our economic problems. To be sure, the economic problem itself—that is, the need to struggle for existence—derives ultimately from the scarcity of nature. If there were no scarcity, goods would be as free as air, and economics, at least in one sense of the word, would cease to exist as a social preoccupation.

And yet if the scarcity of nature sets the stage for the economic problem, it does not impose the only strictures against which men must struggle. For scarcity, as a felt condition, is not solely the fault of nature. If Americans today, for instance, were content to live at the level of Mexican peasants, all our material wants could be fully satisfied with but an hour or two of daily labor. We would experience little or no scarcity, and our economic problems would virtually disappear. Instead, we find in America—and indeed in all industrial societies—that as the ability to increase nature's yield has risen, so has the reach of human wants. In fact, in societies such as ours, where relative social status is importantly connected with the possession of material goods, we often find that "scarcity" as a psychological experience and goad becomes more pronounced as we grow wealthier: our desires to possess the fruits of nature race out ahead of our mounting ability to produce goods.

Thus the "wants" that nature must satisfy are by no means fixed —while, for that matter, nature's yield itself is not a constant, but varies over a wide range, depending on the social application of human energy and skill. Scarcity is therefore not attributable to nature alone but to "human nature" as well; and economics is ultimately concerned not merely with the stinginess of the physical environment, but equally with the appetite of the human temperament.

Hence we must begin a systematic analysis of economics by singling out the functions which social organization must perform to bring human nature into social harness. And when we turn our attention to this fundamental problem, we can quickly see that it involves the solution of two related and yet separate elemental tasks:

1. A society must organize a system for producing the goods and services it needs for its own perpetuation.

2. It must arrange a distribution of the fruits of its production among its own members, so that more production can take place.

These two tasks of economic continuity are, at first look, very simple. But it is a deceptive simplicity. Much of economic history, as we shall see, is concerned with the manner in which various societies have sought to cope with these elementary problems; and what strikes us in surveying their attempts is that most of them were partial failures. (They could not have been total failures, or society would not have survived.) Hence it behooves us to look more carefully into the two main economic tasks to see what hidden difficulties they may conceal.

The Production Problem

What is the difficulty which the production problem poses? What are the obstacles which a society encounters in organizing a system to produce the goods and services it needs?

Since nature is usually stingy, it would seem that the production problem must be essentially one of engineering, or technical efficiency. It would seem to revolve around the effort to economize, to avoid waste and apply social effort as efficaciously as possible.

This is indeed an important task for any society, and a great deal of formal economic thought, as the word itself suggests, is devoted to economizing. Yet this is not the core of the production problem. Long before a society can even concern itself about using its energies "economically," it must first marshall the energies to carry out the productive process itself. That is, *the basic problem of production is to devise social institutions which will mobilize human energy for productive purposes.*

This basic requirement is not always so easily accomplished. For example, in the United States in 1933, the energies of nearly thirteen million people—one quarter of our work force—were not directed into the production process. Although these unemployed men and women were eager to work, although empty factories were available for them to work in, despite the existence of pressing wants, somehow a terrible and mystifying breakdown short-circuited the production process, with the result that an entire third of our previous annual output of goods and services simply disappeared.

We are by no means the only nation which has, on occasion, failed to find work for willing workers. In the very poorest nations, where production is most desperately needed, we frequently find that unemployment is a chronic condition. The streets of the Asian cities are thronged with people who cannot find work. But this, too, is not a condition imposed by the scarcity of nature. There is, after all, an endless amount of work to be done, if only in cleaning the filthy streets or patching up the homes of the poor, building roads, or planting forests. Yet, what seems to be lacking is a social mechanism to put the unemployed to work.

Both these examples point out to us that the production problem is not solely, or perhaps even primarily, a physical and technical struggle with nature. On these "scarcity" aspects of the problem will depend the speed with which a nation may forge ahead and the level of well-being it can reach with a given effort. But the original mobilization of productive effort itself is a challenge to its social organization, and on the success or failure of that social organization will depend the volume of the human effort which can be directed to nature.

Putting men to work is only the first step in the solution of the production problem. Men must not only be put to work; they must be put to work *in the right places*. They must produce the goods and services which society needs. In addition to assuring a large enough quantity of social effort, the economic institutions of society must also assure the *proper allocation of that social effort*.

In a nation such as India or Brazil, where the great majority of the population is born in peasant villages and grows up to be peasant cultivators, the solution to this problem offers little to vex our understanding. The basic demands of society—food and fiber—are precisely the goods which its peasant population "naturally" produces. But in an industrial society, the proper allocation of effort becomes an enormously complicated task. People in the United States demand much more than bread and cotton. They need, for instance, such things as automobiles. Yet no one "naturally" produces an automobile. On the contrary, in order to produce one, an extraordinary spectrum of special tasks must be performed. Some people must make steel. Others must make rubber. Still others must coordinate the assembly process itself. And this is but a tiny sampling of the far from "natural" tasks which must be performed if an automobile is to be produced.

As with the mobilization of its total production effort, society does not always succeed in the proper allocation of its effort. It may, for instance, turn out too many cars or too few. Of greater importance, it may devote its energies to the production of luxuries while the majority of its people are starving. Or it may even court disaster by an inability to channel its productive effort into areas of critical importance. In the early 1950's, for instance, the British suffered a near economic collapse because they were unable to get enough of their workers to mine coal.

Such allocative failures may affect the production problem quite as seriously as a failure to mobilize an adequate quantity of effort, for a viable society must produce not only goods, but the *right* goods. And the allocative question alerts us to a still broader conclusion. It shows us that the act of production, in and of itself, does not fully answer the requirements for survival. Having produced enough of the right goods, society must now *distribute* those goods so that the production process can go on.

The Distribution Problem

Once again, in the case of the peasant who feeds himself and his family from his own crop, this requirement of adequate distribution may seem simple enough. But when we go beyond the most primitive society, the problem is not always so readily solved. In many of the poorest nations of the East and South, urban workers have often been unable to deliver their daily horsepower-hour of work because they have not been given enough of society's output to run their human engines to capacity. Worse yet, they have often languished on the job while granaries bulged with grain and the well-to-do complained of the ineradicable "laziness" of the masses. At the other side of the picture, the distribution mechanism may fail because the rewards it hands out do not succeed in persuading people to perform their necessary tasks. Shortly after the Russian Revolution some factories were organized into communes in which managers and janitors pooled their pay, and from which all drew equal allotments. The result was a rash of absenteeism on the part of the previously better-paid workers and a threatened breakdown in industrial production. Not until the old unequal wage payments were reinstituted did production resume its former course.

As was the case with failures in the production process, distributive failures need not entail a total economic collapse. Societies can exist—and indeed, in the majority of cases, do exist—with badly distorted productive and distributive efforts. It is only rarely, as in the instances above, that maldistribution actively interferes with the actual ability of a society to staff its production posts. More frequently, an inadequate solution to the distribution problem reveals itself in social and political unrest or even in revolution.

Yet this, too, is an aspect of the total economic problem. For if society is to insure its steady material replenishment, it must parcel out its production in a fashion that will maintain not only the capacity but the willingness to go on working. And thus again we find the focus of economic inquiry directed to the study of human institutions. For a viable economic society, we can now see, is not only one which can overcome the stringencies of nature, but one which can contain and control the intransigence of human nature.

THE THREE SOLUTIONS TO THE ECONOMIC PROBLEM

Thus to the economist, society presents itself in an unaccustomed aspect. He sees it essentially as an elaborate mechanism for survival, a mechanism for accomplishing the complicated tasks of production and distribution necessary for social continuity.

But the economist sees something else as well, something which at first seems quite astonishing. Looking not only over the diversity of contemporary societies, but back over the sweep of all history, he sees that man has succeeded in solving the production and distribution problems in but three ways. That is, within the enormous diversity of the actual social institutions which guide and shape the economic process, the economist divines but three overarching *types* of systems which separately or in combination enable humankind to solve its economic challenge. These great systemic types can be called economies run by Tradition, economies run by Command, and economies run by the Market. Let us briefly see what is characteristic of each.

Tradition

Perhaps the oldest and, until a very few years ago, by far the most generally prevalent way of solving the economic challenge has been tradition. It has been a mode of social organization in which both production and distribution were based on procedures devised in the distant past and rigidified as the outcome of a long process of historic trial and error.

Societies based on tradition solve the economic problems very manageably. First, they deal with the production problem—the problem of assuring that the needful tasks will be done—by assigning the jobs of fathers to their sons. Thus a hereditary chain assures that skills will be passed along and that the on-going jobs will be staffed from generation to generation. In ancient Egypt, wrote Adam Smith, the first great economist, "every man was bound by a principle of religion to follow the occupation of his father and was supposed to commit the most horrible sacrilege if he changed it for another."[2] And it was not merely in antiquity that tradition preserved a productive orderliness within society. In our own Western culture, until the fifteenth or sixteenth centuries, the hereditary allocation of tasks was also the main stabilizing force within society. Although there was some movement from country to town and from occupation to occupation, birth usually determined one's role in life. One was born to the soil or to a trade; and on the soil or within the trade, one followed in the footsteps of one's forebears.

Thus tradition has been the stabilizing and impelling force behind a great repetitive cycle of society, assuring that society's work would be done each day very much as it had been done in the past. Even today, among the less industrialized nations of the world, tradition continues to play this immense organizing role. In India, until very recently at least, one was born to a caste which had its own occupation. "Better thine own work is, though done with fault,"; preached the Bhagavad-Gita, the great philosophic moral poem of India, "than doing other's work, even excellently."

Tradition not only provides a solution to the production problem of society, but it also regulates the distribution problem. Take, for example, the Bushmen of the Kalahari Desert in South Africa who depend for their livelihood on hunting prowess. Elizabeth Marshall Thomas, a sensitive observer of these peoples, reports on the manner in which tradition solves the problem of distributing their kill.

The gemsbok has vanished . . . Gai owned two hind legs and a front leg, Tsetchwe had meat from the back, Ukwane had the other front leg, his

2 *The Wealth of Nations* (New York: Modern Library, Inc., 1937), p. 62.

wife had one of the feet and the stomach, the young boys had lengths of intestine. Twikwe had received the head and Dasina the udder.

It seems very unequal when you watch Bushmen divide the kill, yet it is their system, and in the end no person eats more than any other. That day Ukwane gave Gai still another piece because Gai was his relation, Gai gave meat to Dasina because she was his wife's mother . . . No one, of course, contested Gai's large share, because he had been the hunter and by their law that much belonged to him. No one doubted that he would share his large amount with others, and they were not wrong, of course; he did.[3]

The manner in which tradition can divide a social product may be, as the illustration shows, very subtle and ingenious. It may also be very crude and, by our standards, harsh. Tradition has often allocated to women, in nonindustrial societies, the most meager portion of the social product. But however much tradition may accord with or depart from our accustomed moral views, we must see that it is a workable method of dividing society's production.

Traditional solutions to the economic problems of production and distribution are most commonly encountered in primitive agrarian or nonindustrial societies, where in addition to serving an economic function, the unquestioning acceptance of the past provides the necessary perseverance and endurance to confront harsh destinies. Yet even in our own society, tradition continues to play a role in solving the economic problem. It plays its smallest role in determining the distribution of our own social output, although the persistence of such traditional payments as tips to waiters, allowances to minors, or bonuses based on length of service are all vestiges of old traditional ways of distributing goods, as is the differential between men's and women's pay for equal work.

More important is the place which tradition continues to hold, even in America, as a means of solving the production problem— that is, in allocating the performance of tasks. Much of the actual process of selecting an employment in our society is heavily influenced by tradition. We are all familiar with families in which sons follow their fathers into a profession or a business. On a somewhat broader scale, tradition also dissuades us from certain employments. Sons of American middle-class families, for example, do not usually seek factory work, even though factory jobs may pay better than

3 *The Harmless People* (New York: Alfred A. Knopf, Inc., 1959), pp. 49–50.

office jobs, because "bluecollar employment" is not in the middle-class tradition.

Even in our society, which is clearly not a "traditional" one, custom provides an important mechanism for solving the economic problem. But now we must note one very important consequence of the mechanism of tradition. *Its solution to production and distribution is a static one.* A society which follows the path of tradition in its regulation of economic affairs does so at the expense of large-scale rapid social and economic change.

Thus the economy of a Bedouin tribe or a Burmese village is in few essential respects changed today from what it was a hundred or even a thousand years ago. The bulk of the peoples living in tradition-bound societies repeat, in the daily patterns of their economic life, much of the routines which characterized them in the distant past. Such societies may rise and fall, wax and wane, but external events—war, climate, political adventures and misadventures—are mainly responsible for their changing fortunes. Internal, self-generated economic change is but a small factor in the history of most tradition-bound states. Tradition solves the economic problem, but it does so at the cost of economic progress.

Command

A second manner of solving the problem of economic continuity also displays an ancient lineage. This is the method of imposed authority, of economic command. It is a solution based not so much on the perpetuation of a viable system by the changeless reproduction of its ways, as on the organization of a system according to the orders of an economic commander-in-chief.

Not infrequently we find this authoritarian method of economic control superimposed upon a traditional social base. Thus the Pharaohs of Egypt exerted their economic dictates above the time-less cycle of traditional agricultural practice on which the Egyptian economy was based. By their orders, the supreme rulers of Egypt brought into being the enormous economic effort which built the pyramids, the temples, the roads. Herodotus, the Greek historian, tells us how the Pharaoh Cheops organized the task.

[He] ordered all Egyptians to work for himself. Some, accordingly, were appointed to draw stones from the quarries in the Arabian mountains

down to the Nile, others he ordered to receive the stones when transported in vessels across the river. . . . And they worked to the number of
a hundred thousand men at a time, each party during three months. The
time during which the people were thus harassed by toil lasted ten years
on the road which they constructed, and along which they drew the stones;
a work, in my opinion, not much less than the Pyramid.[4]

The mode of authoritarian economic organization was by no
means confined to ancient Egypt. We encounter it in the despotisms
of medieval and classical China which produced, among other
things, the colossal Great Wall or in the slave labor by which many
of the great public works of ancient Rome were built. Of course, we
find it today in the dictates of the communist economic authorities.
In less drastic form, we find it also in our own society, for example,
in the form of *taxes*—that is, in the preemption of part of our
income by the public authorities for public purposes.

Economic command, like tradition, offers solutions to the twin
problems of production and distribution. In times of crises, such
as war or famine, it may be the only way in which a society can
organize its manpower or distribute its goods effectively. Even in
America, we commonly declare martial law when an area has been
devastated by a great natural disaster. On such occasions we may
press people into service, requisition homes, impose curbs on the
use of private property such as cars, or even limit the amount of food
a family may consume.

Quite aside from its obvious utility in meeting emergencies, command has a further usefulness in solving the economic problem.
Unlike tradition, the exercise of command has no inherent effect of
slowing down economic change. Indeed, the exercise of authority is
the most powerful instrument society has for *enforcing economic
change*. One example is, of course, the radical alterations in the
systems of production and distribution which authority has effected
in modern China or Russia. But again, even in our own society, it is
sometimes necessary for economic authority to intervene into the
normal flow of economic life to speed up or bring about change. The
government may, for instance, utilize its tax receipts to lay down a
network of roads which brings a backwater community into the
flux of active economic life. It may undertake an irrigation system

[4] *Histories,* trans. Cary (London: 1901), Book II, p. 124.

which will dramatically change the economic life of a vast region. It may very considerably affect the distribution of income among social classes.

To be sure, economic command which is exercised within the framework of a democratic political process is very different from that which is exercised by strong-arm methods: there is an immense social distance between a tax system controlled by Congress and outright expropriation or labor impressment by a supreme and unchallengeable ruler. Yet whilst the means may be much milder, the *mechanism* is the same. In both cases, command diverts economic effort toward goals chosen by a higher authority. In both cases it interferes with the existing order of production and distribution, to create a new order ordained from "above."

This does not in itself serve to commend or condemn the exercise of command. The new order imposed by the authorities may offend or please our sense of social justice, just as it may improve or lessen the economic efficiency of society. Clearly, command can be an instrument of a democratic as well as of a totalitarian will. There is no implicit moral judgment to be passed on this second of the great mechanisms of economic control. Rather, it is important to note that no society—certainly no modern society—is without its elements of command, just as none is devoid of the influence of tradition. If tradition is the great brake on social and economic change, so economic command can be the great spur to change. As mechanisms for assuring the successful solution to the economic problem, both serve their purposes, both have their uses and their drawbacks. Between them, tradition and command have accounted for most of the long history of man's economic efforts to cope with his environment and with himself. The fact that human society *has* survived is testimony to their effectiveness.

The Market

There is also a third solution to the economic problem—that is, a third solution to the problem of maintaining socially viable patterns of production and distribution. This is the *market organization of society,* an organization which, in truly remarkable fashion, allows society to insure its own provisioning with a minimum of recourse either to tradition or command.

Because we live in a market-run society, we are apt to take for granted the puzzling—indeed, almost paradoxical—nature of the market solution to the economic problem. But assume for a moment that we could act as economic advisers to a society which had not yet decided on its mode of economic organization. Suppose, for instance, that we were called on to act as consultants to one of the new nations emerging from the continent of Africa.

We could imagine the leaders of such a nation saying, "We have always experienced a highly tradition-bound way of life. Our men hunt and cultivate the fields and perform their tasks as they are brought up to do by the force of example and the instruction of their elders. We know, too, something of what can be done by economic command. We are prepared, if necessary, to sign an edict making it compulsory for many of our men to work on community projects for our national development. Tell us, is there any other way we can organize our society so that it will function successfully —or better yet, more successfully?"

Suppose we answered, "Yes, there is another way. Organize your society along the lines of a market economy."

"Very well," say the leaders. "What do we then tell people to do? How do we assign them to their various tasks?"

"That's the very point," we would answer. "In a market economy no one is assigned to any task. The very idea of a market society is that each person is allowed to decide for himself what to do."

There is consternation among the leaders. "You mean there is *no* assignment of some men to mining and others to cattle raising? No manner of selecting some for transportation and others for cloth weaving? You leave this to people to decide for themselves? But what happens if they do not decide correctly? What happens if no one volunteers to go into the mines, or if no one offers himself as a railway engineer?"

"You may rest assured," we tell the leaders, "none of that will happen. In a market society, all the jobs will be filled because it will be to people's advantage to fill them."

Our respondents accept this with uncertain expressions. "Now look," one of them finally says, "let us suppose that we take your advice and let our people do as they please. Now let's talk about something important, like cloth production. Just how do we fix the right level of cloth output in this 'market society' of yours?"

"But you don't," we reply.

"We don't! Then how do we know there will be enough cloth produced?"

"There will be," we tell him. "The market will see to that."

"Then how do we know there won't be *too much* cloth produced?" he asks triumphantly.

"Ah, but the market will see to that too!"

"But what *is* this market that will do all these wonderful things? Who runs it?"

"Oh, nobody runs the market," we answer. "It runs itself. In fact there really isn't any such *thing* as 'the market.' It's just a word we use to describe the way people behave."

"But I thought people behaved the way they wanted to!"

"And so they do," we say. "But never fear. They will want to behave the way you want them to behave."

"I am afraid," says the chief of the delegation, "that we are wasting our time. We thought you had in mind a serious proposal. But what you suggest is madness. It is inconceivable. Good day, sir." And with great dignity the delegation takes its leave.

Could we seriously suggest to such an emergent nation that it entrust itself to a market solution of the economic problem? That will be a problem to which we shall return. But the very perplexity which the market idea would rouse in the mind of someone unacquainted with it may serve to increase our own wonderment at this most sophisticated and interesting of all economic mechanisms. How *does* the market system assure us that our mines will find miners, our factories workers? How does it take care of cloth production? How does it happen that in a market-run nation each person can indeed do as he wishes and, withal, fulfill the needs which society as a whole presents?

Economics and the Market System

Economics, as we commonly conceive it and as we shall study it in much of this book, is primarily concerned with these very problems. Societies which rely primarily on tradition to solve their economic problems are of less interest to the professional economist than to the cultural anthropologist or the sociologist. Societies which solve their economic problems primarily by the exercise of command present interesting economic questions, but here the study of economics is necessarily subservient to the study of politics and the exercise of power.

It is a society which solves its economic problems by the market process that presents an aspect especially interesting to the economist. For here, as we shall see, economics truly plays a unique role. Unlike the case with tradition and command, where we quickly grasp the nature of the economic mechanism of society, when we turn to a market society we are lost without a knowledge of economics. For in a market society it is not at all clear that the problems of production and distribution will be solved by the free interplay of individuals without guidance from tradition or command.

In subsequent chapters of this book we shall analyze these puzzling questions in more detail. But first there is a problem which has surely occurred to the reader. As our hypothetical interview with the leaders of an emergent nation must have suggested, the market solution appears very strange to someone brought up in the ways of tradition or command. Hence the question arises: how did the market solution itself evolve? Was it imposed, full-blown, on our society at some earlier date? Or did it arise spontaneously and without forethought? These are the questions to which we must first turn, as we retrace the evolution of our own market system out of the tradition- and authority-dominated societies of the past.

2

The Pre-Market Economy

Nobody ever saw a dog make a fair and deliberate exchange of one bone for another with another dog," wrote Adam Smith in the *Wealth of Nations*. "Nobody ever saw one animal by its gestures and natural cries signify to another, this is mine, that yours; I am willing to give this for that."[1]

Smith was writing about "a certain propensity in human nature . . . ; the propensity to truck, barter, and exchange one thing for another." Whether or not such a propensity exists as a universal characteristic of humankind is perhaps less likely than Smith believed, but he was certainly not mistaken in putting the act of exchange at the very center of his scheme of economic life. For there can be no doubt that exchange, buying and selling, lies at the very heart of a market society such as he was describing. And so, as we now begin to study the rise of the market society, what could be

[1] Smith, *op. cit.*, p. 13.

18

more natural than to commence by tracing the pedigree of markets themselves?

It comes as something of a surprise, perhaps, to discover how very ancient is that pedigree. Men have traded with one another at least as far back as the last Ice Age. We have evidence that the mammoth-hunters of the Russian steppes obtained Mediterranean shells in trade, as did also the Cro-Magnon hunters of the central valleys of France. In fact, on the moors of Pomerania in northeastern Germany, archeologists have come across an oaken box, replete with the remains of its original leather shoulder strap, in which were a dagger, a sickle head, and a needle—all of Bronze Age manufacture. According to the conjectures of experts, this was very likely the sample kit of a prototype of the traveling salesman—an itinerant representative who collected orders for the specialized production of his community.[2]

And as we proceed from the dawn of civilization to its first organized societies, the evidences of trade and of markets increase rapidly. As Miriam Beard has written:

Millennia before Homer sang, or the wolf suckled Romulus and Remus, the bustling damkars [traders] of Uruk and Nippur . . . were buckling down to business. Atidum the merchant, in need of enlarged office facilities, was agreeing to rent a suitable location from Ribatum, Priestess of Shamash, for one and one-sixth shekels of silver per year—so much down and the rest in easy installments. Abu-wakar, the rich shipper was delighted that his daughter had become Priestess of Shamash and could open a real estate office near the temple. Ilabras was writing to Ibi: "May Shamash and Marduk keep thee! As thou knowest, I had issued a note for a female slave. Now the time to pay is come."[3]

Thus at first glance it seems as if we can discover evidences of a market society deep in the past. But these disconcerting notes of modernity must be interpreted with caution. If markets, buying-and-selling, even highly organized trading bodies, were well-nigh ubiquitous features of ancient society, they must not be confused

---

[2] *Cambridge Economic History of Europe* (London: Cambridge University Press, 1952), II, p. 4.

[3] *A History of the Business Man* (New York: The Macmillan Company, 1938), p. 12.

with the equally ubiquitous presence of a *market society*. Trade existed as an important adjunct to society from earliest times, but the fundamental impetus to production, or the basic allocation of resources among different uses, or the distribution of goods among social classes was largely divorced from the marketing process. That is, *the markets of antiquity were not the means by which those societies solved their basic economic problems.* They were external to the great processes of production and distribution rather than integral to them; they were "above" the critical economic machinery rather than within it. As we shall see, between the deceptively contemporary air of many markets of the distant past and the reality of our contemporary market economy lay an immense distance over which society would take centuries to travel.

THE ECONOMIC ORGANIZATION OF ANTIQUITY

We must ourselves traverse that distance if we are to understand how contemporary market society came into being and, indeed, if we are to understand what it is. For only by immersing ourselves in the societies of the past, only by seeing how they did, in fact, solve their economic problems, can we begin to see clearly what is involved in the evolution of the market society which is our own environment.

Needless to say, it would make an enormous difference to us, as general observers, which of the many pre-market societies of the past we visited. Between the monolithic temple-states of Sumer and Akkad and the "modernity" of classical Greece or Rome is in itself a cultural journey of fantastic distance. Yet, traveling only as economic historians, we will find that it makes much less difference in which of the societies of antiquity we light. For as we examine these societies, we can see that underlying their profound dissimilarities of art or political rule or religious belief, there are equally profound similarities of economic structure, similarities we call less to mind because they are in the "background" of history and rarely adorn its more exciting pages. But these identifying characteristics of economic organization are the ones which now interest us as we turn our gaze to the past. What is it that we see?

The Agricultural Foundation of Ancient Societies

The first, and perhaps the most striking, impression is the overwhelmingly agricultural aspect of all these economies.

In a sense, of course, all human communities, no matter how industrialized, live off the soil: all that differentiates the "agricultural" society from the "industrial" is the number of the non-agricultural population which its food growers can support. Thus an American farmer, working a large acreage with abundant equipment, maintains twenty-six nonfarmers; while an Asian peasant, tilling his tiny plot with little more than a stick-plow, is often hard pressed to sustain his own family.

Over all of antiquity the capacity of the agricultural population to sustain a nonfarming population was very limited. Exact statistics are unreliable, but we can project backwards to the situation which prevailed in all these ancient nations by looking at the under-developed regions of the world today where the levels of technique and the productivity of agriculture bear a close—too close—re-semblance to antiquity. Thus in India, in Egypt, in the Philippines, Indonesia, Brazil, Colombia, Mexico, we find that it takes two farm families to support one nonfarm family, while in tropical Africa a recent survey tells us: "The productivity of African agriculture is still so low that it takes anywhere from two to ten people—men, women, and children—to raise enough food to supply their own needs and those of *one* additional—non-food-growing—adult."[4]

Antiquity was not *that* badly off; indeed at times it produced impressive agricultural outputs. But neither was it remotely comparable to American farm productivity with its enormous capacity to support a nonagricultural population. All ancient economic societies were basically rural economies. This did not preclude, as we shall see, a very brilliant and wealthy urban society nor a truly impressive network of international trade. Yet the typical economic personage of antiquity was neither trader nor urban dweller. He was a tiller of the soil, and it was in his rural communities that the economies of antiquity were ultimately anchored.

But this must not lead us to assume that economic life was therefore comparable to that of a modern agricultural community like

---

[4] George H. T. Kimble, *Tropical Africa* (New York: Twentieth Century Fund, 1960), I, 572. (Italics added.)

Denmark or New Zealand. Contemporary farmers, like businessmen, are very much bound up in the web of transactions characteristic of a market society. They sell their output on one market; they buy their supplies on another. The accumulation of money, and not wheat or corn, is the object of their efforts. Books of profit and loss regularly tell them if they are doing well or not. The latest news of agricultural technology is studied and put into effect if it is profitable.

None of this properly describes the "farmer" of ancient Egypt, of antique Greece or Rome, or of the great Eastern civilizations. The tiller of the soil was a peasant, and a peasant is a social creature very different from a farmer. He is not technologically alert but, on the contrary, clings with stubborn persistence—and often with great skill —to his well-known ways. He must, since a small error might mean starvation. He does not buy the majority of his supplies but, to a large extent, fashions them himself; similarly, he does not produce for a "market," but principally for himself. Finally, he is often not even free to consume his own crop, but typically he must hand over a portion—a tenth, a third, half or even more—to the owner of his land.

For in the general case, the peasant of antiquity did not own his land. We hear of the independent citizen-farmers of classical Greece and republican Rome, but these were exceptions to the general rule in which peasants were but tenants of a great lord. And even in Greece and Rome, the independent peasantry tended to become swallowed up as the tenantry of huge commercial estates. Pliny mentions one such enormous estate or latifundium (literally: broad farm) which boasted a population of 4,117 slaves, 7,200 oxen, and 257,000 other animals.

Hence the peasant, who was the bone and muscle of the economies of antiquity, was in himself a prime example of the nonmarket aspect of these economies. Although some cultivators freely sold a portion of their own crop in the city market places, the great majority of agricultural producers scarcely entered the market at all. For many of these producers—especially when they were slaves—this was, accordingly, an almost cashless world, where a few coppers a year, carefully hoarded and spent only for emergencies, constituted the only link with a world of market transactions.*

---

* This is not, let us note, only an ancient condition. Traveling in Morocco,

Thus whereas the peasant's legal and social status varied widely in different areas and eras of antiquity, in a broad view the tenor of his economic life was singularly constant. Of the web of transactions, the drive for profits of the modern farmer, he knew little or nothing. Generally poor, tax-ridden and oppressed, prey to nature's caprices and to the exploitation of war and peace, bound to the soil by law and custom, the peasant of antiquity—as the peasant today who continues to constitute the agricultural backdrop to the civilizations of the East and South—was dominated by the economic rule of tradition. His main stimulus for change was command—or, rather, obedience. Labor, patience, and the incredible endurance of the human being was his contribution to civilization.

The Economic Life of the Cities

The basic agricultural cast of ancient society and its typical exclusion of the peasant-cultivator from an active market existence makes all the more striking another common aspect of economic organization in antiquity. This is the diversity, vitality, and ebullience of the economic life of the cities.

Whether we turn to ancient Egypt, classical Greece, or Rome, we cannot help but be struck by this contrast between the relatively static countryside and the active city. In Greece, for example, a whole panoply of goods passed across the docks of the Piraeus: grain from Italy, metal from Crete and even Britain, books from Egypt, perfume from still more distant origins. Isocrates, in the *Panegyricus,* boasts: "The articles which it is difficult to get, one here, one there, from the rest of the world; all these it is easy to buy in Athens." So, too, Rome developed a thriving foreign and domestic commerce. By the time of Augustus, 6,000 loads of ox-towed barges were required to feed the city annually,[5] while in the city forum a crowd of speculators converged as on "an immense stock exchange."[6]

Thus something which at least superficially approximated our own society was visible in many of the larger urban centers of an-

John Gunther reported of the local peasant-serfs: "formerly they got no wages—what would they need money for—but this is changing now." *Changing now*—in 1953! (*Inside Africa*, New York: Harper & Brothers, 1955, p. 104.)

[5] *Cambridge Economic History of Europe*, II, p. 47.

[6] W. C. Cunningham, *An Essay on Western Civilization* (New York: 1913), p. 164.

tiquity. And yet we must not be beguiled into the conclusion that this was a market society similar to our own. For in at least two respects the differences were profound.

The first of these was the essentially restricted character and scope of the market function of the city. Unlike the modern city which is not only a receiver of goods shipped in from the hinterlands, but also an important exporter of goods and services back to the countryside, the cities of antiquity tended to assume an economically parasitic role vis-à-vis the rest of the economy. Much of the trade which entered the great urban centers of Egypt, Greece, and Rome (over and above the necessary provisioning of the city masses) was in the nature of luxury goods for its upper classes, rather than raw materials to be worked and then sent out to a goods-consuming economy. The cities were the vessels of civilization; but as centers of economic activity, a wide gulf separated them from the country, making the cities enclaves of economic life rather than nourishing components of integrated rural-urban economies.

Even more important was a second difference between the ancient city economies and a contemporary market society. This was their reliance on *slave labor*.

For slavery on a massive scale was a fundamental pillar of nearly every ancient economic society. In Greece, for instance, the deceptively modern air of the Piraeus masks the fact that much of the purchasing power of the Greek merchant was provided by the labor of 20,000 slaves who labored, under sickening conditions, in the silver mines of Laurentium. At the height of "democratic" Athens, it is estimated that at least one-third of its population were slaves. In Italy of 30 B.C., some 1,500,000 slaves—on the latifundia, in the galleys, the mines, the "factories," the shops—provided a major impetus in keeping the economic machinery in motion.[7] Seneca even tells us that a proposal that they wear special dress was voted down lest recognizing their own number, they might know their strength.

Slaves were not, of course, the only source of labor. Groups of free artisans and workmen, often banded together in "collegia" or fraternal bodies, also serviced the Roman city, as did similar free workmen in Greece and elsewhere. In many cities, especially latter-day Rome, a mass of unemployed (but not enslaved) laborers provided

---

[7] K. J. Beloch, *Die Bevölkerung der griechisch-römischen Welt* (Leipzig: 1886), p. 478.

a source of casual work. Yet, without the motive power of the slave it is doubtful if the brilliant city economies of the past could have been sustained. And this brings us to the central point. It is that the flourishing market economy of the city rested atop an economic structure run by tradition and command. Nothing like the free exercise and interplay of self-interest guided the basic economic effort of antiquity. If an astonishingly modern urban market structure greets our eye, we must not forget that its merchants are standing on the shoulders of innumerable peasants and slaves.

Wealth and Power

The presence of great agglomerations of urban wealth amid the far poorer rural setting alerts us to another characteristic of ancient economic society. This is the special relationship between its wealth and its underlying economic organization.

In any society, wealth implies that a *surplus* has been wrung from nature, that a social organization has not alone solved its economic production problem but has achieved a margin of effort above that required for its own existence. Perhaps what first astonishes us when we regard the civilizations of the ancient world is the size of surplus which could be got from a basically poor peasant population. The temples of the ancient Assyrian kings, the extraordinary treasures of the Aztecs, the pyramids and pleasure craft of the Pharaohs of Egypt, the Acropolis of Athens and the magnificent roads and architecture of Rome all testify to the ability of an essentially agricultural civilization to achieve a massive surplus, to pry considerable amounts of labor loose from the land, support it at whatever low level, and put it to work building for posterity.

But the stupendous achievements of the past testify as well to something else. The surplus productive potential which society manages to achieve (whether by technology or by adroit social organization) can be applied in many directions. If the surplus is applied to agricultural improvements, such as irrigation ditches or dams, it is apt to increase the bounty of the harvest still further. If it is applied to the tools and equipment of the city workman, it is apt to raise his ability to produce. Or the surplus may be used to support a large standing army, or a nonworking religious order, or a class of courtiers and idle nobility.

Thus the social form taken by the accumulation of wealth reveals a great deal. "To whom does the surplus of society accrue?" is a question which invariably sheds important light on the structure of that society.

To whom did the wealth of antiquity accrue? At first glimpse it seems impossible to answer in a phrase. Emperors, nobles, religious orders, merchant traders—all enjoyed the wealth of antiquity at one time or another. But at second look, an interesting and significant generalization becomes possible: most wealth did not go to those who played a strictly *economic* role. Although there are records of clever slaves in Egypt and Rome who became wealthy, and rich merchants and bankers are visible throughout the annals of antiquity, theirs was not the primary route to wealth. On the whole, *in ancient civilization wealth was the reward for political, military, or religious power or status, and not for economic activity.*

There was a reason for this. Societies tend to reward most highly the activities they value most highly; and in the long and turbulent centuries of antiquity, political leadership, religious tutelage, and military prowess were unquestionably more necessary for social survival than trading expertise. In fact, in many of these societies, economic activity itself was disdained as essentially ignoble. As Aristotle wrote in his *Politics,* "in the best-governed polis . . . the citizens may not lead either the life of craftsmen or of traders, for such a life is devoid of nobility and hostile to perfection of character." It was a theme on which Cicero would later expand in his essay *De Officiis* (Book I).

The toil of a hired worker, who is paid only for his toil and not for artistic skill, is unworthy of a free man and is sordid in character. For in his case, money is the price of slavery. Sordid too is the calling of those who buy wholesale in order to sell retail, since they would gain no profits without a great deal of lying. . . . Trade on a small retail scale is sordid, but if it is on a large wholesale scale including the import of many wares from everywhere and their distribution to many people without any misrepresentation, it is not to be too greatly censured. . . .

Especially, added the great lawyer, "if those who carry on such trade finally retire to country estates, after being surfeited or at least satisfied with their gains."

Over and above the lesser social function of the merchant compared with the general, the consul, or the priest, this disdain of wealth obtained from "ignoble" economic activity reflected an economic fact of great importance: society had not yet integrated the production of wealth with the production of goods. Wealth was still a surplus to be seized by conquest or squeezed from the underlying agricultural population; it was not yet a natural adjunct of a system of continuously increasing production in which some part of an expanding total social output might accrue to many classes of society.

And so it would be for many centuries. Until the smallest as well as the largest activities of society would receive their price tag, until purchases and sales, bids and offers would penetrate down to the lowest orders of society, the accumulation of wealth would always remain more a matter of political, military, or religious power than of economics. To sum it up: *in pre-market societies, wealth tends to follow power; not until the market society will power tend to follow wealth.*

"Economics" and Social Justice in Antiquity

Before we move on to view the economic system of antiquity in transition and evolution, we must ask one more question. What did contemporary economists think of it?

And the answer we find is an interesting one: there were no contemporary "economists." Historians, philosophers, political theorists, writers on manners and morals abounded during the long span of history we here call "antiquity," but economists, as such, did not exist. The reason is not far to seek. The economics of society—that is, the mode by which society organized itself to meet the basic tasks of economic survival—were hardly such as to provoke the curiosity of a thoughtful man. There was little or no "veil" of money to pierce, little or no complexity of contractual relationship in the market place to unravel, little or no economic rhythm of society to interpret. As the harvest flourished, as the justice or injustice of the tax gathering system varied, as the fortunes of war and politics changed, so went the lot of the peasant proprietor, the slave, the petty craftsman, and trader. As relative military strength rose or fell, as individual merchants fared luckily or otherwise, as the arts prospered or declined, so went the pulse of trade. As his prowess in war or politics permitted, as his chance at ransoms, local monopolies, or marriage dictated, so fared the individual acquisitor of wealth. In all of this there was little to tax the analytic powers of social observers.

If there was a problem of economics—aside from the eternal problems of poor harvests, fortunes of war, etc.—it was inextricably mingled with the problem of political justice. As far back as the early Assyrian tablets, we have records of social reformers who sought to alleviate taxes on the peasantry, and throughout the Bible —indeed, down through the Middle Ages—a strain of primitive communism, of egalitarian sharing, runs through the background of religious thought. In the Book of Leviticus, for example, there is mentioned the interesting custom of the *jubilee* year, one year in each fifty in which the Israelites were to "return to each man unto his possession."* But despite the fact that religion was concerned with riches and poverty, and thus with the distributive problem of economics, the span of antiquity saw little or no systematic inquiry into the *social system* which produced riches or poverty. If riches were an affront, this was due to the personal failings of greedy men; and if social justice were to be obtained, it must be achieved by personal redistribution, by alms and charity. The idea of an "economic" study of society, as contrasted with a political or moral one, was conspicuous largely by its absence.

There was, however, one exception which we should note. Aristotle, the great pupil of Plato, turned his powerful scrutiny to economic affairs, and with him the systematic study of economics, as such, truly begins. Not that Aristotle, any more than the majority of the Church fathers, was a radical social reformer. Much is summed up in his famous sentence: "From the hour of their birth, some are marked out for subjection, others for rule." But the student of the history of economic thought turns first to Aristotle for questions whose treatment he can subsequently trace down through the present time: questions such as "What is value?" "What is the basis of exchange?" "What is interest?"

We will not linger here over Aristotle's formulations of these ideas. But one point we might note, for it accords with what we have already seen of the attitude of antiquity to economic activity itself.

---

* That is, lands which had been forfeited in debt, etc., were to be restored to their original owners. Judging from the wrath of the later prophets such as Amos, however, the injunction must have been observed largely in the breach.

When Aristotle examined the economic process, he differentiated it into two branches—not production and distribution, as we have done, but *use* and *gain*. More specifically, he differentiated between *oeconomia*—whence "economics," and *chrematistike*, from which we have no precise derivative term. By *oeconomia* the Greek philosopher meant the art of household management, the administration of one's patrimony, the careful husbanding of resources. *Chrematistike*, on the other hand, implied the use of nature's resources or of human skill for acquisitive purposes: *Chrematistike* was trade for trade's sake, economic activity which had as its motive and end not use, but profit. Aristotle approved of *oeconomia* but not of *chrematistike*, and within the scope of the essentially limited market structure of antiquity, where the city trader all too frequently exploited the country peasant, it is not hard to see why. The much more difficult problem of whether a market society, in which *everyone* strives for gain, might warrant approval or disapproval never appears in Aristotle's writings, as it never appeared in ancient history. The market society with its genuinely perplexing questions of economic order and economic morality had yet to come into being. Until it did, the philosophy needed to rationalize that order was understandably lacking.

ECONOMIC SOCIETY IN THE MIDDLE AGES

Our conspectus of economic organization has thus far scanned only the great civilizations of antiquity. Now we must turn in somewhat closer focus to a society far nearer in time and, what is more important, immediately precedent to ours in terms of social evolution. This is the vast expanse of history we call the Middle Ages, an expanse which stretches over and describes the Western world, from Sweden to the Mediterranean, "beginning" with the fall of Rome and "ending" with the Renaissance.

Modern scholarship emphasizes more and more the diversity which characterizes that enormous span of time and space, a diversity not alone of social appearance from century to century but of contrast from locality to locality within any given period. It is one thing to speak of "life" in the Middle Ages if one has in mind a

tenth century peasant community in Normandy (where, it is estimated, the average inhabitant probably never saw more than two or
three hundred persons in his lifetime or commanded a vocabulary
of more than six hundred words),[8] and another if we mean the
worldly city of Florence about which Boccaccio wrote so engagingly.

Even more relevant for our purposes is the need to think of the
Middle Ages in terms of economic variety and change. The early
years of feudal economic life are very different from the middle or
later years, particularly insofar as general well-being is concerned.
The commencement of feudalism coincided with a period of terrible
retrenchment, deprivation, depopulation—during the fifth century
the population of Rome actually fell from 1,500,000 to 300,000. But
by the twelfth century, towns had again expanded (after 600 years!)
to the limits of their old Roman walls and even spilled out beyond;
and by the beginning of the fourteenth century, a very considerable
prosperity reigned in many parts of Europe.* Then came a series of
catastrophes: a ghastly two-year famine in 1315; thereafter, in 1348,
the Black Death which carried off between a third and two-thirds of
the urban population; a century-long devastating struggle between
England and France and among the petty principalities of Germany
and Italy. All of these misfortunes pulled back the level of economic
existence to dreadful depths. Neither stasis nor smooth linear progress, but enormous and irregular secular tides mark the long history
of feudalism, and they caution us against a simplistic conception of
its development.

Our purpose, however, is not to trace these tides but rather to
form a generalized picture of the economic *structure* which, beneath
the swings of fortune, marks the feudal era as a unique way-station
of Western economic history. And here we can begin by noting the
all-important development which underlay the genesis of that economic structure. *This was the breakdown of large-scale political
organization.*

For as Rome "fell" and as successive raids and invasions from
north, east, and south tore apart the European countryside, the great

---

[8] George G. Coulton, *Medieval Village, Manor and Monastery* (New York:
Harper & Brothers, Torchbooks, 1960), p. 15.

* There is some evidence that in England around the year 1500, real wages
achieved a level that they would not again surpass until *1900*. (*Economica*, November, 1956, pp. 296–314.)

administrative framework of law and order was replaced by a patch-work quilt of small-scale political entities. Even in the ninth century when Charlemagne's Holy Roman Empire assumed such impressive dimensions on the map, beneath the veneer of a unified "state" there was, in fact, political chaos: neither a single language nor a coordinated central government, nor a unified system of law, coinage, or currency, nor, most important, any consciousness of "national" allegiance bound the statelets of Charlemagne's day into more than temporary cohesion.

We note this striking difference between antiquity and the Middle Ages to stress the tremendous economic consequences that came with political dissolution. As safety and security gave way to local autarky and anarchy, long voyages of commodities became extremely hazardous, and the once vigorous life of the great cities impossible. As a common coin and a common law disappeared, merchants in Gaul could no longer do business with merchants in Italy, and the accustomed network of economic connections was severed or fell into disuse. As disease and invasion depopulated the countryside, men turned of necessity to the most defensive forms of economic organization, to forms aimed at sheer survival through self-sufficiency. A new need arose, a need to compress the viable organization of society into the smallest possible compass. For centuries it would be this very insularity of economic life, this extreme self-reliance, which would be the economic hallmark of the Middle Ages.

The Manorial Organization of Society

The need for self-sufficiency brought with it a new basic unit of economic organization: *the manorial estate.*

What was such an estate like? Typically, it was a large tract of land, often including many thousands of acres, which was "owned" by a feudal lord, spiritual or temporal.* The word "owned" is properly in quotation marks. For the manor was not first and foremost a piece of economic property as such. Rather, it was a social and political entity in which the lord of the manor was not only land-

---

* That is, the lord might be the abbot or the bishop of the locality, or he might be a secular personage, a baron who came into his possessions by inheritance or by being made a knight and given lands for exceptional service in battle or for other reasons.

lord, but protector, judge, police chief, administrator. Although himself bound into a great hierarchy in which each lord was some other lord's servant (and where even the pope was *servus servorum Dei*), the feudal noble was, within the confines of his own manor, quite literally "lord of the land." He was also undisputed owner and master of many of the people who lived on the land, for the serfs (or villeins) of a manor, although not slaves, were in many respects as much the property of the lord as were his (or their) houses, flocks, or crops.

At the focal point of the estate was the lord's homestead, a great manor house, usually armed against attack from marauders, walled off from the surrounding countryside, and sometimes attaining the stature of a genuine castle. In the enclosed courtyard of the manor were workshops in which cloth might be spun or woven, grapes pressed, food stored, simple ironwork or blacksmithing work performed, coarse grain ground. Extending out around the manor was a patchwork of fields, typically subdivided into acre or half-acre "strips," each with its own cycle of crops and rest. Half or more of all of these belonged directly to the lord; the remainder "belonged," in various senses of that legal term, to the hierarchy of free, half-free, and unfree families who made up an estate.

The exact meaning of the word "belonged" hinged on the obligations and rights accruing to a serf, a freeman, or whatever other category one might be born into. Note however that even a freeman who "owned" his land could not sell it to another feudal lord. At best, his ownership meant that he could not himself be displaced from his land short of extraordinary circumstances. A lesser personage than a freeman did not even have this security. A typical serf was literally tied to "his" plot of land. He could not, without specific permission and, usually, without specific payment, leave his homestead for another, either within the domain of the manor or within that of another. With his status came, as well, a series of obligations which lay at the very core of the manorial economic organization. These consisted of the necessity to perform labor for the lord—to till his fields, to work in his shops, to provide him with a portion of one's own crop. From manor to manor, and from age to age, the labor-dues varied: in some localities they amounted to as much as four or even five days of labor a week, which meant that only by the labor of a serf's wife or children could his own fields be maintained. And, finally, the serfs owed small money-payments: head taxes, like the *chevage;* death-duties, like the *heriot;* or *merchet,* a marriage fee, or dues to use the lord's mill or his ovens.

There was, however, an extremely important *quid pro quo* for all of this. If the serf gave the lord his labor and much of the fruits of his toil, in exchange the lord provided some things which the serf alone could not have obtained.

The most important of these was a degree of physical security. It is difficult for us to reconstruct the violent tenor of much of feudal life, but one investigator has provided a statistic which may serve to make the point. Of the sons of English dukes born in 1330–1479, *46 per cent* died violent deaths. Their life expectancy when violent death was excluded was 31 years; when violent death was included, it was but 24 years.[9] The peasant, although not a warrior and therefore not occupationally exposed to the dangers of continual combat, assassination, etc., was preeminently fair prey for the marauding lord, defenseless against capture, unable to protect his poor possessions against destruction. Hence we can begin to understand why even free men became serfs by "commending" themselves to a lord who, in exchange for their economic, social, and political subservience, offered them in return the invaluable cloak of his military protection.

In addition, the lord offered a certain element of *economic* security. In times of famine, it was the lord who fed his serfs from the reserves in his own manorial storehouses. And, although he had to pay for it, the serf was *entitled* to use the lord's own beasts and equipment in cultivating his own strips as well as those of the lord himself. In an age when the average serf possessed almost no tools himself, this was an essential boon.[10]

These facts should not incline us to an idyllic picture of feudal life. The relation between lord and serf was often and even usually

[9] T. H. Hollingsworth, "A Demographic Study of the British Ducal Families," *Population Studies,* XI (1957–1958). I am indebted to Dr. Goran Ohlin for this reference.

[10] For a picture of life among the various classes in medieval Europe, one might turn to Eileen Power's *Medieval People* (Garden City, N.Y.: Anchor Books, 1954), a scholarly but charming account of the reality of human existence which lies behind history. For a sense of the violent tenor of the times, see J. Huizinga, *The Waning of the Middle Ages* (Garden City, N.Y.: Anchor Books, 1954), Ch. I.

exploitative in the extreme. Yet we must see that it was also mutually supportive. Each provided for the other services essential for
existence in a world where over-all political organization and stability had virtually disappeared.

The Economics of Manorial Life

Despite the extreme self-sufficiency of manorial life, there is much
here that resembles the economic organization of antiquity.

To begin with, like those earlier societies, this was clearly a form
of economic society organized by tradition. Indeed, the hand of custom—the famous "ancient customs" of the medieval manor court
which served frequently as the counsel for the otherwise undefended
serf—was never stronger. Lacking strong unified central government,
even the exercise of command was relatively weak. As a result, the
pace of economic change, of economic development, although by no
means lacking, was extremely slow during the early years of the
medieval period.

Second, even more than with antiquity, this was a form of society
which was characterized by a striking absence of money transactions.
Unlike the latifundium of Rome, which sold its output to the city,
the manor supplied only itself, and perhaps a local town. Hence little
money changed hands. No manorial estate was ever quite so self-
sufficient that it could disperse with monetary links with the outside
world. Even serfs bought some commodities, and the lord, on occasion, had to buy considerable supplies which he could not produce
for himself. But as Henri Pirenne, an authority on medieval economic history, has put it

. . . the tenants paid their obligations to their lord in kind. Every serf,
and every owner of a *mansa,* owed a fixed number of days of labour and
a fixed quantity of natural products or of goods manufactured by himself,
corn, eggs, geese, chickens, lambs, pigs, and hempen, linen or woollen cloth.
It is true that a few pence had also to be paid, but they formed such a small
proportion of the whole that they cannot prevent the conclusion that the
economy of the domain was a natural economy. It was a natural economy
because it was not an exchange economy . . . since it did not engage in
commerce it had no need to make use of money. . . .[11]

11 *Economic and Social History of Medieval Europe* (New York: Harcourt,
Brace & World, Inc., Harvest Book ed.), p. 105.

Town and Fair

It would, however, be a misrepresentation of medieval life to conclude that cash and cash transactions and the bargaining of a market society were wholly foreign to it. Rather, as was the case with antiquity, we must think of medieval economic society as consisting of a huge, static, virtually moneyless foundation of agricultural production atop which flourished a considerable variety of more dynamic activities.

For one thing, in addition to manors, there also existed the shrunken descendants of Roman towns (with, as we shall later see, the nuclei of new towns) and these small cities obviously required a network of markets to serve them. Every town had its stalls to which peasants brought some portion of their crop for sale. More important, towns were clearly a different social unit from manors, and the laws and customs of the manors did not apply to their problems. Even when towns fell under manorial protection, little by little, townspeople won for themselves freedom from feudal obligations of labor and, more important, from feudal obligations of law.* In contrast to the "ancient customs" of the manor, a new, evolving "law of merchants" regulated much of the commercial activity within the town walls.

Another locus of active economic life was the *fair*. The fair was a kind of traveling market which established itself in fixed localities, for fixed dates, in which merchants from all over Europe conducted a genuine international exchange. Held usually but once a year, the great fairs were tremendous occasions, a mixture of social holiday, religious festival, and a time of intense economic activity. At some fairs, like those at Champagne in France or Stourbridge in England, a wide variety of merchandise was brought for sale: silks from the Levant, books and parchments, horses, drugs, spices. Anyone who has ever been to the Flea Market, the famous open-air bazaar outside of Paris, or to a country fair in New England or the Middle West has savored something of the atmosphere of such a market. One can imagine the excitement which fairs must have engendered in the still air of medieval life.

---

* Hence the saying "City air makes men free"; for the serf who escaped to a city and remained there a year was usually considered to have passed from the jurisdiction of his lord to that of the city burghers.

Guilds

And finally, within the towns themselves, we find the tiny but highly important centers of medieval "industrial" production. For even at its grandest, the manor could not support every craft needed for its maintenance, much less its extension. The services or products of glaziers and masons, expert armorers and metal-workers, fine weavers and dyers had to be bought when they were needed, and typically they were to be found in the medieval institutions, as characteristic of town life as the manors themselves were of life in the country.

These institutions were the *guilds*—trade, professional, and craft organizations which hearkened back to Roman origins. Such organizations were the "business units" of the Middle Ages; in fact, one could not usually set oneself up in "business" unless one belonged to a guild. Thus the guilds were a kind of union, but not a union of workers so much as of managers. The dominant figures in the guild were the guild masters—independent manufacturers, working in their own houses and banding together to elect their own guild government which then laid down the rules concerning the internal conduct of affairs. Under the master guildsmen were their few journeymen (from the French *journé* or day), who were paid by the day, and their half-dozen or so apprentices, ten to twelve years old, who were bound to them for periods of three to twelve years as their legal wards. In time, an apprentice could become a journeyman and then, at least in medieval romance, graduate to the status of a master craftsman on completion of his "masterpiece."

Any survey of medieval town life delights in the color of guild organization: the broiders and glovers, the hatters and scriveners, the shipwrights and upholsterers, each with its guild hall, its distinctive livery, and its elaborate set of rules. But if life in the guilds and at the fairs provides a sharp contrast with the stodgy life on the manor, we must not be misled by surface resemblances into thinking that it represented a foretaste of modern life in medieval dress. It is a long distance from the guild to the modern business firm, and it is well to fix in mind some of the differences.

In the first place, the guild was much more than just an institution for organizing production. While most of its regulations concerned wages and conditions of work and specifications of output, they also dwelt at length on "noneconomic" matters: on the charitable contributions expected from each member, on his civic role, on his appropriate dress, and even on his daily deportment. Guilds were the regulators of not only production but of social conduct: when one member of the mercer's guild in London "broke the hed" of another in an argument over some merchandise, both were fined £10 and bonded for £200 not to repeat the disgrace. In another guild, members who engaged in a brawl were fined a barrel of beer, to be drunk by the rest of the guild.

But between guild and modern business firm there is a much more profound gulf than this pervasive paternalism. *Unlike a modern firm, the purpose of a guild was not first and foremost to make money.* Rather, it was to preserve a certain orderly way of life—a way which envisaged a decent income for its master craftsmen but which was certainly not intended to allow any of them to become a "big" businessman or a monopolist. On the contrary, guilds were specifically designed to ward off any such outcome of an uninhibited struggle among their members. The terms of service, the wages, the route of advancement of apprentices and journeymen were all fixed by custom. So, too, were the terms of sale: a guild member who cornered the supply of an item was guilty of *forestalling,* for which rigorous penalties were invoked, and one who bought wholesale to sell at retail was similarly punished for the faults of *engrossing* or *regrating.* Thus competition was strictly limited and profits were held to prescribed levels. Advertising was forbidden, and even technical progress in advance of one's fellow guildmen was considered disloyal.

In the great cloth guilds of Florence in the fourteenth century, for instance, no merchant was permitted to tempt a buyer into his shop or to call out to a customer standing in another's doorway, nor even to process his cloth in a manner different from that of his brethren. Standards of cloth production and processing were subject to the minutest scrutiny. If a scarlet dye, for instance, were found to be adulterated, the perpetrator was condemned to a crushing fine and, failing payment, to loss of his right hand.[12]

Surely the guilds represent a more "modern" aspect of feudal life than the manor, but the whole temper of guild life was still far re-

---

[12] G. Renard, *Histoire du Travail à Florence* (Paris: 1913), pp. 190 ff.

moved from the goals and ideals of modern business enterprise. There was no free play of price, no free competition, no restless probing for advantage. Existing on the margin of a relatively moneyless society, the guilds perforce sought to take the risks out of their slender enterprises. Their aim was not increase, but preservation, stability, orderliness. As such, they were as drenched in the medieval atmosphere as the manors.

Medieval Economics

Beyond even these differences, we must note a still deeper chasm between medieval economic society and that of a market economy. This is the gulf between a society in which economic activity is still inextricably mixed with social and religious activity, and one in which economic life has, so to speak, emerged into a special category of its own. In our next chapter we shall be talking about the ways in which a market society creates a special sphere of economic existence. But as we complete our introduction to medieval economic society, the main point to which we should pay heed is that no such special sphere then existed. *In medieval society, economics was a subordinate and not a dominant aspect of life.*

And what was dominant? The answer is, of course, that in economic matters as in so many other facets of medieval life, the guiding ideal was religious. It was the Church, the great pillar of stability in an age of disorder, which constituted the ultimate authority on economics, as on most other matters.

But the economics of medieval Catholicism was concerned not with the credits and debits of successful business operation so much as with the credits and debits of the souls of business operators. As R. H. Tawney, one of the great students of the problem, has written

. . . the specific contributions of medieval writers to the technique of economic theory were less significant than their premises. Their fundamental assumptions, both of which were to leave a deep imprint on social thought of the sixteenth and seventeenth centuries, were two: that economic interests are subordinate to the real business of life, which is salvation; and that economic conduct is one aspect of personal conduct, upon which, as on other parts of it, the rules of morality are binding. Material riches are necessary . . . since without them men cannot support themselves and help one another . . . But economic motives are suspect. Because they are powerful appetites men fear them, but they are not mean enough to applaud them. Like other strong passions, what they need, it is thought, is not a clear field, but repression . . .[13]

Thus what we find throughout medieval religious thought is a pervasive uneasiness with the practices of economic society. Essentially, the Church's attitude toward trade was wary and nicely summed up in the saying: *Homo mercator vix aut numquam Deo placere potest*—the merchant can scarcely or never be pleasing to God.

We find such a suspicion of business motives in the Church's concern with the idea of a "just price." What was a just price? It was selling a thing for what it was worth, and no more. "It is wholly sinful," wrote Thomas Aquinas, "to practise fraud for the express purpose of selling a thing for more than its just price, inasmuch as a man deceives his neighbor to his loss."[14]

What *was* a thing "worth"? Presumably, what it cost to acquire it or make it. But suppose a seller had himself paid too much for an article? Then what was a "just price" at which he might resell it? Or suppose a man paid too little? Was he then in danger of spiritual loss, offsetting his material gain?

These were the questions over which the medieval "economist-theologians" mulled, and they testify to the mixture of economics and ethics which is characteristic of the age. But they were not merely theoretical questions. We have records of the dismay which economic theology caused to the actual participants in the economic process. One St. Gerald of Aurillac in the tenth century, having bought an ecclesiastical garment in Rome for an unusually low price, learned from some itinerant merchants that he had picked up a "bargain" and, rather than rejoicing, hastened to send back to the seller an additional sum, lest he fall into the sin of avarice.[15]

St. Gerald's attitude is no doubt exceptional. Yet if the injunction to charge fair prices did not succeed in staying men's appetites for gain, it did stay their unbridled enthusiasm. Men in ordinary business frequently stopped to assess the condition of their moral bal-

13 *Religion and the Rise of Capitalism* (New York: Harcourt, Brace & World, Inc.), p. 31.

14 A. E. Monroe, ed., "Summa Theologica" in, *Early Economic Thought* (Cambridge, Mass.: Harvard University Press, 1924), p. 54.

15 Henri Pirenne, *Economics and Social History of Medieval Europe* (New York: Harcourt, Brace & World, Inc., Harvest Books, 1956), p. 27.

ance sheets. Whole towns would, on occasion, repent of usury and pay a heavy amend, or merchants like Gandoufle le Grand would, on their deathbeds, order restitution made to those from whom interest had been extracted. Men of affairs in the twelfth and thirteenth centuries occasionally inserted codicils in their wills urging their sons not to follow their footsteps into the snares of trade, or they would seek to make restitution for their commercial sins by charitable contributions. One medieval merchant of London founded a divinity scholarship with £14 "forasmoche as I fynde myn conscience aggrugged that I have deceived in this life divers persons to that amount."[16]

Thus the theological cast of suspicion injected a wholly new note into the money-making process. For the first time it associated the making of money with *guilt*. Unlike the acquisitor of antiquity who unashamedly reveled in his treasures, the medieval profiteer counted his gains in the knowledge that he might be imperiling his soul.

Nowhere was this disapproval of money-making more evident than in the Church's horror of usury—lending money at interest. Money-lending had, since Aristotle's day, been regarded as an essentially parasitic activity, an attempt to make a "barren" commodity, money, yield a return. But what had always been a vaguely disreputable and unpopular activity became, under Church scrutiny, a deeply evil one. Usury was decreed to be a *mortal* sin. At the Councils of Lyons and Vienne in the thirteenth and fourteenth centuries, the usurer was declared a pariah of society, to whom no one, under pain of excommunication, might rent a house, whose confession might not be heard, whose body might not have Christian burial, whose very will was invalid. Anyone even defending usury was to be suspected of heresy.

All these powerful Churchly sentiments were produced not merely by theological scruples. On the contrary, many of the Church's injunctions against both usury and profiteering arose from the most secular of realities. Famine, the endemic scourge of the Middle Ages, brought with it the most heartless economic gouging; loans commanded 40 and 60 per cent—for bread. Much of the dislike of profit-seeking and interest-taking rose from its identification with just such ruthless practices, with which medieval times abounded.

16 S. L. Thrupp, *The Merchant Class in Medieval London* (Chicago: University of Chicago Press, 1948), p. 177. Also Renard, *op. cit.,* pp. 220 ff.

Finally, another, perhaps even more fundamental, reason under-lay the disrepute of gain and profit. This was the essentially static organization of economic life itself. Let us not forget that that life was basically agricultural and that agriculture, with its infinite com-plexity of peasant strips, was far from efficient. To quote once more from Henri Pirenne

. . . the whole idea of profit, and indeed the possibility of profit, was incompatible with the position occupied by the great medieval land-owner. Unable to produce for sale owing to the want of a market, he had no need to tax his ingenuity in order to wring from his men and his land a surplus which would merely be an encumbrance, and as he was forced to consume his own produce, he was content to limit it to his needs. His means of existence was assured by the traditional functioning of an organization which he did not try to improve.[17]

And what was true of the country was also true of the city. The idea of an *expanding* economy, a *growing* scale of production, an *increasing* productivity was as foreign to the guild master or fair-merchant as to the serf and lord. Medieval economic organization was conceived as a means of reproducing, but not enhancing, the material well-being of the past. Its motto was perpetuation, not progress. There is little wonder that in such a static organization, profits and profit-seeking were essentially disturbing rather than useful economic phenomena.

The Prerequisites of Change

We have traced the broad outlines of the economic organization of the West roughly up to the tenth or twelfth century. Once again it is wise to emphasize the diversity of currents concealed within a landscape we have too often been forced to treat as undifferentiated. At best, our journey into antiquity and the Middle Ages can give us a few glimpses of the prevailing flavor of the times, a sense of the ruling economic climate, of the main institutions and ideas by which men organized their economic efforts.

But one thing is certain. We are still very far from the temper and tempo of modern economic life. The few stirrings we have witnessed in the gray world of the manor and the town are but the harbingers

17 *Op. cit.,* p. 63.

of a tremendous change which, over the course of the next centuries, would dramatically alter the basic form of economic organization itself, replacing the old ties of tradition and command with new ties of market transactions.

We shall have to wait until our next chapter to witness the actual process of change itself. But perhaps it will help us put into focus both what we have already seen and what we are about to witness if we anticipate our line of advance. We now have an idea of a pre-market society, a society in which markets exist but which does not yet depend on a market mechanism to solve the economic problem. What changes will be required to transform such a society into a true market economy?

1. *The monetization of economic life will have to proceed to its ultimate conclusion.*

One prerequisite of a market society should by now be clear: a market society must involve the process of exchange, of buying and selling, at every level of society. But for this to take place men must have the wherewithal to enter a market; that is, they must have cash. And, in turn, if society is to be permeated with cash, men must earn money for their labors. In other words, *for a market society to exist, nearly every task must have a monetary reward.*

Even in our highly monetized society we do not pay for *every* service: most conspicuously not for the housekeeping services of a wife. But all through the pre-market era, the number of unpaid services—the amount of work performed by law without monetary compensation—was vastly larger than in our society. Slave labor was, of course, unpaid. So was most serf labor. Even the labor of apprentices was remunerated more in kind, in food and lodging, than in cash. Thus at least 60 or 70 per cent of the actual working population of an ancient or medieval economy labored without anything resembling full payment in money.

Clearly, in such a society the possibilities for a highly involved exchange economy were limited. But a still more important consequence must be noted. The absence of a widespread monetization of tasks meant the absence of a widespread *market for producers.* Nothing like the flow of "purchasing power" which dominates and directs our own productive efforts could be forthcoming in a society in which money incomes were the exception rather than the rule.

2. *The pressures of a free play of market "demand" will have to take over the regulation of the economic tasks of society.*

All through antiquity and the Middle Ages, as we have seen, it was tradition or command which solved the economic problem. These were the forces which directed men to their tasks and these were the forces which regulated the distribution of social rewards. But in a market society, another means of control must rise to take their place. *An all-encompassing flow of money demand, itself stemming from the total monetization of all economic tasks, must become the great propulsive mechanism of society.* Men must go to their tasks not because they are ordered there, but because they will make money there; and producers must decide on the volume and the variety of their output not because the rules of the manor or the guild so determine, but because there is a market demand for particular things. From the top to the bottom of society, in other words, a new marketing orientation must take over the production and distribution tasks. The whole replenishment, the steady provisioning, the very progress of society must now be subject to the guiding hand of a universal demand for labor and goods.

3. *A new attitude toward economic activity will be needed.*

For such a society to function, men must be free to seek gain. The suspiciousness and unease which surrounded the ideas of profit, of change, of social mobility must give way to new ideas which would encourage those very attitudes and activities. In turn this meant, in the famous words of Sir Henry Maine, that the *society of status* must give way to the *society of contract,* that the society in which men were born to their stations in life must give way to a society in which they were free to define those stations for themselves.

Such an idea would have seemed to the medieval mind without any possible rationale. The idea that a general free-for-all should determine men's compensations, with neither a floor to prevent them from being ground down nor a ceiling to prevent them from rising beyond all reason, would have appeared senseless—even blasphemous. If we may listen again to R. H. Tawney

To found a science of society upon the assumption that the appetite for economic gain is . . . to be accepted, like other natural forces . . . would have appeared to the medieval thinker as hardly less irrational or less immoral than to make the premise of social philosophy the unrestrained operation of such necessary human attributes as pugnacity or the sexual instinct.[18]

Yet some such freeing of the quest for economic gain, some such aggressive competition in the new contractual relationship of man to man would be essential for the birth of a market society.

What forces would ultimately drive the world of medieval economic organization into a world of money, of universal markets, of profit-seeking? The stage is now set for us to attempt to answer this profoundly important and difficult question. Let us turn to a consideration of the causes capable of effecting so vast a change.

[18] *Op. cit.*, pp. 31–32.

3

The Emergence of the Market Society

*T*radition, changelessness, order—these were the key concepts of economic society in the Middle Ages, and our preceding chapter introduced us to this unfamiliar and static way of economic life. But our purpose in this chapter is different. It is no longer to describe those factors which preserved the economic stability of medieval society, but to identify those forces which eventually burst it asunder.

Once again we need a word of caution. Our chapter spans an im-mense variety of historical experience. We must beware of thinking that the forces of change which dominate this chapter were identical from region to region or from century to century, or that the transition which they effected was uniform throughout the broad expanse of Europe. On the contrary, the great evolution which we will witness in these pages was not sharp and clear, but muddy and irregular. At the same time that the first evidences of a truly modern market society were already beginning to manifest themselves in the medieval cities of Italy or Holland, the most archaic forms of feudal relationship persisted in the agricultural sectors of these nations, and indeed in the city life of other nations. We must bear in mind that the historic processes of this chapter extended from the tenth to the seventeenth (and even eighteenth and nineteenth) centuries and manifested themselves in no two countries in precisely the same way.

With these cautions in mind, now let us turn to the great evolution itself. What agents were powerful enough to effect the major historic changes needed to bring about a market society?

The Itinerant Merchant

We meet the first of these forces of change in an unexpected guise. It is a small irregular procession of armed men, jogging along one of the rudimentary roads of medieval Europe: standard bearer with colors in the lead, then a military chief, then a group of riders carrying bows and swords, and finally a caravan of horses and mules laden with casks and bales, bags and packs.

Someone unacquainted with medieval life might easily take such a troop for part of the baggage train of a small army. But he would be mistaken. These were not soldiers but merchants, the traveling merchants whom the English of the twelfth century called "piepowers," from *pieds poudreux,* dusty feet. No wonder they were dusty; many of them came immense distances along routes so bad that we know of one instance where only the intervention of a local ecclesiastical lord prevented the "road" from being plowed up as arable land. In their bags and packs were goods which had somehow made a perilous journey across Europe, or even all the way from Arabia or India, to be sold from town to town, or from halt to halt, as these merchant adventurers wound their way across the medieval countryside.

And adventurers they were indeed. For in the fixed hierarchies of the great manorial estates of Europe there was no natural place for these unlanded peddlers of goods, with their unfeudal attributes of calculation and (often very crude) bookkeeping and their natural insistence on trade in money. The traveling merchants ranked very low in society. Many of them, without doubt, were the sons of serfs, or even runaway serfs themselves. Yet since no one could prove their bondage, they had, if only by default, the gift of "freedom." It is no wonder that in the eyes of the nobility, the merchants were upstarts and a disturbing element in the normal pattern of things.

Yet no one would have dispensed with their services. To their brightly canopied stalls at the fairs flocked the lords and ladies of the manors as well as the Bodos and Ermentrudes of the fields. After all, where else could one buy pepper, or purple dye, or acquire a guaranteed splinter from the Cross? Where else could one buy the marvelous cloths woven in Tuscany or learn such esoteric words, derived from the Arabic, as "jar" or "syrup"? If the merchant was a disturbing leaven in the mix of medieval life, he was also the pinch of active ingredient without which the mixture would have been very dull indeed.

We first note the traveling merchant in Europe in the eighth and ninth century, and we can follow his progress until the fourteenth and fifteenth century. By this time, largely through the merchants' own efforts, commerce was sufficiently organized no longer to require these itinerant journeyers.* For what these travelers brought, together with their wares, was the first breath of commerce and commercial intercourse to a Europe which had sunk to an almost tradeless and self-sufficient manorial stagnation. Even to towns as minuscule and isolated as Forcalquier in France—a dot on the map without so much as a road to connect its few hundred souls to the outer world—these hardy traders beat their path: we know from a primitive book of accounts that in May, 1331, thirty-six itinerant merchants visited Forcalquier to transact business at the home and "shop" of one Ugo Teralh, a notary.[1] And so, in a thousand isolated communities, did they slowly weave a web of economic interdependence.

Urbanization

An important by-product of the rise of the itinerant merchant was the slow urbanization of medieval life, the creation of *new* towns

---

* Records of an order for goods placed on the occasion of a funeral of a Swedish nobleman in 1328 include saffron from Spain or Italy, caraway seed from the Mediterranean, ginger from India, cinnamon from Ceylon, pepper from Malabar, anise from southern Europe, and Rhine and Bordeaux wines. The order was placed for *immediate* delivery from one local merchant, despite the fact that Sweden was then a laggard and even primitive land. Cf. Fritz Rörig, *Mittelalterliche Weltwirtschaft* (Jena: 1933), p. 17. (I am again indebted to Dr. Goran Ohlin for this reference.)

[1] *Cambridge Economic History of Europe,* II, pp. 325–326.

and villages. When the traveling merchants stopped, they naturally chose the protected site of a local castle or burg. And so we find growing up around the walls of advantageously situated castles—in the *focis burgis,* whence *faubourg,* the French word for "suburb"— more or less permanent trading places, which in turn became the inner core of small towns. Nestled close to the castle wall for protection, the new burgs were still not "of" the manor. The inhabitants of the burg—the burgesses, burghers, bourgeois—had at best an anomalous and insecure relation to the manorial world within. As we have seen, there was no way of applying the time-hallowed rule of "ancient customs" in adjudicating their disputes, since there *were* no ancient customs in the commercial quarters. Neither were there clear-cut rules for their taxation or for the particular degrees of fealty they owed their local masters. Worse yet, some of the growing towns began to surround themselves with walls. By the twelfth century, the commercial burg of Bruges, for example, had already swallowed up the old fortress like a pearl around a grain of sand.

Curiously, it was this very struggle for existence in the interstices of feudal society which provided much of the impetus for the development of a new social and economic order within the city. In all previous civilizations, cities had been the outposts of central government. Now, for the first time, they existed as independent entities outside the main framework of social power. As a result, they were able to define for themselves—as they *had* to define for themselves—a code of law and social behavior and a set of governing institutions which were eventually to displace those of the feudal countryside.

The process was long drawn out, for the rate of growth of towns was often very slow. In the nearly two centuries between 1086 and 1279, for example, the town of Cambridge, England, added an average of but one house *per year.*[2] Yet if growth was slow, it was steady; and in other locales it was much faster. During the 1,000 years of the Middle Ages nearly 1,000 towns were fathered in Europe, a tremendous stimulus to the commercialization and monetization of life, for each town had its local marts, its local toll gates, often its local mint; its granaries and shops, its drinking places and inns, its air of "city life" which contrasted so sharply with that of the

[2] George Gordon Coulton, *Medieval Panorama* (London: Meridian Books Ltd., 1955), p. 285.

country. The slow spontaneous growth of urban life was a major factor in introducing a marketing flavor to European economic life.

The Crusades

The rise of the itinerant merchant and the town were two great factors in the slow evolution of a market society out of medieval economic life; a third factor was the Crusades.

It is an ironic turn to history that the Crusades, the supreme religious adventure of the Middle Ages, should have contributed so much toward the establishment of a society to which the Church was so vigorously opposed. If we consider the Crusades, however, not from the point of view of their religious impulse, but simply as great expeditions of exploration and colonization, their economic impact becomes much more understandable.*

The Crusades served to bring into sudden and startling contact two very different worlds. One was the still slumbering society of European feudalism with all its rural inertia, its aversion to trade, and its naïve conceptions of business; the other was the brilliant society of Byzantium and Venice, with its urban vitality, its unabashed enjoyment of money-making, and its sophisticated business ways. The Crusaders, coming from their draughty castles and boring manorial routines, thought they would find in the East only untutored heathen savages. They were astonished to be met by a people far more civilized, infinitely more luxurious, and much more money-oriented than they.

One result was that the simple-minded Crusaders found themselves the pawns of commercial interests which they little understood. During the first three Crusades, the Venetians, who provided ships, gulled them as shamelessly as country bumpkins at a fair. The fact that they were fleeced, however, did not prevent the Crusaders from reaching the Holy Land, albeit with inconclusive results. But in the notorious Fourth Crusade (1202–4) Dandolo, the wily 94 year-old Doge of Venice, managed to subvert the entire religious expedition into a gigantic plundering operation for Venetian profit.

* We might note here some of the complex interaction of the process we are watching. For the Crusades were not only a cause of European economic development, but also a *symptom* of the development which had previously taken place.

First Dandolo held up the voyagers for an initial transportation price of 85,000 silver marks, an enormous sum for the unmoneyed nobility to scrape up. Then, when the funds had been found, he refused to carry out his bargain until the Crusaders agreed to attack the town of Zara, a rich commercial rival of Venice. Since Zara was a *Christian,* not an "infidel" community, Pope Innocent III was horrified and suggested that the attack be directed instead against heathen Egypt. But Egypt was one of Venice's best customers, and this horrified Dandolo even more. The Crusaders, stranded and strapped, had no choice: Zara soon fell—after which, at Dandolo's urging, Christian Constantinople was also sacked. The "heathen" Orient was never reached at all, but Venice profited marvelously.

It was not only Venice which gained, however. The economic impact on the Crusaders themselves was much more formidable than the religious. On many this impact was disastrous, as knights who had melted down their silver plate to join the Crusades came back penniless to their manor houses. To others, however, the Crusades brought a new economic impetus. When in 1101, for example, the Genoese raided Caesarea, a Palestinian seaport, 8,000 soldiers and sailors reaped a reward of some forty-eight *solidi* each, plus two pounds of pepper—and thus were 8,000 petty capitalists born.[3] And in 1204 when Constantinople fell, not only did each knight receive twenty marks in silver as his share of the booty, but even the squires and archers were rewarded with a few marks each.

Thus the Crusades provided an immense fertilizing experience for Europe. The old, landed basis of "wealth" came into contact with a new moneyed basis which proved much more powerful. Indeed, the old conception of life itself was forcibly revised before a glimpse of an existence not only wealthier, but gayer and more vital. As a means of shaking a sluggish society out of its rut, the Crusades played an immense role in speeding along the economic transformation of Europe.

The Growth of National Power

Yet another factor in the slow commercialization of economic life was the gradual amalgamation of Europe's fragmented economic and political entities into larger wholes. As the disintegration of

[3] *Cambridge Economic History of Europe,* II, p. 306.

economic life following the break-up of the old Roman Empire had shown, a strong economic society requires a strong and broad political base. Hence as political Europe began its slow process of reknitting, once again its economic tempo began to rise.

One of the most striking characteristics of the Middle Ages, and one of its most crippling obstacles to economic development, was the medieval crazy-quilt of compartmented, isolated areas of government. Over a journey of a hundred miles, a traveling merchant might fall under a dozen different sovereignties, each with different rules, regulations, laws, weights, measures, money. Worse yet, at each border there was apt to be a toll station. At the turn of the thirteenth and fourteenth centuries there were said to be more than thirty toll stations along the Weser River and at least thirty-five along the Elbe; along the Rhine, a century later, there were more than sixty such toll stations, mostly belonging to local ecclesiastical princes: Thomas Wykes, an English chronicler, described the system as "the raving madness of the Teutons." But it was not only a German disease. There were so many toll stations along the Seine in France in the late fifteenth century that it cost half its final selling price to ship grain 200 miles down the river.[4] Indeed, among the European nations, England alone enjoyed an internally unified market during the middle and late Middle Ages. This was one powerful contributory factor to England's emergence as the first great European economic power.

The amalgamation of Europe's fragmented markets was essentially a political as well as an economic process; it followed the gradual centralization of power which changed the map of Europe from the infinite complexity of the tenth century to the more or less "modern" map of the sixteenth. Here, once again, the burgeoning towns played a central and crucial role. It was the city burghers who became the allies of the nascent monarchies, thereby disassociating themselves still further from their local feudal lords while, in turn, supplying the shaky monarchs with an absolutely essential prerequisite for kingship: cash.

Thus monarch and bourgeois combined to bring about the slow growth of centralized governments, and from centralized government, in turn, came not alone a unification of law and money but a direct stimulus to the development of commerce and industry as

4 *Cambridge Economic History of Europe,* II, pp. 134–135.

well. In France, for example, manufacturing was promoted by royal patronage of the famous Gobelin tapestry and Sèvres porcelain works, and business was created for innumerable craftsmen and artisans by the demands of the royal palaces and banquet halls. In other fields, growing national power also imparted a new encouragement: navies had to be built, armies had to be equipped, and these new "national" armed forces, many of whom were mercenaries, had to be paid. All this set into faster motion the pumps of monetary circulation.

Another economic impetus given by the gradual consolidation of political power was the official encouragement of exploration. All through the long years of the Middle Ages a few intrepid adventurers, like Marco Polo, had beat their way to remote regions in search of a short route to the fabled riches of India; and as a matter of fact, by the early fourteenth century the route to the Far East was well enough known so that silk from China cost but half the price of that from the Caspian area, only half the distance away.

Yet the network of all these hazardous and brave penetrations beyond Europe formed only the thinnest of spider webs. There still remained the systematic exploration of the unknown, and this awaited the kingly support of state adventurers. Columbus and Vasco da Gama, Cabral and Magellan did not venture on their epoch-making journeys as individual merchants (although they all hoped to make their fortunes thereby) but as adventurers in fleets bought with, and equipped by, royal money, bearing the royal mark of approval, and sent forth in hope of additions to the royal till.

The economic consequences of those amazing adventures were incalculably great. For one thing, they opened up an invigorating flow of precious metals into Europe. Gold and silver, coming from the great Spanish mines in Mexico and Peru, were slowly redistributed to other nations as Spain paid in gold specie for goods it bought abroad. As a result, prices rose throughout Europe—between 1520 and 1650 alone, it is estimated that they increased 200 to 400 per cent, bringing about both stimulus and stress to industry, but setting in motion a great wave of speculation and commerce.

In addition, of course, the longer-run results of exploration brought an economic stimulus of still greater importance. The establishment of colonies in the sixteenth and seventeenth centuries and the subsequent enjoyment of trade with the New World provided a tremendous boost in propelling Europe into a bustling commercial society. The discovery of the New World was, from the beginning, a catalytic and revolutionizing influence on the Old.

The Change in Religious Climate

The forces of change that we have thus far summarized were actually visible. At any time during the long transition from a non-market into a market society we could have witnessed with our own eyes the traveling merchants, the expanding towns, the Crusades, the evidences of a growing national power. Yet these were not the only forces which undermined the feudal system and brought into being its commercial successor. There were, as well, powerful but invisible currents of change, currents which affected the intellectual atmosphere, the beliefs, and attitudes of Europe. One of these, of special importance, was a change in the religious climate of the times.

In our last chapter we saw how deeply the Catholic church was imbued with theological aversions to the principle of gain—and especially to interest-taking or usury. An amusing story of the times sums up the position of the Church very well. Humbertus de Romanis, a monk, tells of someone who found a devil in every nook and cranny of a Florentine cloister, although in the market place he found but one. The reason, Humbertus explains, was that it took only one to corrupt a market place, where every man harbored a devil in his own heart.[5] In such a disapproving climate, it was hard for the commercial side of life to thrive.

To be sure, for all its fulminations against gain and usury, the Church itself grew in time to a position of commanding economic importance. Through its tithes and benefices it was the largest collector and distributor of money in all of Europe; and in an age in which banks and safe deposit boxes did not exist, it was the repository of much feudal wealth. Some of its sub-orders, such as the Knights Templar, became immensely wealthy and served as banking institutions, lending to needy monarchs on stiff terms. Nonetheless, all of this faintly disreputable activity was undertaken despite, and not because of, the Church's deepest convictions. For

5 Beard, *op. cit.*, p. 160.

behind the ecclesiastical disapproval of wealth-seeking was a deep-seated theological conviction, a firm belief in the transient nature of this life on earth and the importance of preparing for the Eternal Morrow. The Church lifted its eyes and sought to lift the eyes of others above the daily struggle for existence. It strove to minimize the importance of life on earth and to denigrate the earthly activities to which an all too weak flesh succumbed.

What changed this dampening influence on the zest for wealth-making? According to the theories of the German sociologist Max Weber and the English economic historian, R. H. Tawney, the underlying cause lay in the rise of a new theological point of view contained in the teachings of the Protestant reformer, John Calvin (1509–1564).

Calvinism was a harsh religious philosophy. Its core was a belief in *predestination,* in the idea that from the beginning God had chosen the saved and the damned, and that nothing man could do on earth could alter that inviolable writ. Furthermore, according to Calvin, the number of the damned exceeded by a vast amount the number of the saved, so that for the average person the chances were great that this earthly prelude was but the momentary grace given before eternal Hell and Damnation commenced.

Perhaps only a man of Calvin's iron will could have borne life under such a sentence. For we soon find that in the hands of his followers in the Lowlands and England, the inexorable and inscrutable quality of the original doctrine began to be softened. Although the idea of predestination was still preached, it was now allowed that in the tenor of one's worldly life there was a *hint* of what was to follow. Thus the English and Dutch divines taught that whereas even the saintliest-seeming man might end in Hell, the frivolous or wanton one was certainly headed there. Only in a blameless life lay the slightest chance of demonstrating that Salvation was still a possibility.

And so the Calvinists urged a life of rectitude, severity and, most important of all, diligence. In contrast to the Catholic theologians who tended to look upon worldly activity as vanity, the Calvinists sanctified and approved of endeavor as a kind of index of spiritual worth. Indeed in Calvinist hands there grew up the idea of a man *dedicated* to his work: "called" to it, as it were. Hence the fervid pursuit of one's calling, far from evidencing a distraction from religious ends, came to be taken as evidence of a dedication to a religious life. The energetic merchant was, in Calvinist eyes, a *Godly* man, not an ungodly one; and from this identification of work and worth, it was not long before the notion grew up that the more successful a man, the more worthy he was. Calvinism thus provided a religious atmosphere which, in contrast to Catholicism, encouraged wealth-seeking and the temper of a businesslike world.

Perhaps even more important than its encouragement in seeking wealth was the influence of Calvinism on the *use* of wealth. By and large the prevailing attitude of the prosperous Catholic merchants had been that the aim of worldly success was the enjoyment of a life of ease and luxury, while Catholic nobility displayed on occasion a positively grotesque disdain for wealth. In an orgy of gambling which gripped Paris at the end of the seventeenth century we hear of a prince who sent his mistress a diamond worth 5,000 *livres* and had it pulverized and sprinkled over her reply when she rejected it as being too small. The same prince eventually gambled away an income of 600,000 *livres* a year. A *maréchal* whose grandson turned up his nose at a gift of a purse of gold threw it into the street: "Let the street cleaner have it then."[6]

The Calvinist manufacturer or trader had a very different attitude toward wealth. If his religion approved of diligence, it most emphatically did not approve of indulgence. Wealth was to be accumulated and put to good use, not frittered away.

Calvinism promoted an aspect of economic life of which we have hitherto heard very little: *thrift*. It made saving, the conscious abstinence from the enjoyment of income, a virtue. It made investment, the use of saving for productive purposes, an instrument of piety as well as profit. It even condoned, with various *quids* and *quos*, the payment of interest. In fact, Calvinism fostered a new conception of economic life. In place of the old ideal of social and economic stability, of knowing and keeping one's "place," it brought respectability to an ideal of struggle, of material improvement, of economic growth.

Economic historians still debate the precise degree of influence which may properly be attributed to "the Protestant Ethic" in

[6] Werner Sombart, *Luxury and Capitalism* (New York: Columbia University Press, 1938), pp. 120 ff. Also Thirion, *La Vie Privé des Financiers au XVIIIe Siècle* (Paris: 1895), p. 292.

bringing about the rise of a new gain-centered worldly philosophy. After all, there was nothing much that a Calvinist would have been able to teach an Italian Catholic banker about the virtues of a businesslike approach to life. Yet, looking back on the subsequent course of economic progress, it is striking that without exception it was the Protestant countries with their "Puritan streak" of work and thrift which forged ahead in the economic race. As one of the powerful winds of change of the sixteenth and seventeenth centuries, the new religious outlook undoubtedly provided a highly favorable stimulus for the evolution of the market society.

The Breakdown of the Manorial System

The enumeration of all these currents does not exhaust the catalogue of forces bearing against the old fixed economic order in Europe. The list could be expanded and infinitely refined.* Yet, with all due caution we can now begin to comprehend the immense coalition of events—some as specific as the Crusades, some as diffuse as a change in religious ideals—which jointly cooperated to destroy the medieval framework of economic life and to prepare the way for a new dynamic framework of market transactions.

One important aspect of this profound alteration was the gradual *monetization of feudal obligations.* In locality after locality we can trace the conversion of the old feudal payments in *kind*—the days of labor or chickens or eggs which a lord received from his tenants— into payments of *money* dues and money rents with which they now discharged their obligations to him.

A number of causes lay behind this commutation of feudal payments. One was the growing urban demand for food, as city populations began to swell. In concentric circles around the cities, money filtered out into the countryside, at one and the same time raising

* An extremely important influence (to which we will specifically turn in our next chapter) was the rise of a new interest in technology, founded on scientific inquiry into natural events. Another important causative factor was the development of modern business concepts and techniques. The German economic historian Werner Sombart has even said that if he were forced to give a single date for the "beginning" of modern capitalism he would choose 1202, the year in which appeared the *Liber Abbaci,* a primer of commercial arithmetic. Similarly, the historian Oswald Spengler has called the invention of double-entry bookkeeping in 1494 an achievement worthy of being ranked with that of Columbus and Copernicus.

the capacity of the rural sector to buy urban goods and whetting its desire to do so. At the same time, in a search for larger cash incomes to buy a widening variety of goods, the nobility looked with increasing favor on receiving its rents and dues in money rather than in kind. In so doing, however, it unwittingly set into motion a cause for the further serious deterioration of the manorial system. Often the old feudal services were converted into *fixed* sums of money payments. This temporarily eased the cash position of the lord, but soon placed him in the squeeze which always hurts the creditor in times of inflation. And even when dues were not fixed, rents and money dues lagged sufficiently behind the growing monetary needs of the nobility, so that still further feudal obligations were monetized to keep the lord in cash. But as prices rose and the monetized style of life expanded still further, these too failed to keep him solvent.

The result was that the rural nobility, which now depended increasingly on rents and dues for its income, steadily lost its economic power.* Indeed, beginning in the sixteenth century we find a new class coming into being—the impoverished nobility. In the year 1530 in the Gevaudan district of France, we find that 121 lords had an aggregate income of 21,400 *livres,* but one of these seigneurs accounted for 5,000 *livres* of the sum, another for 2,000—and the rest averaged but a mean 121 *livres* apiece.⁷ In fact, the shortage of cash afflicted not only the lesser nobility but even the monarchy itself. Maximilian I, Emperor of the Holy Roman Empire, on occasion even lacked the cash to pay for the overnight lodgings of his entourage on tour; and when he married two of his grandchildren to the children of the King of Hungary, all the trappings of the weddings—2,000 caparisoned horses, jewels, and gold and silver plate—were borrowed from merchant bankers to whom Maximilian had written wheedling letters begging them not to forsake him in his moment of need.

Clearly, the manorial system was incompatible with a cash economy; for while the nobility was pinched between rising prices and costs and static incomes, the merchant classes, to whom cash

---

* This process of economic decline was considerably enhanced by the ineptitude of the nobility as managers of their estates. The descendants of the Crusaders were not much more businesslike than their ancestors.

⁷ *Cambridge Economic History of Europe,* I, pp. 557–558.

naturally gravitated, steadily increased their power. In the Gevaudan district, for example, where the richest lord had his income of 5,000 *livres,* the richest town merchants had incomes up to 65,000 *livres.* In Germany, while Maximilian scratched for cash, the great banking families of Augsburg commanded incomes far larger than Maximilian's entire kingly revenue. In Italy, the Gianfigliazzi of Florence, who began as "nobodies" lending money to the Bishop of Fiesole, ended up stripping him of his possessions and leaving him a pauper; while in Tuscany, the lords who looked down their noses at usurers in the tenth century lost their estates to them in the twelfth and thirteenth. All over Europe men of mean social standing turned the monetary economy to good account. One Jean Amici of Toulouse made a fortune in English booty during the Hundred Years War; Guillaume de St-Yon grew rich by selling meat at rapacious prices to Paris; and Jacques Coeur, the most extraordinary figure of all, rose from merchant to King's coiner, then to King's purchasing agent, then to financier not for, but *of,* the King, during the course of which he accumulated a huge fortune estimated at 27 million *écus.*

THE EMERGENCE OF THE ECONOMIC ASPECT OF LIFE

We can discern an immense process of change which literally revolutionized the economic organization of Europe. Whereas in the tenth century, cash and transactions were only peripheral to the solution of the economic problem, by the sixteenth and seventeenth centuries cash and transactions were already beginning to provide the very molecular force of social cohesion.

But over and above this general monetization of life, another and perhaps even more profound change was taking place. This was the emergence of a separate *economic* sphere of activity visible within, and separable from, the surrounding matrix of social life. It was the creation of a whole aspect of society which had never previously existed, but which was thenceforth to constitute a commanding facet of human existence.

In antiquity and feudal times, as we have seen, one could not easily separate the economic motivations or even the economic actions of the great mass of men from the normal round of existence itself. The peasant following his immemorial ways was hardly conscious of acting according to "economic" motives; indeed, he did not: he heeded the orders of his lord or the dictates of custom. Nor was the lord himself economically oriented. His interests were military or political or religious, and not basically oriented toward the idea of gain or increase. Even in the towns, as we have seen, the conduct of ordinary business was inextricably mixed with non-economic concerns. The undeniable fact that men were acquisitive, not to say avaricious, did not yet impart its flavor to life in general; the making of money, as we have been at some pains to indicate, was a peripheral rather than a central concern of ancient or medieval existence.

With the monetization of daily activity, however, a genuinely new element of life came slowly to the fore. Labor, for example, emerged as an activity quite different from the past. No longer was "labor" part of an explicit social relationship in which one man (serf or apprentice) worked for another (lord or guildmaster) in return for at least an assurance of subsistence. Labor was now a mere quantum of effort, a "commodity" to be disposed of on the market place for the best price it could bring, quite devoid of any reciprocal responsibilities on the part of the buyer, beyond the payment of wages. If those wages were not enough to provide subsistence—well, that was not the buyer's responsibility. He had bought his "labor," and that was that.

This emergence of "pure" labor—labor as a quantity of effort detached from a man's life and bought on the market in fixed quantities—was followed also in respect to two other main elements of economic life. One of these was land. Formerly conceived as the territory of a great lord, as inviolable as the territory of a modern nation-state, land was now also seen in its economic aspect as something to be bought or leased for the economic return it yielded. An estate which was once the core of political and administrative power became a "property" with a market price, available for any number of uses, even as a site for a factory. The dues, the payments in kind, the intangibles of prestige and power which once flowed from the ownership of land gave way to the single return of *rent;* that is, to a money return derived from putting land to *profitable* use.

The same transformation became true of property. As it was conceived in antiquity and throughout most of the Middle Ages, property was a sum of tangible wealth, a hoard, a treasury of plate, bullion, or jewels. Very logically, it was realized in the form of luxurious homes, in castles and armaments, in courtly robes and trappings. But with the monetization and commercialization of society, property, too, became expressible in a monetary equivalent: a man was now "worth" so many *livres,* or *écus,* or pounds, or whatever. Property became *capital,* manifesting itself no longer in specific goods, but as an abstract sum of infinite flexibility whose value was its capacity to earn *interest* or *profits.*

None of these changes, it should be emphasized, was planned, clearly foreseen, or for that matter, welcomed. It was not with equanimity that the feudal hierarchies saw their prerogatives nibbled away by the mercantile classes. Neither did the tradition-preserving guildmaster desire his own enforced metamorphosis into a "capitalist," a man of affairs guided by market signals and beset by competition. But perhaps for no social class was the transition more painful than for the peasant, caught up in a process of history which dispossessed him from his livelihood and made him a landless laborer.

The Enclosures

This process, which was particularly important in England, was the *enclosure movement,* a by-product of the monetization of feudal life. Starting as early as the thirteenth century, the landed aristocracy, increasingly squeezed for cash, began to view their estates not merely as the ancestral fiefs, but as sources of cash revenue. In order to raise larger cash crops, they began to "enclose" the pasture which had previously been deemed "common land." Communal grazing fields which had in fact always belonged to the lord, despite their communal use, were now claimed for the exclusive benefit of the lord and turned into sheepwalks. Why sheepwalks? Because a rising demand for woolen cloth was making sheep-raising a highly profitable occupation. The medieval historian Eileen Power writes:

The visitor to the House of Lords, looking respectfully upon that august assembly, cannot fail to be struck by a stout and ungainly object facing the throne—an ungainly object upon which in full session of Parliament, he will observe seated the Lord Chancellor of England. The object is a woolsack, and it is stuffed as full of pure history as the office of the Lord

Chancellor itself. . . . The Lord Chancellor of England is seated upon a woolsack because it was upon a woolsack that this fair land rose to prosperity.[8]

The enclosure process in England proceeded at an irregular pace which reached twin climaxes in the sixteenth and again in the late eighteenth and early nineteenth centuries:* By its end, some ten million acres, nearly *half* the arable land of England, had been "enclosed"—in its early Tudor days by the more or less high-handed conversion of the "commons" to sheep-raising; in the final period, by the forced consolidation of tenants' strips and plots into tracts suitable for large-scale commercial farming. Presumably there was fair compensation.

From a strictly economic point of view, the enclosure movement was unquestionably salutary in that it brought into productive employment land which had hitherto yielded only a pittance. Indeed, particularly in the eighteenth and nineteenth centuries, enclosure was the means by which England "rationalized" its agriculture and finally escaped from the inefficiency of the traditional manorial strip system. But there was another, crueler side to enclosure. As the common fields were enclosed, it became ever more difficult for the tenant to support himself. At first slowly, then with increasing rapidity, he was pressed off the land, until in the fifteenth and sixteenth centuries, when the initial enclosure of the commons reached its peak, as many as three-fourths to nine-tenths of the tenants of some estates were simply turned off the farm. Whole hamlets were thus wiped out. Sir Thomas More described it savagely in Book I of his *Utopia:*

Your sheep that were wont to be so meek and tame, and so small eaters, now, as I hear say, be become so great devourers and so wild, that they eat up and swallow down the very men themselves. They consume, destroy and devour whole fields, houses and cities. For look in what parts of the realm doth grow the finest, and therefore dearest wool, there noblemen and gentlemen, yea and certain abbots, holy men Got wot, not con-

---

[8] *Medieval People* (Garden City, New York: Anchor Books, 1954), p. 125.

* In other European nations the enclosure process also took place, with varying degrees of severity. In France and Italy, the small-holder peasant persisted long after he had virtually ceased to exist in England; in Germany, a process of dispossession of unusual cruelty resulted in a series of peasant uprisings and "wars."

tenting themselves with the yearly revenues and profits that were wont to grow to their forefathers and predecessors of their land . . . leave no ground for tillage, they enclose all into pastures, they throw down houses, they pluck down towns and leave nothing standing, but only the church to make of it a sheep house. . . .

The enclosure process provided a powerful force for the dissolution of feudal ties and the formation of the new relationships of a market society. By dispossessing the peasant, it "created" a new kind of labor force—landless, without traditional sources of income, however meagre, impelled to find work for wages wherever it might be available.

From the agricultural proletariat came in turn the urban proletariat, although there was, in addition, a process of proletarianization *within* the cities as guild structures gave way to more "business-like" firms. But many of the landless peasantry who had been evicted from the great estates wended their way cityward in search of work. Population increases further augmented their numbers. As a result, we find England, from Elizabethan times on, plagued with the problem of the "wandering poor." One not untypical proposal of the eighteenth century was that they be confined in what a reformer candidly termed "Houses of Terror."

Thus did the emergence of a market-oriented system grind into being a "labor force," and though the process of adjustment for other classes of society was not so brutal, it, too, exacted its social price. Tenaciously the guildmasters fought against the invasion of their protected trades by manufacturers who trespassed on traditional preserves or who upset established modes of production with new machinery. Doggedly the landed nobility sought to protect their ancient privileges against the encroachment of the moneyed *nouveaux riches.*

Yet the process of economization, breaking down the established routines of the past, rearranging the power and prestige of all social classes, could not be stopped. Ruthlessly it pursued its historic course and impartially it distributed its historic rewards and sacrifices. Although stretched out over a long period, it was not an evolution but a slow revolution which overtook European economic society. Only when that society had run its long gauntlet, suffering one of the most wrenching dislocations of history, would the world of transactions appear "natural" and "normal" and the categories of "land," "labor," and "capital" became so matter-of-fact that it would be difficult to believe they had not always existed.

The Factors of Production

Yet, as we have seen, free, wage-earning, contractual labor, rentable, profit-producing land, and fluid, investment-seeking capital were not at all "natural" and "normal" but were *creations* of the great transformation of a pre-market into a market society. Economics calls these three creations the *factors of production,* and much of economics is concerned with analyzing the manner in which these three basic constituents of the productive process are combined by the market mechanism.

What we must realize at this stage of our inquiry, however, is that "land," "labor," and "capital" do not exist as eternal categories of *social* organization. Admittedly, they are categories of *nature,* but these eternal aspects of the productive process—the soil, human effort, and the artifacts which can be applied to production—do not take on, in every society, the specific separation which distinguishes them in a market society. In pre-market economies, land, labor, and capital are inextricably mixed and mingled in the figure of slave and serf, lord and guildmaster—none of whom enters the production process as the incarnation of a specific economic function offered for a price. The slave is not a "worker," the guildmaster is not a "capitalist," nor is the lord a "landlord." Only when a social system has evolved in which labor is sold, land is rented, capital is freely invested do we find the categories of economics emerging from the flux of life.

Modern economics thus describes the manner in which a certain kind of society, with a specific history of acculturation and institutional evolution, solves its economic problems. It may well be that in another era there will no longer be "land," "labor," and "capital": If, for example, a pure communist society ever evolves, the method by which the social product will be assured or distributed need not bear any more relation to our present system of wage payments or rental incomes or profit-shares than our own system bears to its feudal predecessor. In that case, "economics" as we know it will have to be revised to correspond to the new social relationships by which the production and distribution problems will be solved.

But the emergence of a market society, with its new factors of production, was not yet the only creation of the forces of change we have examined in this chapter. Along with the new relationships of man to man in the market place, there arose a new form of *social control* to take over the guidance of the economy from the former aegis of tradition and command.

The Preconditions of Market Operation

What was this new form of control? Essentially, it was a pattern of social behavior, of normal, everyday action which the new market environment imposed on society. And what was this pattern of behavior? In the language of the economist, it was the drive to maximize one's income (or to minimize one's expenditures) by concluding the best possible bargains on the market place. In ordinary language, it was the drive to buy cheap and sell dear.

The market society had not, of course, invented this drive. Perhaps it did not even intensify it. But it did make it a *ubiquitous* and *necessitous* aspect of social behavior. Although men may have *felt* acquisitive during the Middle Ages or antiquity, they did not, in fact, enter into market transactions for the basic economic activities of their livelihoods. And even if they did (when a peasant sold his few eggs at the town market), rarely was the transaction a matter of overriding importance for his continued existence. Market transactions in a fundamentally nonmarket society were thus a subsidiary activity, a means of supplementing a livelihood which, however sparse, was largely independent of buying or selling.

With the monetization of labor, land, and capital, however, transactions became *universal* and *critical* activities. Now everything was for sale, and the terms of transactions were anything but subsidiary to existence itself. To a man who sold his labor on a market, in a society which assumed no responsibility for his upkeep, the price at which he concluded his bargain was all-important. So it was with the landlord and the budding capitalist. For each of these a good bargain could spell riches—and a bad one, ruin. Thus the pattern of economic maximization was generalized throughout society and given an inherent urgency which made it a powerful force for shaping human behavior.

The new market society did more than merely bring about an environment in which men were forced to follow their economic self-interest. It brought into being at the same time a social environment in which men could be *controlled* in their economic activities. With the generalized drive to maximize income, it was now possible to direct the application of men's energies in various directions by raising or lowering the rewards offered for different tasks. If more effort was needed in the making of shoes, the market mechanism raised the rewards for land, labor, and capital employed in shoe manufacture. Or if society, operating through that market mechanism, wished to diminish the amount of social energy employed in making hats, it had but to lower the rewards—wages, rents, profits— of hat manufacture, and there would ensue an exodus of the factors of the production from hat-making toward other, more profitable fields. In the universalized presence of a drive toward income maximization, society possessed a powerful tool for *allocating its resources.*

Note, however, that this regulatory device required more than just the drive of self-interest. Equally necessary was a mobility of the factors of production. To the extent that labor was tied to its manorial estates or to its guild establishments, or that guildmasters were forbidden to expand their scales of operation or to venture into new endeavors, the control mechanism would not work. In that case, raising rewards for shoes or lowering rewards for hats could not bring about any substantial increase or decrease in the distribution of social effort.

An essential part of the evolution of the market society was thus not only the monetization of life but the mobilization of life—that is, the dissolution of those ties of place and station which were the very cement of feudal existence. And this essential requirement of mobility leads to a further point. Mobility meant that any job or activity was now open to all comers. Competition appeared. The traditional compartmented division of feudal labor had to give way to a universal rivalry among employments. No longer was each employment a protected haven for apprentice and guildmaster alike. Now any worker and any employer could be displaced from his task by a competitor who would do the job more cheaply.

The Workings of Competition

For those who *were* displaced, the institution of competition must have seemed a harsh and unjust one; but for society as a whole, it provided an essential safeguard. Having freed the drive for economic self-interest from the limitations of feudalism, society seemed in danger of being endlessly gouged by profiteering merchants or demanding workmen—the very fear of the medieval social philosopher.

What competition did, however, was to *contain* the economic drive. By pitting seller against seller, it made it impossible for any single participant to gain a strategic position for his own advantage. Even though every seller in a competitive market would *like* to charge monopolistic prices, the presence of a crowd of eager competitors at his elbow, each ready to steal away the lucrative business of the next by shading his price, assured society that ultimate selling prices would be no more than the minimum required to make continued production possible.

Competition not only prevented the seller from using his economic power to general social disadvantage, but it also assured a similar restraint on the buyer. No single purchaser could force prices below the cost of production, for other eager buyers would quickly outbid him. And this competitive mechanism worked not only in the market for commodities but in the market for factors, as well. Clearly, no laborer could ask for more than the "going" wage if he wanted to secure employment. But neither would he have to take less from any single wage-cutting employer, for he could always find better wages elsewhere.

Even if all employers in, say, the shoe trade paid lower wages than employers in the hat trade, again competition would provide the remedy. For labor would then leave the shoe trade for the hat trade, thereby bringing about a shortage of workers in the shoe plants and a surplus in hats. Wages would therefore rise in the shoe trade as manufacturers sought to bid labor back into their plants, and they would decline in hats.

And now we begin to see the complex nature of the price control mechanism provided by the competitive struggle. Across the market, buyer and seller faced one another in a contest wherein every buyer sought to pay as little as possible and every seller sought to gain as much as possible. But this was not merely a tug of war about the outcome of which one could say very little. On the contrary, because sellers were themselves engaged in a contest with one another, and because buyers were engaged in a similar contest, the outcome of the tug of war was quite predictable. While prices of goods might sway back and forth, the interaction of supply and demand operated to bring them always back toward *costs of production*.* And while incomes of factors in different employments might fluctuate temporarily upward or downward, again the competitive mechanism operated always to bring the rewards for similar tasks into a common alignment.

Only one final point remains to be noted. We have seen how a competitive market economy operated to fulfill the wants of society. But who was to say what its wants were?

In pre-market economies such a question does not pose subtle problems. The "wants" of such societies are either codified by ageless tradition or specifically formulated by its rulers. But in a market society, the specification of wants takes on a new dimension. It now consists of the demands of everyone who has the wherewithal to enter the market. The "wants" of society are thus expressed by millions of daily orders placed on the market by an entire community. As these orders enter the market place they affect the prices at which goods sell. Thus shifts in prices become, in effect, signals to producers, rising prices betokening an increase in demand and an actual or prospective increase in rewards; falling prices signaling the opposite.

In this way the market society catapults the consumer into a position of extraordinary importance. On his ability and willingness to buy hinges the schedule of demands which confront society's producers. If consumers do not want a good or service, or if they do not wish to buy it at its offered price, that good or service will go unsold. In that case, the production effort needed to supply it will not pay for itself and will soon terminate. *In a market society, the consumer is the ultimate formulator of the pattern of economic activity.* He is now the sovereign of the economic process—sovereign not as an individual, but as a member of an entire society which collectively guides and controls the on-going productive effort of society.

* These costs are necessarily very different, depending on whether a long or a short period of time is involved. A competitive price for fish on a particular day will depend on the size of the catch and the appetites of the customers at the dock, but in the long run it will adjust itself to the basic costs of fishing as a continuing industry and to the established tastes of consumers of food.

The Market Mechanism in Theory

It may help us if we stop for a moment and capsulize what we have learned:

1. The market mechanism provides a method of solving the production and distribution problems of society, with a minimum of recourse to tradition or command. It does so by utilizing the motive of economic self-interest, or maximization of income, in a society based on the monetization of tasks and the mobility of the factors of production.
2. The motive of self-interest serves to drive the factors of production into those employments where they will fare best. By raising or lowering rewards (wages or profits or rents), labor, capital, and land can be directed to whatever uses society desires.
3. In addition to the motive of self-interest, a market society depends for control on the institution of competition—that is, on the removal of the pre-market rigidities of social organization. Competition protects the consumer by driving prices down toward costs of production. It also tends to prevent rewards in one field from being out of line with rewards in another.
4. In a market society, the consumer exercises a final sovereignty in determining the goods which will be produced. It is his collective spending on the market place which gives the price signals that guide society's producers.

What we have just summarized is very far from a rigorous analysis of the "laws of the market." But it begins to give us a *theoretical* understanding of how the market system works. It tells us how a very "pure" market system—one in which there are no immobilities, no special privileges, no interferences from outside—imposes its social controls upon the economic process.

More than that, our analysis alerts us to the fact that without a grasp of theory we cannot fully comprehend the evolution of history itself, including that history going on under our very noses as daily life. Deprived of the elucidating tool of theory, economic reality is all detail and bewilderment. We cannot bring it into focus unless we have some way of reducing its endless variety of events into some kind of orderly *relationship*. Theory, and only theory, gives us this powerful insight. It sketches out for us an imaginary world in which the causal connections among things are highlighted in bold relief, thereby enabling us to look for and understand these causal relationships in the hurly-burly of actual life.

Does the market really work as this first introduction to theory suggests? Much of the rest of this book will be devoted to that very question—that is, to what extent the outcome of the market process in actuality corresponds with its outcome in a "pure" market system. But we are not yet ready to consider that problem. We have as yet traced the market only to its first half-formed appearance when the "theory" of a market was still far from formulated in men's minds. Let us therefore return to our historical narrative as the market system begins to evolve into capitalism itself.

The Market System and the Rise of Capitalism

The slow evolution of the market system cannot be considered merely as the rise of a new mechanism of social control. It must also be seen as the evolution of a new socio-economic organization of society, a new structure of law, of political organization, of social institutions, of ideas.

A market society could not coexist with a form of legal organization which, for example, did not recognize the freedom of the individual to contract for employment as he wished. Nor could it exist under a code of law which barely recognized "private property" as we know it. Neither could it flourish under a political system in which privilege accrued to birth rather than to achievement, or in which the landed nobility by law and usage possessed the main power to regulate society's affairs. Feudalism as a legal, political, and social organization had to give way to another form of society with a very different set of laws, customs, and political institutions.

We call that other form of society *capitalism,* and the long process of change which we have studied in its economic aspects can be given a wider interpretation as the evolution (and revolution) of feudalism into capitalism. The student of government notes the growth of political representation on the part of the middle classes, a growth culminating in the overthrow of feudal power in the French Revolution and its more gradual erosion in England. So, too, a student of law notes the rise of the law of contract, or the decline of the legal restrictions of serfdom or in the legal prerogatives of the aristocracy. Without a study of these changes, we cannot fully comprehend the manner in which capitalism arose from feudalism. Yet without an understanding of the deeper-seated economic changes which took place, so to speak, spontaneously and without conscious human intervention, the accompanying legal and political changes cannot themselves be understood.

Many of those necessary changes did not take place until the sixteenth and seventeenth centuries, or even later. After all, serfdom was not formally abolished in France until 1789, and in Germany until a half century later. Even by 1700, the market society had not yet reached a stage in which capitalism was a fully realized legal and political entity. Although "land," "labor," and "capital" had come into being; although a highly monetized society characterized France and England and Holland; although the merchant classes were strong and rich, these still lacked a final achievement of economic "freedom," a final throwing off of traditional bonds and restrictions on labor and capital, a final loosening of controls and commands from above. In England in the late 1700's, no master hatter could employ more than two apprentices, or no master cutler more than one, and these and similar guild regulations would not vanish until the medieval Statute of Artificers would be repealed in 1813. Likewise in France an immense web of regulations bound the would-be capitalist. Rules and edicts, many of them seeking to standardize production, laid down the exact number of threads to be woven into the cloths of the French textile manufacturers, and to disregard these laws was to risk pillorying—first for the cloth, then for the manufacturer.

By the mid-seventeenth century we find the great revolution of the market but half-complete—or rather, we find the underlying process of monetization and commercialization now contained uncomfortably within a frame of social organization not yet fully adapted to it.

We call this stage of pre-capitalism *mercantilism,* but we must not think of mercantilism solely as a time in which a nascent capitalism was held back by an outmoded social and economic order. On the contrary, it was also a time when the final achievement of capitalism was powerfully stimulated and accelerated. For the policies of mercantilism were devoted to building up national economic strength—in part by subsidy, in part by urging the rising manu-facturer to expand. In France, Colbert, finance minister to Louis XIV, told the butterfly court of Versailles that the greatness of the country depended on its wealth, its wealth on its work, and its work on the encouragement of those industrial, commercial, and agri-cultural producers who were, in the main, regarded with supercilious disdain. With this end in mind he struggled to encourage the rising bourgeoisie and to promote the interests of manufacture and com-merce in general.

He did so in a curiously self-defeating way, with a web of regula-tions, tariffs, and ordinances which suffocated the entrepreneurial impulse at the same time that it sought to foster it; and the social benefits of his economic policy were largely vitiated by the necessity to abide by a feudal system of taxation which was harsh, iniquitous, and corrupt. Yet, as in no previous period, the seeds for subsequent growth were deliberately sown all through the mercantile era: Frederick the Great complained in the margin of one of his edicts that his commoners had to be dragged to their profits "by their noses and ears."[9]

And one significant anomaly is also to be remarked. Despite the multiplicity of regulations which mercantilism imposed, it was also during these years—perhaps because of the very difficulties of regula-tion—that the idea of a totally free and unhampered market began to gain acceptance. The words "Laissez-faire, laissez passer" (Let manufacture, let circulation go unhindered) were first voiced by a French mercantilist official, weary of seeking to impose a bureau-cratic "orderliness" on the market. They would soon be the slogan of the new capitalist world.

A full-scale review of economic history must study European mercantilism at length, for it is a critical era of economic history, an era in which industrial growth was first launched as a deliberate act of national economic policy. Yet it was, so to speak, a position of unstable rest, not fully emancipated from the past, not fully entrant upon the future. The basic elements of capitalism had been created and waited for a full trial. That trial was soon to come, first in England, later throughout Europe and in the United States. We shall soon watch this major chapter of economic history unfold.

9 A. Lowe, *Economics and Sociology* (London: George Allen & Unwin, 1935), p. 23.

4

The Industrial Revolution

*H*eretofore, in our survey of economic history, we have concentrated attention almost entirely on two main currents of economic activity: agriculture and commerce. Yet there was, from earliest days, a third essential source of economic wealth—industry—which we have purposely let slip by unnoticed. For in contrast to agriculture and commerce, industrial manufacture did not leave a major imprint on economic society itself. As a peasant, a serf, a merchant, or a guildsman, the actors in the economic drama directly typified the basic activities of their times, but this would not have been true of someone in industry. Such a person as a "factory worker"—indeed, the very idea of an *industrial* "proletarian"—was singularly absent from the long years before the late seventeenth century.

Let us note as well that the "industrial capitalist" was also lacking. Most of the money makers of the past gained their fortunes by trading, or transporting, or lending—not by making. It is amusing—

more than amusing: instructive—to mark the best ways of getting rich enumerated by Leon Battista Alberti, a fifteenth-century architect, musician, and courtier. They are: (1) wholesale trade; (2) seeking for treasure trove; (3) ingratiating oneself with a rich man to become his heir; (4) usury; (5) the rental of pastures, horses and the like. A seventeenth-century commentator adds to this: royal service, soldiering, and alchemy. Manufacturing is conspicuously absent from both lists.[1]

Granted, in ancient Greece Demosthenes had a cabinet and an armor "factory"; and from long before his time, in ancient Egypt we even have the attendance record of workers in "factories" for the production of cloth. Yet it is clear that this form of production was far less important than either agriculture or commerce in shaping the economic texture of the times. For one thing, the typical scale of manufacture was small. Note that the very word "manufacture" (from the Latin *manus*, hand, and *facere*, to make) implies a system of hand, rather than machine, technology. Demonsthenes' enterprises, for example, employed no more than fifty men. It is true that from time to time we do come across quite large manufacturing operations; already in the second century A.D. a Roman brickworks employed forty-six foremen; and by the time we reach the seventeenth century, enterprises with several hundred workers are not unheard of. Yet such operations were the exception rather than the rule. In 1660, for instance, a steelmaker in France needed no more than three tons of pig iron a year for his output of swords, or sickle blades, or artistic cutlery. Similarly, most guild operations, as we have seen, were small. As late as 1843, a Prussian census showed only sixty-seven working people for every hundred masters.[2] Most "industry" was carried on, in the past, as it is carried on today in the East and Near East, in the backs of small shops or the dim cellar of a house; in a shed behind a bazaar or in the scattered homes of workers to whom materials would be supplied by an organizing "capitalist."

[1] Werner Sombart, *The Quintessence of Capitalism* (New York: E. P. Dutton & Co., Inc., 1915), pp. 34–35.

[2] *Cambridge Economic History of Europe*, II, p. 34; John U. Nef, *Cultural Foundations of Industrial Civilization* (New York: Harper & Brothers, Torchbooks, 1960), p. 131; R. H. Tawney, *Equality*, 4th ed. (London: Macmillan & Co., Ltd., 1952), p. 59.

The Pace of Technical Change

In addition to the smallness of the scale of industry, another aspect of the times delayed industrial manufacture from making known its social presence. This was the absence of any sustained interest in the development of an *industrial technology*. Throughout antiquity and the Middle Ages, little of society's creative energy was directed toward a systematic improvement of manufacturing techniques. It is indicative of the disinterest attached to productive technology that so simple and important an invention as the horsecollar had to await the Middle Ages for discovery:[3] the Egyptians, Greeks, and Romans, who were capable of a magnificent technology of architecture, were simply not fundamentally concerned with the techniques of everyday production itself. Even well into the Renaissance and Reformation, the idea of industrial technology hardly attracted serious thought. Leonardo da Vinci, for example, whose fecund mind played with inventions of the most varied kind, was primarily interested in machines for war or for amusement, and very few of the ideas that flowed from his designing pen had application to production itself.

There was good reason for this prevailing indifference: in the societies of the pre-market world, the necessary economic base for any large-scale industrial manufacture was totally lacking. In economies sustained by the labor of peasants, slaves, and serfs, economies in which the stream of money was small and the current of economic life, accidents of war and nature aside, relatively changeless from year to year, who could dream of a process in which avalanches of goods would be turned out? The very idea of industrial production on the large scale was inconceivable in an unmonetized, static society.*

For all these reasons, the pace of industrialization was slow. It is a question whether Europe in the year 1200 was significantly more technologically advanced than it had been in the year 200 b.c. The widespread use of waterpower in industry, for instance, did not appear until the fifteenth century, and it would be still another

---

[3] E. M. Jope, in *History of Technology*, eds. Charles J. Singer, *et al.* (New York: Oxford University Press, 1956), II, 553.

* Even today, one sees the difficulties of the unmonetized, static, underdeveloped societies in finding an *industrial*-minded, rather than *commercial*-minded, entrepreneurial group.

century before windmills provided a common means of tapping the energy of nature. The mechanical clock dates from the thirteenth century, but not for 200 years would significant improvements be made in instruments for navigation, surveying, or measuring. Movable type, that indispensable forerunner of mass communication, did not appear until 1450.

In short, despite important pockets of highly organized production, notably in the thirteenth century Flanders cloth industry and in Northern Italian towns, not until the mid-fifteenth century can we discern the first signs of a general groundswell of industrial technology, and even in that day it would have been impossible to foresee that one day industry would be the dominant form of productive organization. As a matter of fact, as late as the eighteenth century, when manufacturing had already begun to reach respectable proportions as a form of social endeavor, it was not generally thought of as inherently possessing any but secondary importance. Agriculture, of course, was the visible foundation of the nation itself. Trading was regarded as useful insofar as it brought a nation gold. But, at best, industry was seen as a handmaiden of the others, providing the trader with the goods to export, or serving the farmer as a secondary market for the products of the earth.*

What finally conspired to bring manufacturing into a position of overwhelming prominence?

It was a complex concatenation of events which finally brought about that eruption we call The Industrial Revolution. As with the Commercial Revolution and the Mercantile era which preceded it and formed its indispensable preparation, it is impossible in a few pages to do justice to the many currents which contributed to that final outburst of industrial technology. But if we cannot trace the process in detail, we can at least gain an idea of its impetus and of the main forces behind it if we turn now to England around 1750. Here, for the first time, industrial manufacture as a major form of economic activity began to work its immense social transformations. Let us observe the process as it took place.

* It was in the mid-eighteenth century that the French doctor François Quesnay propounded one of the first systematic explanations of economic production and distribution. It is noteworthy that in his system (called *Physiocracy*) only the farmer was regarded as a producer of net worth; and the manufacturer, while his utility was not ignored, was nonetheless relegated to the "sterile" (i.e., non-wealth-producing) classes.

England in 1750

Why did the Industrial Revolution originally take place in England and not on the continent? To answer the question we must look at the background factors which distinguished England from most other European nations in the eighteenth century.

The first of these factors was simply that England was relatively wealthy. In fact, a century of successful exploration, slave-trading, piracy, war, and commerce had made her the richest nation in the world. Even more important, her riches had accrued not merely to a few nobles, but to a large upper-middle stratum of commercial bourgeoisie. England was thus one of the first nations to develop, albeit on a small scale, a prime requisite of an industrial economy: a "mass" consumer market. As a result, a rising pressure of demand inspired a search for new techniques.*

Second, England was the scene of the most successful and thorough-going transformation of feudal society into commercial society. A succession of strong kings had effectively broken the power of the local nobility and had made England into a single unified state. As part of this process, we also find in England the strongest encouragement to the rising mercantile classes. Then too, as we have seen, the enclosure movement, which gained in tempo in the seventeenth and eighteenth centuries, expelled an army of laborers to man her new industrial establishments.

Third, England was the locus of a unique enthusiasm for science and engineering. The famous Royal Academy, of which Newton was an early president, was founded in 1660 and was the immediate source of much intellectual excitement. Indeed, a popular interest in gadgets, machines, and devices of all sorts soon became a mild national obsession: *Gentlemen's Magazine,* a kind of *New Yorker* of the period, announced in 1729 that it would henceforth keep its readers "abreast of every invention"—a task which the mounting flow of inventions soon rendered quite impossible. No less important was an enthusiasm of the British landed aristocracy for scientific farming: English landlords displayed an interest in matters of crop

---

* Very typically, the Society for the Encouragement of Arts and Manufactures (itself a significant child of the age) offered a prize for a machine that would spin six threads of cotton at one time, thus enabling the spinner to keep up with the technologically more advanced weaver. It was this which led, at least in part, to Arkwright's spinning jenny, of which we shall hear more shortly.

rotation and fertilizer which their French counterparts would have found quite beneath their dignity.

Then there were a host of other background causes, some as fortuitous as the immense resources of coal and iron ore on which the British sat; others as purposeful as the development of a national patent system which deliberately sought to stimulate and protect the act of invention itself. In many ways, England was "ready" for an Industrial Revolution. But perhaps what finally translated the potentiality into an actuality was the emergence of a group of new men who seized upon the latent opportunities of history as a vehicle for their own rise to fame and fortune.

The Rise of the New Men

One such, for instance, was John Wilkinson. The son of an old-fashioned small-scale iron producer, Wilkinson was a man possessed by the technological possibilities of his business. He invented a dozen things: a rolling mill and a steam lathe, a process for the manufacture of iron pipes, and a design for machining accurate cylinders. Typically, he decided that the old-fashioned leather bellows used in the making of iron itself were not efficient, and so he determined to make iron ones. "Everybody laughed at me," he later wrote. "I did it and applied the steam engine to blow them and they all cried: 'Who could have thought of it?' "[4]

He followed his success in production with a passion for application: everything must be made of iron: pipes, bridges, even ships. After a ship made of iron plates had been successfully launched, he wrote a friend: "It answers all my expectations, and has convinced the unbelievers, who were nine hundred and ninety nine in a thousand. It will be a nine-days wonder, and afterwards, a Columbus' egg."

But Wilkinson was only one of many. The most famous was, of course, James Watt, who, together with Matthew Boulton, formed the first company for the manufacture of steam engines. Watt was the son of an architect, shipbuilder, and maker of nautical instruments. At thirteen he was already making models of machines, and by young manhood he was an accomplished artisan. He planned to

[4] Paul Mantoux, *The Industrial Revolution in the Eighteenth Century*, 2nd ed. (New York: Harcourt, Brace & World, Inc., 1928), pp. 313 ff.

settle in Glasgow, but the guild of hammermen objected to his making mathematical instruments—the last remnants of feudalism thus
coming into an ironic personal conflict with the man who, more
than any other, would create *the* invention that would destroy guild
organization. At any rate, Watt found a haven at the university and
there, in 1764, had his attention turned to an early and very unsatisfactory steam engine invented by Newcomen. In his careful and
systematic way, Watt experimented with steam pressures, cylinder
designs, and valves, until by 1796 he had developed a truly radical
and (by the standards of those days) extraordinarily powerful and
efficient engine. Interestingly, Watt could never have done so well
with his engines had not Wilkinson perfected a manner of making
good piston-cylinder fits. Previously, cylinders and pistons were
made of wood and rapidly wore out. Typically, too, it was Wilkinson who bought the first steam engine to be used for purposes other
than pumping: it blew the famous iron bellows.

There was needed, however, more than Watt's skill. The new
engines had to be produced and sold, and the factory that made
them had to be financed and organized. Watt at first formed a partnership with John Roebuck, another iron magnate, but it shortly
failed. Thereafter luck came his way. Matthew Boulton, already a
wealthy and highly successful manufacturer of buttons and buckles,
took up Roebuck's contract with Watt, and the greatest combination
of technical skill and business acumen of the day was born.

Even then the firm did not prosper immediately. Expenses of development were high, and the new firm was not out of debt for twelve
years. Yet from the beginning, interest was high. By 1781 Boulton
was able to claim that the people of London, Birmingham, and
Manchester were all "steam mill mad"; and by 1786, when two
steam engines were harnessed to fifty pairs of millstones in the largest flour mill in the world, all of London came to see and marvel.

The steam engine was the greatest single invention, but by no
means the sole mainstay, of the Industrial Revolution. Hardly less
important were a group of textile inventions, of which the most
famous was Arkwright's jenny.

Arkwright's career is, in itself, interesting. A barber, he plied his
trade near the weaving districts of Manchester and so heard the cry-
ing need for a machine that would enable the cottage spinners to
keep up with the technically more advanced weavers. Good fortune

threw him into contact with a clockmaker named John Kay, whom he hired to perfect a machine that Kay had already begun with another employer-inventor. What happened thereafter is obscure: Kay left the business accused of theft and embezzlement, and Arkwright appeared as the "sole inventor" of a spinning jenny in 1769.

He now found two rich hosiers, Samuel Need and Jedediah Strutt, who agreed to set up business with him to produce jennies, and in 1771 the firm built its own spinning mill. It was an immense success; by 1779 it had several thousand spindles, more than 300 workmen, and ran night and day. Within not many years Arkwright had built an immense fortune for himself and founded an even more immense textile industry for England. "O reader," wrote Carlyle, looking back on his career, "what a historical phenomenon is that bag-cheeked, pot-bellied, much enduring, much inventing barber! . . . It was this man that had to give England the power of cotton."[5]

The Industrial Entrepreneur

It is interesting, as we watch the careers of these New Men to draw a few generalizations concerning them. For these were an entirely new class of economically important persons. Peter Onions, who invented the puddling process, was an obscure foreman; Arkwright was a barber, Benjamin Huntsman, the steel pioneer, was originally a maker of clocks; Maudslay, who invented the automatic screw machine, was a bright young mechanic at the Woolwich Arsenal. None of the great industrial pioneers came of noble lineage; and with few exceptions, such as Matthew Boulton, none even possessed money capital. In agriculture, the new revolutionary methods of scientific farming enjoyed aristocratic patronage and leadership, especially from the famous Sir Jethro Tull and Lord Townshend; but in industry, the lead went to men of humble origin and descent.

Let us note, therefore, that this required a social system flexible enough to permit the rise of such obscure "adventurers." It is not until we see the catalytic effect of unleashing and harnessing the energies of talented men in the lower and middle ranks of the social order that we begin to appreciate the immense liberating effect of the preceding economic and political revolutions. In the medieval hierarchy the meteoric careers of such new men would have been

[5] Mantoux, *op. cit.*, p. 225.

unthinkable. In addition, the new men were the product of the unique economic preparation of England itself. They were, of course, the beneficiaries of the rising demand and the technical inquisitiveness of the times. Beyond that, many of the small manufacturers were, themselves, former small proprietors who had been bought out during the late period of the enclosure movement and who determined to use their tiny capital in the promising area of manufacture.

Many of these new men made great sums of money. A few, like Boulton and Watt, were modest in their wants. Despite an iron-clad patent, they charged for their engines only the basic cost of the machine and installation plus one-third the saving in fuel which the customer got. Some, like Josiah Wedgwood, founder of the great china works, actually refused, on principle, to take out patents. But most of them did not display such fine sensibilities. Arkwright retired a multi-millionaire living in ostentatious splendor; Huntsman, Wilkinson, Samuel Walker (who began life as a nailsmith and stole the secret of cast steel)—all went on to roll up huge fortunes.* Indeed, Wilkinson's iron business became a minor industrial state with a credit stronger than many German and Italian principalities. It even coined its own money, and its copper and silver tokens (with a profile and legend of John Wilkinson, Ironmaster) were much in use between 1787 and 1808.

Beyond mere avarice, the manufacturers have been described by the economic historian, Paul Mantoux, as "tyrannical, hard, sometimes cruel: their passions and greeds were those of upstarts. They had the reputation of being heavy drinkers and of having little regard for the honour of their female employees. They were proud of their newly acquired wealth and lived in great style with footmen, carriages and gorgeous town and country houses."[6]

Pleasant or unpleasant, the personal characteristics fade beside one overriding quality. These were all men interested in expansion, in growth, in investment for investment's sake. All of them were identified with technological progress, and none of them disdained

---

* In contrast to the manufacturers, the inventors did not usually fare successfully. Many of them, who did not have Watt's good fortune in finding a Boulton, died poor and neglected, fruitlessly suing for stolen inventions, unpaid royalties, ignored claims.

6 Mantoux, *op. cit.*, p. 397.

the productive process. An employee of Maudslay's once remarked, "It was a pleasure to see him handle a tool of any kind, but he was *quite splendid* with an 18-inch file."[7] Watt was tireless in experimenting with his machines; Wedgwood stomped about his factory on his wooden leg scrawling, "This won't do for Jos. Wedgwood," wherever he saw evidence of careless work. Richard Arkwright was a bundle of ceaseless energy in promoting his interests, jouncing about England over execrable roads in a post chaise driven by four horses, pursuing his correspondence as he traveled.

"With us," wrote a French visitor to a calico works in 1788, "a man rich enough to set up and run a factory like this would not care to remain in a position which he would deem unworthy of his wealth."[8] This was an attitude entirely foreign to the rising English industrial capitalist. His work was its own dignity and reward; the wealth it brought was quite aside. Boswell, on being shown Watt and Boulton's great engine works at Soho, declared that he never forgot Boulton's expression as the latter declared, "I sell here, sir, what all the world desires to have—Power."[9]

The New Men were first and last *entrepreneurs*—enterprisers. They brought with them a new energy, as restless as it proved to be inexhaustible. In an economic, if not a political, sense, they deserve the epithet "revolutionaries," for the change they ushered in was nothing short of total, sweeping, and irreversible.

Industrial and Social Repercussions

The first and most striking element of that change was a sharp rise in the output of the newly industrialized industries. The import of raw cotton for spinning weighed 1,000,000 pounds in 1701; 3 million pounds in 1750; 5 million in 1781. That was a respectable rate of increase. But then came the sudden burst in textile technology. By 1784 the figure was over 11 million pounds; by 1789 it was three times greater yet, and still it grew: to 43 million pounds in 1799; 56 million in 1800; 60 million in 1802. In a century, cloth production had grown 3000 per cent![10]

[7] Lewis Mumford, *Technics and Civilization* (New York: Harcourt, Brace & World, Inc., 1934), p. 210.

[8] Mantoux, *op. cit.*, p. 404.

[9] H. R. Fox Bourne, *English Merchants* (London: 1866), p. 119.

[10] Mantoux, *op. cit.*, p. 258.

So was it with much else where the new technology penetrated. The output of coal increased tenfold in forty years; that of pig iron leaped from 68,000 tons in 1788 to 1,347,000 tons in 1839.[11]

The first impact of the Industrial Revolution was an immense quickening of the pace of production in the new industrial sector of the economy, an effect which we find repeated in every nation which goes through an "industrial revolution." In France, for example, the impact of industrial techniques did not make its influence felt until about 1815: between that date and 1845, the French output of pig iron grew fivefold; her coal production, sevenfold; her rate of importation, tenfold.[12]

The Industrial Revolution, itself, did not immediately exert a comparable leverage on the *over-all* increase of output. The industrial sector, to begin with, was small; and the phenomenal rates of increase in those industries where its leverage was first and most fruitfully applied were by no means mirrored in every industry. What is of crucial importance, however, is that the Industrial Revolution ushered in the technology by which large-scale, sustained growth was eventually to take place. This is a process into which we must look more carefully at the end of this chapter.

But first we must pay heed to another immediate and visible result of the English Industrial Revolution itself. We can characterize it as the transformation of an essentially commercial and agricultural society into one in which industrial manufacture became the dominant mode of organizing economic life. To put it more concretely, the Industrial Revolution was characterized by *the rise of the factory to the center of social as well as economic life.* After 1850, the factory was the key economic institution of England, the economic institution which shaped its politics, its social problems, the character of daily life—just as decisively as the manor or the guild had done a few centuries earlier.

It is difficult for us today to realize the pace of change or the quality of change which this rise of factory work brought about. Until the mid-eighteenth century, Glasgow, Newcastle, and the Rhondda Valley were mostly waste or farm land, and Manchester in

---

[11] J. L. and B. Hammond, *The Rise of Modern Industry* (New York: Harcourt, Brace & World, Inc., 1937), p. 160.

[12] A. Dunham, *The Industrial Revolution in France, 1815–48* (New York: 1955), p. 432.

1727 was described by Daniel Defoe as "a mere village." Forty years later there were a hundred integrated mills and a whole cluster of machine plants, forges, leather and chemical works in the area. A modern industrial city had been created.

Already by the 1780's the shape of the new environment was visible. A French minerologist visiting England in 1784 wrote:

[The] creaking, the piercing noise of the pulleys, the continuous sound of hammering, the ceaseless energy of the men keeping all this machinery in motion, presented a sight as interesting as it was new. . . . The night is so filled with fire and light that when from a distance we see, here a glowing mass of coal, there darting flames leaping from the blast furnaces, when we hear the heavy hammers striking the echoing anvils and the shrill whistling of the air pumps, we do not know whether we are looking at a volcano in eruption or have been miraculously transported to Vulcan's cave. . . .[13]

The factory provided not merely a new landscape but a new and far-from-congenial social habitat. In our day, we have become so used to urban-industrial life that we forget what a wrench is the transition from farm to city. For the peasant, this transfer requires a drastic adjustment. No longer does he work at his own pace, but at the pace of a machine. No longer are slack seasons determined by the weather, but by the state of the market. No longer is the land, however miserable its crop, an eternal source of sustenance close at hand, but only the packed and sterile earth of the industrial site.

It is little wonder that the English laborer, still more used to rural than urban ways, feared and hated the advent of the machine. Throughout the early years of the Industrial Revolution workmen literally attacked the invading army of machinery, burned and wrecked factories. During the late eighteenth century, for instance, when the first textile mills were built, whole hamlets rose in revolt rather than work in the mills. Headed by a mythical General Ludd, the Luddites constituted a fierce but fruitless opposition to industrialism. In 1813, in a mass trial which ended in many hangings and transportations, the movement came to an end.*

---

[13] Mantoux, *op. cit.*, p. 313.

* Even in our day, however, we use the word "Luddite" to describe an attempt to "fight back" at the threat of machinery.

Distasteful as was the advent of the factory itself, even more distasteful were the conditions within it. Child labor, for instance, was commonplace and sometimes began at age four; hours of work were generally dawn to dusk; abuses of every kind were all too frequent. A Committee of Parliament appointed in 1832 to look into conditions gives this testimony from a factory overseer.

Q. At what time in the morning, in the brisk time, did these girls go to the mills?

A. In the brisk time, for about six weeks, they have gone at three o'clock in the morning and ended at ten or nearly half past at night.

Q. What intervals were allowed for rest and refreshment during those nineteen hours of labour?

A. Breakfast a quarter of an hour, and dinner half an hour, and drinking a quarter of an hour.

Q. Was any of that time taken up in cleaning the machinery?

A. They generally had to do what they call dry down; sometimes this took the whole time at breakfast or drinking.

Q. Had you not great difficulty in awakening your children to the excessive labour?

A. Yes, in the early time we had to take them up asleep and shake them.

Q. Had any of them any accident in consequence of this labour?

A. Yes, my eldest daughter . . . the cog caught her forefinger nail and screwed it off below the knuckle.

Q. Has she lost that finger?

A. It is cut off at the second joint.

Q. Were her wages paid during that time?

A. As soon as the accident happened the wages were totally stopped.[14]

It was a grim age. The long hours of work, the general dirt and clangor of the factories, the lack of even the most elementary safety

[14] Tawney, Bland and Brown, *English Economic History, Selected Documents* (London: George Bell & Sons, Ltd., 1914), p. 510.

precautions, all combined to give early industrial capitalism a reputation from which, in the minds of many people of the world, it has
never recovered. Worse yet were the slums to which the majority of
workers returned after their travail. A government commissioner
reports on one such workers' quarter in Glasgow called "the wynds."

The wynds comprise a fluctuating population of from 15,000 to 30,000
persons. This quarter consists of a labyrinth of lanes, out of which number-
less entrances lead into small square courts, each with a dunghill reeking
in the centre. . . . In some of these lodging-rooms (visited at night), we
found a whole lair of human beings littered along the floor, sometimes
fifteen and twenty, some clothed and some naked; men, women, and
children huddled promiscuously together. Their bed consisted of musty
straw intermixed with rags. There was generally little or no furniture in
these places; the sole article of comfort was a fire. Thieving and prostitu-
tion constitute the main sources of revenue of this population.[15]

Early Capitalism and Social Justice

Without question, the times were marked by tremendous social
suffering. But it is well, in looking back on the birth years of industrial capitalism, to bear several facts in mind:

1. *It is doubtful if the poverty represented a deterioration in life
for the masses in general.* In at least some sections of England, industrialism brought immediate benefits. Wedgwood (an exception-
ally good employer, it is true) used to tell his employees to ask their
parents for a description of the country as *they* first knew it and to
compare their present state. So, too, the twelve-hour day in Arkwright's mills was a two-hour *improvement* over previous Manchester standards. Furthermore, the existing poverty was not by any
means new. As we know from Hogarth's etchings, long before the
Industrial Revolution, "Gin Lane" already sported its pitiful types.
As one reformer of the mid-nineteenth century wrote, those whose
sensibilities were revolted by the sight of suffering factory children
thought "how much more delightful would have been the gambol
of free limbs on the hillside; the sight of the green mead with its
spangles of buttercups and daisies; the song of the bird and the hum-
ming of the bee . . . [but] we have seen children perishing from

15 William Johnston, *England As It Is* (London: 1851), pp. 81–82.

sheer hunger in the mud hovel or in the ditch by the wayside."[16]

2. *Much of the harsh criticism to which early industrial capitalism was subjected derived not so much from its economic but from its political accompaniments.* For coincident with the rise of capitalism, and indeed contributory to it, was a deepseated change in the vantage point of political criticism. New ideas of democracy, of social justice, of the "rights" of the individual charged the times with a critical temper of mind before which *any* economic system would have suffered censure.

To be sure, the political movements by which capitalism was carried to its heights were not working-class movements, but middle-class, bourgeois movements: the rising manufacturers in England and France had little "social conscience" beyond a concern for their own rights and privileges. But the movement of political liberalism which they set into motion had a momentum beyond the narrow limits for which it was intended. By the first quarter of the nineteenth century, the conditions of the working classes, now so exposed to public view in the new factory-slum environment, had begun to curry public sympathy.

Thus, one of the unexpected consequences of the Industrial Revolution was a sharp reorientation of political ideas. In the creation of an industrial working class and an industrial environment, the Revolution bequeathed a new economic framework to politics. Karl Marx and Friedrich Engels were to write in 1848 that "all history" was the history of class struggle, but never did that struggle emerge so nakedly into the open as after the industrial environment had been brought into being.

Equally important was that the rise of political liberalism not only roused feelings of hostility toward the prevailing order, but initiated the slow process of amelioration. *From the outset, a reform movement coincided with capitalism.* In 1802, pauper apprentices were finally limited to a twelve-hour day and barred from night work. In 1819, the employment of children under nine was prohibited in cotton mills; in 1833, a 48- to 69-hour week was decreed for workers under eighteen (who comprised about 75 per cent of all cotton mill workers), and a system of government inspection of factories

[16] Friedrich Hayek, ed., *Capitalism and the Historians* (Chicago: University of Chicago Press, 1954), p. 180.

was inaugurated; in 1842, children under ten were barred from the coal mines; in 1847 a 10-hour daily limit (later raised to 10½) was set for children and women.

The nature of the reforms is, itself, eloquent testimony to the conditions of the times, and the fact that the reforms were bitterly opposed and often observed in the breech is testimony to the prevailing spirit. Yet capitalism, unlike feudalism, was from the beginning subject to the corrective force of democracy. Karl Marx, drawing on the material of his times, drew a mordant picture of the capitalist process in all its economic squalor, but he overlooked (or shrugged off) this countervailing force whose power was steadily to grow.

3. The most important effect of the Industrial Revolution we have left for last: *This was its long-term leverage on economic well-being.* The ultimate impact of the Industrial Revolution was to usher in a rise of living standards on a mass scale unlike anything that the world had ever known before.

This did not happen overnight. In 1840, according to the calculations of Arnold Toynbee, Sr., the wage of an ordinary laborer came to eight shillings a week, which were six shillings less than he needed to buy the bare necessities of life.[17] He made up the deficit by sending his children or his wife, or both, to work in the mills. If, as we have noted, some sections of the working class gained from the early impact of industrialization, others suffered a *decline* from the standard of living enjoyed in 1795 or thereabouts. A Committee of Parliament in the 1830's, for example, discovered that a hand-weaver at that earlier date could have bought more than three times as many provisions with his wages as at the later date. Although not every trade suffered equally, the first flush of the Industrial Revolution brought its hardships to bear full force, while its benefits were not as immediately noticeable.

By 1870, however, the long-run effects of the Industrial Revolution were beginning to make themselves felt. The price of necessaries had by then risen to fifteen shillings, but weekly earnings had crept up to meet and even exceed that sum. Hours were shorter, too. At the Jarrow Shipyards and the New Castle Chemical Works, the workweek had fallen from 61 to 54 hours; and even in the notoriously long-worked textile mills, the stint was down to "only" 57

[17] *The Industrial Revolution* (Boston: Beacon Press, Inc., 1956), p. 113.

hours. It was still a far cry from an abundant society, much less an "affluent" one, but the corner had been turned.

THE INDUSTRIAL REVOLUTION IN THE PERSPECTIVE OF THEORY

We have reviewed very briefly the salient historic features of the rise of industrial capitalism. Now we must reflect back on the great economic and social changes we have witnessed and ask a pertinent economic question: *How did the process of industrialization raise material well-being?* To answer the question, we must leave for a while the study of economic history, and return to economic theory, to elucidate systematically what we have thus far described, but have not yet analyzed for a full understanding.

Let us begin by asking what is necessary for a rise in the economic well-being of a society. The answer is not difficult. If we are to enjoy a greater material well-being, generally speaking, we must produce more. This is particularly true when we begin at the stage of scarcely-better-than-subsistence which characterized so much of Europe before the Industrial Revolution. For such a society to raise the standard of living of its masses, the first necessity is unquestionably higher production. Despite all the inequities of distribution which attended the society of serf and lord, capitalist and child-employee, underlying the meanness of the times was one over-riding reality: this was scarcity. There was simply not enough to go around, and if somewhat less lopsided distributive arrangements might have lessened the *moral* indignity of the times, they would not have contributed much to a massive improvement in basic economic well-being. Even assuming that the wage of the city laborer and the income of the peasant could have been doubled had the rich been deprived of their share—and this is an extravagant assumption—still, the characteristic of rural and urban life would have been its poverty.

We must add only one important qualification to this emphasis on increased output as the prerequisite of economic improvement. It will not help over-all living standards if a country produces more while its population is growing even faster than its increased output. The production of goods and services must rise *faster* than population if individual well-being is to improve.

How does a society raise its *per capita* output?

The Industrial Revolution gives us our clue. *The key to higher output lies in enhancing the human energies of the community with the leverage of industrial capital.* Our analytic understanding of growth must begin by looking further into this extraordinary power which capital possesses.

Capital and Productivity

We have already frequently used the word "capital," but we have not yet defined it. We can see that in a fundamental sense, capital consists of anything which can enhance man's power to perform economically useful work. An unshaped stone is capital to the cave man who can use it as a hunting implement. A hoe is capital to a peasant; a road system is capital to the inhabitants of a modern industrial society. Knowledge is capital, too—indeed, perhaps the most precious part of society's stock of capital.

When economists talk of capital, however, they usually confine their meaning to *capital goods*—the stock of tools, equipment, machines, and buildings which society produces in order to expedite the production process.* All these capital goods have one effect in common on the productive process: they all operate to make human labor more productive. They make it possible for a worker to produce more goods in an hour (or a week, or a year) than he could produce without the aid of that capital. Capital is therefore a method of raising per capita *productivity,* which is an individual's output in a given span of time. For example, in a forty-hour week a typical modern worker using power-driven mechanical equipment can physically outproduce three men working seventy hours a week with the simpler tools of a half century ago. To put it differently, in one day a modern worker will turn out as much output as his counterpart of 1900 in a full week—not because the modern worker works harder, but because he has at his command thousands of dollars

* Is money capital? It certainly is to the individual who possesses it. But it is not capital for society as a whole. For money only represents *claims* to society's real wealth, which is its goods and services. If an individual's money disappears, he loses his claim on those goods and services, and we can indeed say that he has lost his "capital." But if *all* money disappeared, we could not say that society had lost its claim on its own wealth. It would only have to devise another system of tickets.

worth of capital equipment rather than the few hundred dollars worth available to a worker in 1900.

Why does capital make labor so much more productive?

The most important reason is that capital goods enable man to use principles and devices such as the lever and the wheel, heat and cold, combustion and expansion in ways that the unaided body cannot. Capital gives men mechanical and physico-chemical powers of literally trans-human dimensions. They magnify enormously his muscular strength; they refine his powers of control; they endow him with endurance and resilience far beyond those of the flesh and bone. In using capital, man utilizes the natural world as a supplement to his own feeble capacities.

Another reason for the augmentation of production lies in the fact that capital facilitates the *specialization of man's labor*. A team of men working together, each man tending to one job alone in which he is expert, can usually outproduce the same number of men, each of whom does a variety of jobs. The prime example is, of course, the auto production line in which a thousand men cooperate to produce an immensely larger output of cars than could be achieved if each man built a car by himself. Auto assembly lines, of course, use prodigious quantities of capital in the overhead conveyor belts, the inventories of parts on hand, the huge factory with its power system, and so on. And while not all specialization of labor depends on capital, capital is usually necessary for the large-scale industrial operations in which specialization becomes most effective.

In our next chapter we will return to these important matters in the context of the development of modern industry. In this chapter, while we are discussing the basic question of the rise of industry itself, there is a still more fundamental problem to be disposed of. This is the question of how capital is made in the first place, of how a society generates the capital equipment it needs in order to grow.

A Model Economy

In a rich, already industrialized economy such as our own, the capital building process seems to present few conceptual problems: we just use our industrial equipment to make more industrial equipment. If we ask the question of a *poor* society, however, a society in which 70 or 80 per cent of the people work the soil to produce a

Thus we see how inextricably linked are the acts of saving and investment: saving is the releasing of resources from consumption; investment is the employment of these resources in making capital. Indeed, from society's point of view, saving and investment are only two sides of the same coin. Why do we then separate them in economic discourse? The reason is that different people may perform the saving and investing functions. Those who release the resources may not be (and, in fact, usually are not) the same individuals as those who gather up those resources for investment purposes. But we can also see that every act of investment requires the presence of released resources.*

This does not mean that investment necessarily entails a *diminution* of consumption. A rich society does not feel its normal, recurrent saving as a "pinch" on its spending. A society with unemployed factors can put its idle resources to work building capital without diminishing its expenditure on consumption. (It is still saving, of course, insofar as it is not using those newly employed resources to make consumption goods.) But—and this is a crucial point—when a *fully employed* society builds more capital, it *must* curtail its consumption. In this case, there is nowhere whence the needed capital-building resources can come but from their erstwhile consumption employments.

We can see this situation very clearly in our model economy. As we shift resources into the expanding capital sector, we must necessarily take them away from the consumption sector. As farmers leave the fields to man the new hoe-and-spade machines, food production will fall until the new spades and hoes are actually produced. We have had to enforce a *reduction* in living standards in order to mount the investment effort by which, in time, standards will exceed their former level.

Let us go on still further. We can now see that the *rate* at which our model economy can invest—that is, the size of the yearly addition it can make to its spade-building sector—depends on its capacity to save. If its living standards are already close to the margin of existence, it will not be able to transfer much labor from consumption-effort to capital-building effort. However badly it may wish for more tools, however productive those tools would prove to be, it cannot

---

* Note, however, that an act of saving—i.e., an abstention from consumption—does not *automatically* bring about an act of purposive investment. This leads to serious problems to which we shall turn in Chapter 6.

invest beyond the point at which its remaining consumption activity would no longer be adequate to maintain subsistence. At the other extreme, if a society is well-to-do, it may be able to abstain from a great deal of current consumption effort to provide for the future. Accordingly, its growth will be fast. *It is a hard economic reality that the amount of construction for the future can never exceed the amount of resources and effort which are unused or which can be released from consumption in the present.*

Growth in Early Capitalism

This seems to imply that the process of economic growth must perforce be very slow for a poor economy. And indeed, in Chapter 7, when we study the plight of the underdeveloped countries today, we shall discover this to be true. How then did England manage to bring about so rapid an increase in its stock of industrial capital beginning in 1750?

The answer is a complex one and illustrates very well the "distance" between theory and actuality. England, in 1750, resembled our model economy only to some degree, and the exceptions proved of major importance. For one thing, England *had* unemployed resources and therefore did not face a squeeze so drastic as the one we imposed on our imaginary society. For another, the scientific revolution in agriculture enabled England to maintain and even to raise its output of food, despite (and also because of) the exodus of its dispossessed peasants from the lands. But most important of all was the fact of the Industrial Revolution itself. All during England's early capital building period, new inventions were raising the output of its capital-building sector and in particular of its fast-growing machine-tool sector. England did not start from the impoverished and barely self-sustaining level of our model, but from a much more advanced level from which rapid additions to its capital stock were possible.

Yet England experienced difficulties enough in launching its Great Transformation. And as we can now see, many of these difficulties were the direct consequences of the problems which our model highlighted for us. The industrialization process of the eighteenth and nineteenth centuries did, indeed, necessitate a vast amount of saving —that is, of the releasing of consumption—and much of the social hardship of the time can be traced to this source.

For who did the saving? Who abstained from consumption? The manufacturers, themselves (for all their ostentatious ways) were among those who plowed back a substantial portion of their profits into more investment. Yet the real savers were not the manufacturers so much as another class—the industrial workers. Here, in the low level of industrial wages, the great sacrifice was made—not voluntarily, by any matter of means, but made just the same. From the resources they could have consumed was built the industrial foundation for the future.

We can also see something which is perhaps even more significant. This is the fact that England *had* to hold down the level of its working class consumption in order to free its productive effort for the accumulation of capital goods. In point of historic actuality, the "holding-down," was accomplished largely by the forces of the market place—with a liberal assist, to be sure, from the capitalists and from a government quick to oppose the demands of labor in the interests of its upper classes. But social inequities aside, the hard fact remains that had industrial wages risen very much, a vast demand for consumers goods would have turned the direction of the English economy away from capital-building, toward the satisfaction of current wants. This would certainly have redounded to some extent to the immediate welfare of the English worker. At the same time, however, it would have *postponed* the day when society's over-all productive powers were capable of generating an aggregate output of very large size.

This bitter choice must be confronted by every industrializing society. To assuage the needs of today or to build for tomorrow is *the* decision which a developing society must make. As we shall see in our final chapter, it is a decision which lies behind much of the political and economic agony of a large part of the world today.

Incentives for Growth

There remains but one last question. We have gained some insight into the mechanics of growth, but we have not yet answered the question: how are these mechanics brought about? How does society arrange the reallocation of its factors of production into the creation of the capital it needs?

This query brings us again to a consideration of our original division of economic societies into three types: traditional, command, and market. It also leads to some very important conclusions.

The first of these is obvious: it is that tradition-bound societies are not apt to grow. In such societies there is *no* direct social means of inducing the needed reallocation of factors. Worse yet, there are often strong social and religious barriers which create obstacles to the needed shifts in employment.

The situation is very different, however, when we turn to command societies. We have seen a striking use of command as the industrializing agency in modern times. In at least two countries, the Soviet Union and Communist China, command has been the mechanism for a genuinely startling leap from peasanthood into (or toward) industrialization.

In Chapter 7 we shall return to the Russian experience. Meanwhile, let us not forget that command was one of the principal ways by which Europe began its industrialization. In the state-directed establishment of shipyards and armories, the construction of royal palaces and estates, tapestry works and chinaware factories, a very important organizing impetus was given to the creation of an industrial sector in France and England. It is true, of course, that in those days, command was never so ruthlessly applied nor so widely directed as with the Communist states. But however much milder the dosage, the medicine was in essence the same: the *initial* transfer of labor from the traditional pursuits of the land to the new tasks of the factory depended on a commanding authority which ordered the new pattern into being.*

The Market as a Capital-Building Mechanism

But command was by no means the main agency for the final industrialization of the West. Rather, the organizing force which put men to work in making capital equipment was the market.

* As Barbara Ward has written in *India and the West:* "A developing society must at some point begin to save, even though it is still poor. This is the tough early stage of growth which Marx encountered in Victorian England and unfortunately took to be permanent. It is a difficult phase in any economy—so difficult that most societies got through it by *force majeure.* . . . No one asked the British laborers moving into the Manchester slums whether they wanted to save. . . . The Soviet workers who came to Sverdlovsk and Magnitogorsk from the primitive steppes had no say in the scale or the condition of their work. Nor have the Chinese in their communes today."

How did the market achieve this remarkable transformation? It achieved its purposes by the lure of monetary rewards. It was the hope of *profits* that lured manufacturers into turning out more capital goods. It was the attraction of better *wages* (or simply of *any* wages) that directed workers into the new plants. It was the signal of rising prices which encouraged, and falling prices which discouraged, the production of this or that particular capital good.

And what, we may next ask, opened the prospect of profits large enough to induce enterpreneurs to risk their savings in new capital goods? The answer brings us full circle to the focal point of this chapter. For the answer is to be found primarily in the body of technological advance which constituted the core of the Industrial Revolution.

Not that every new invention brought with it a fortune for its pioneering promoters, or that every new product found a market waiting for it. The path of technical advance is littered with inventions born "too soon" and with enterprises founded with great hopes and closed down six months later. But looking back over the vast process of capital accumulation which, beginning in the late eighteenth century, lifted first England and then America into the long flight of industrial development, there is little doubt that the impelling force was the succession of inventions and innovations which successively opened new aspects of nature to human control. Steam power, the cheap and efficient spinning and weaving of cloth, the first mass production of iron, and later steel—these were the great breakthroughs of industrial science that opened the way for the massive accumulation of capital. And once the great inventions had marked out the channel of advance, secondary improvements and subsidiary inventions took on an important supporting role. To the enterpriser with a cost-cutting innovation went the prize of a market advantage in costs and a correspondingly higher profit. More than that, once one pioneer in a field had gained a technical advantage, competition quickly forced everyone else in the field to catch up as quickly as they could. Most of the cost-cutting innovations involved adding machinery to the production process—and this in turn boosted the formation of capital.

Capitalism as a whole proved an unparalleled machine for the accumulation of capital. In its development we find the first economic system in history in which economic growth became an *integral* part of daily life. As Marx and Engels were to write in the *Communist Manifesto:* "The bourgeoisie, during its scarce one hundred years, has created more massive and more colossal productive forces than have all preceding generations together." And the compliment, all the more meaningful coming from the two arch-enemies of its social order, was true.

5

The Impact of Industrial Technology

*W*ith this chapter, we enter a new major period of economic history. Formerly we have dealt largely with the past, giving only an occasional glance to later echoes of the problems we have encountered. Commencing with this chapter, our focus turns toward and into the actual present. We have reached the stage of economic history whose nearest boundary is our own time. Simultaneously, our point of geographic focus shifts. As economic history enters the mid-nineteenth century, the dynamic center of events comes increasingly to be located in the United States. Not only do we now begin to enter the modern world, but the economic trends in which we will be interested take us directly into our own society.

What will be the theme of this chapter? Essentially it will be a continuation of a motif we began with the Industrial Revolution—the impact of technology on economic society. Looking back, we can see that the burst of inventions which marked "the" Revolution was not in any sense the completion of an historic event. Rather, it was merely the inception of a process of technological change which would continually accelerate down to the present time.

We can distinguish three or even four stages of this continuous process. The "first" Industrial Revolution was largely concentrated in new textile machinery, improved methods of coal production and iron manufacture, revolutionary agricultural techniques, and steam power. It was succeeded in the middle years of the nineteenth century by a "second" Industrial Revolution: a clustering of industrial inventions centering on steel, on railroad and steamship transportation, on agricultural machinery, and chemicals. By the early years of the twentieth century there was a third wave of inventions: electrical power, automobiles, the gasoline engine. In our own time there is a fourth: the revolution of electronics, air travel, automation, and, of course, nuclear energy.

It is difficult, perhaps impossible, to exaggerate the impact of this continuing industrial revolution. Now advancing rapidly, now slowly; now on a broad front, now on a narrow salient; now in the most practical of inventions, again in the purest of theoretical discoveries, the cumulative application of science and technology to the productive process was *the* great change of the nineteenth and twentieth centuries. The initial Industrial Revolution was thus in retrospect a kind of discontinuous leap in human history; a leap as important as that which had lifted the first pastoral settlements above the earlier hunting communities. We have already noted that in the factory the new technology brought a new working place for man, but its impact was vastly greater than that alone. The enormously heightened powers of transportation and communication, the far more effective means of wresting a crop from the soil, the hugely enhanced ability to apply power for lifting, hauling, shaping, binding, cutting—all this conspired to bring about a literal remaking of the human environment, and by no means an entirely benign one.

The Impact of One Invention

In this book we cannot do more than inquire into some of the economic consequences of the incursion of industrial technology into modern society, but it may help us gain some insight into the dimensions of that penetrative process if we follow for a short distance the repercussions of a single invention.

Let us therefore look in on the Paris Exposition of 1867, where curious visitors are gathered around an interesting exhibit: a small engine in which illuminating gas and air are introduced into a combustion chamber and ignited by a spark. The resulting explosion pushes a piston; the piston turns a wheel. There is but one working stroke in every four, and the machine requires a large flywheel to regularize its movement, but as the historian Allan Nevins writes, the effect of the machine "was comparable to the sudden snapping on of an electric globe in a room men had been trying to light with smoky candles."[1] It was the world's first internal combustion engine.

It was not long before the engine, invented by Dr. N. A. Otto of Germany, was a regular feature of the American landscape. Adapted to run on gasoline, a hitherto uninteresting by-product of kerosene manufacture, it was an ideal stationary power plant. Writes Nevins, "Soon every progressive farm, shop, and feed-mill had its one-cylinder engine chugging away, pumping water, sawing wood, grinding meal, and doing other small jobs."[2] by 1900 there were more than 18,500 internal combustion engines in the United States; and whereas the most powerful model in the Chicago World's Fair in 1893 was 35 horsepower, at the Paris Exposition seven years later it was 1,000 horsepower.

In itself the internal combustion engine was an extraordinary means of increasing and diffusing and making mobile a basic requirement of material progress: power. And soon the new engine opened the way for a yet more startling advance. In 1886, Charles E. Duryea of Chicopee, Massachusetts had already decided that the gasoline engine was a far more promising power source than steam for a self-propelling road vehicle. By 1892 he and his brother had produced the first gas-powered "automobile," a weak and fragile toy. The next model in 1893 was a better one, and by 1896 the Duryea brothers actually sold thirteen cars. In that same year, a thirty-two-

[1] *Ford, the Times, the Man, the Company* (New York: Charles Scribner's Sons, 1954), I, p. 96.

[2] *Study in Power, John D. Rockefeller* (New York: Charles Scribner's Sons, 1953), II, p. 109.

year-old mechanic called Henry Ford sold his first "quadricycle." The history of the automobile industry had begun.

Its growth was phenomenal. By 1905 there were 121 establishments making automobiles, and 10,000 wage earners were employed in the industry. By 1923 the number of plants had risen to 2,471, making the industry the largest in the country. In 1960 its annual payroll was as large as the national income of the United States in 1890. Not only that, but the automobile industry had become the single greatest customer for sheet steel, zinc, lead, rubber, leather. It was the buyer of one out of every three radios produced in the nation. It absorbed twenty-five billion pounds of chemicals a year. It was the second largest user of engineering talent in the country, bowing only to national defense. It was the source of one-sixth of all the patents issued in the nation and the object of one-tenth of all consumer spending in the country. In fact, it has been estimated that no less than one job out of every seven and one business out of every six owed their existences directly or indirectly to the car.

Even this impressive array of figures by no means exhausts the impact of the internal combustion engine and its vehicular mounting. Because of the existence of the car, some fifty thousand towns managed to flourish without rail or water connections, an erstwhile impossibility. Seven out of ten workers no longer lived within walking distance of their places of employment but drove to work. Of the nation's freight tonnage, 76 per cent no longer moved by rail but by truck. To an extraordinary extent, our entire economy was "mobilized"—which is to say, dependent for its very functioning on the existence of wheeled, self-propelled transportation. If by some strange occurrence our automotive fleet were put out of commission —say by a spontaneous change in the nature of the gasoline molecule, rending it incombustible—the effect would be as grave and as socially disastrous as a catastrophic famine in the Middle Ages.

The General Impact of Technology

We dwell on the impact of the car, not because it was the most significant of technological changes. Before the car, there had been the startling economic transformation of the train, and after it would come the no less totally transforming effects of electronic communication. Rather, we touch on the profound economic implications of the automobile to illustrate the diffuse effects of all in-dustrial technology—effects which economics often cannot measure and which exceed its normal area of study but which must, nonethe-less, be borne in mind as the ever-present and primary reality of the technological revolution itself. Let us mention a few of these general effects on the society in which we live.

The first has been a *vast increase in the degree of urbanization of society*. To an extraordinary extent (as we shall see in our next chapter) technology has enhanced the ability of the farmer to sup-port the nonfarmer. As a result, society has more and more taken on the aspects and problems of the city rather than the country. In 1790 only twenty-four towns and cities in all of the United States num-bered more than 2,500, and together they accounted for only 6 per cent of the population. By 1860 the 392 biggest cities held 20 per cent of the population; and by the late 1950's, 168 great metropolitan areas from Boston through Washington, D.C., along the eastern seaboard had become virtually one huge, loosely connected city with 60 per cent of the nation's people. Industrial technology has literally refashioned the human environment, bringing with it all the gains —and all the terrible problems—of city life on a mass scale.

Second, *the steady growth of industrial technology has radically lessened the degree of economic independence of the average citizen.* In our opening chapter we noted the extreme vulnerability of the "unsupported" inhabitant of a modern society, dependent on the work of a thousand others to sustain his own existence. This, too, we can now trace to the effect of the continuing industrial revolu-tion. Technology has not only moved men off the soil and into the city, but has vastly increased the specialized nature of work. Unlike the "man of all trades" of the early nineteenth century—the farmer who could perform so many of his necessary tasks himself—the typical factory worker or office worker is trained and employed to do only one small part of a social operation which now achieves stagger-ing complexity. Technology has vastly increased the degree of economic interdependence of the modern community and has made the solution of the economic problem hinge on the smooth coordi-nation of an ever-widening network of delicately connected activities.

Third, and stemming from these changes, *the expansion of in-dustrial technology has profoundly altered the kinds of skills de-manded of the economic population.* It is obvious that the inventory of skills we possessed in 1800 would never suffice to operate the social "machine" of 1960. But even in the much shorter time span since 1900, the required distribution of skills has significantly changed, as the table below shows.

OCCUPATIONAL DISTRIBUTION OF THE LABOR FORCE
1900–1960

	% of Labor Force	
	1900	1960
Managerial & Professional		
Professional & technical workers	4.1	11.8
Managers, officials & proprietors (nonfarm)	5.9	10.9
White Collar		
Clerical workers	3.1	14.9
Sales workers	4.8	6.5
Blue Collar		
Skilled workers & foremen	10.3	12.9
Semi-skilled workers	12.8	18.6
Unskilled workers	12.4	4.9
Household & other service workers	8.9	12.7
Farm		
Farmers and farm managers	20.0	4.2
Farm laborers	17.6	2.6

Source: 1900 figures calculated from *Historical Statistics of the United States,* Series D 72-122, p. 74; 1960 figures from *Stat. Abstract 1960,* p. 216. Totals do not add to 100% owing to rounding.

Note how different is our profile of occupations today from the not too distant past. We have already commented on the sharp drop in the number of people needed to feed the nation, but we can also see a shift within the "blue collar" group from unskilled to skilled and semi-skilled jobs, as more people labor with capital equipment than with their hands. In addition, as the sharp increase in the number of managers and clerical workers indicates, a swifter and more complex production process requires ever more people to coordinate and oversee the actual making of goods. In 1899 there was one "nonproduction" employee for every thirteen production workers; in 1954, one for every four. And finally we note that the sheer volume of production makes selling a much more important and complicated task and enforces a rise in the number of persons whose jobs are concerned with the distribution of goods rather than their output.

What we have seen by no means covers the over-all impact of technology on the structure—much less the operation—of our economic society, but it will serve as a useful backdrop against which to proceed. We shall return again to the general impact of technology. It is now time to look more deeply into its more immediate and specific manifestation—the startling increases in production which it made possible.

The Effect on Output

In our last chapter, we began an investigation into one of the most important problems in economics: the power of industrial capital to raise output. Now we must pursue the problem further by following the actual effect of the continuing industrial revolution on production. Let us begin by acquainting ourselves with some of the statistics of output in the United States over the past century.

The table on p. 108 gives us a first view of the trend. Here is the output record of an assortment of goods and services by twenty-year intervals over the last century.

A first glance cannot fail to be impressive: fivefold, tenfold, even thousandfold increases in output are visible in our table. Some items have latterly declined; note, for instance, the dip in coal production before the onslaughts of oil. But the main line of march is clear enough.

Yet, how representative are these items? Which of their many rates of increase should we take as reflecting the nation as a whole? Clearly, a larger sampling of the national output would soon involve us in a hopeless mass of statistics. A table comprising thousands of items would be necessary to give us a panorama of production, and the eye would fail before the task. If we want to grasp the over-all trend of national output, we must find a more convenient way of doing so. How shall we derive it?

Gross National Product

Perhaps we should begin by admitting that there is no fully satisfactory way of measuring economic growth in a dynamic economy. And for a very good reason: we are not measuring com-

PRODUCTION OF SELECTED COMMODITIES AND SERVICES IN THE UNITED STATES

(Year indicated or nearest available date)

	1860	1880	1900	1920	1940	1959
Corn (1,000 bu.)	838,793	1,706,673	2,661,978	3,070,604	2,457,146	4,361,170
Wheat (1,000 bu.)	173,105	502,257	599,315	843,277	814,646	1,128,151
Bituminous coal (1,000 tons)	9,057	50,757	212,316	568,667	460,772	410,446
Petroleum (1,000 bbls.)	500	26,286	63,621	442,929	1,353,214	2,574,590
Copper (short tons)	8,064	30,240	303,059	612,275	878,086	830,435
Cement (1,000 bbls.)	1,100	2,073	17,231	97,079	132,864	351,653
Steel capacity (1,000 tons)		(est.) 900	23,276	60,220	81,619	147,634
Paper and paperboard (1,000 tons)	n.a.*	n.a.	2,782	7,671	16,557	34,051
Number of nonfarm houses built (1 family or more)	n.a.	n.a.	189,000	247,000	602,600	1,379,000
Av. no. daily local telephone calls, Bell System (in thou.)		237	4,773	31,836	79,040	204,491
Pieces of mail handled (millions)	n.a.	3,747	7,130	23,055	27,749	61,247
Total horsepower, prime movers (1,000 h.p.)	13,763	26,314	65,045	453,450	2,759,018	7,143,723**

* Not available.
** 1955.
Source: *Historical Statistics of the United States; United States Statistical Abstract, 1960.*

parable things. Output not only grows but *changes;* new items appear, old ones disappear; quality, style, durability, all vary from year to year. At best, any measurement must be an approximation, a general guideline to the past.

For the reasons we have just given, economists use a different yardstick from the one above, a yardstick which concerns not just the tonnages and barrels and bushels of physical production, but the *values* of those outputs—that is, the actual amount of money for which the bushels, barrels, and tons of output were sold. We can imagine a gigantic cash register which rings up a sum every time a final good or service is sold in the economy. At the end of the year, the total on the cash register would tell us the total value of the final output of all kinds of goods and services in the nation. This sum is called *Gross National Product* (or GNP, as it is often abbreviated).

Note that we talk about sales of only *final* goods. This is because we do not want to double-count in measuring total output. For example, some wheat is sold to millers who process it into flour which is sold to bakers, who, in turn, bake it into bread for sale in a grocery store. If we counted the value of the sale of wheat, and then of the sale of flour, and then of the sale of bread, we should be counting the wheat and the flour more than once. Wheat and flour are products which enter into the final good, bread. Therefore, their value is already included when we simply take the value of bread. Most goods incorporate many such products bought in an earlier stage of production: a car, for instance, includes steel and rubber and upholstery, all of which were produced and sold to the automobile manufacturing company. Whatever they cost is included in the price the customer pays for a car.

The only way to be reasonably sure that we are not double-counting when we sum up the nation's production is to include the value of *final products* only.

What are these final products? Economists class them into four general categories:

1. *Consumption goods.* These are the goods and services bought by individuals for their private use and enjoyment. They include such items as food and clothing, doctors' bills, travel expenses, etc. They do not, however, include individuals' purchases of new houses.

2. *Gross domestic private investment.* This covers additions to our stock of real wealth. Here we find not only private purchases of houses, but commercial construction, business purchases of capital goods of all kinds, and additions to inventories.
3. *Net exports.* This category measures the value of goods and services produced here and sold abroad, less the value of goods and services produced abroad and sold here. In other words, it represents the net disposal of our production to foreign buyers.
4. *Government purchases.* Here we find that portion of our annual output which is bought by local, state or federal government: purchases and pay for the armed forces, school teachers' salaries, road construction, etc.

In our next chapter, we shall see that this division of GNP into main component parts serves a very useful function, for these categories of output often behave differently as the economy grows. For the moment, however, it is enough that we understand the basic make-up of GNP as a measuring stick for the over-all trend of output.

The Trend of Gross National Product

What does Gross National Product look like over the period we have been studying? The first line of figures in the next table gives us the value of our GNP over the twenty-year intervals of our previous scrutiny. Still, the figures do not give us much of a basis for comparison, since the *prices* in which GNP is toted up each year are not the same. Clearly, if prices are higher in one year than another, Gross National Product will be a bigger number, even though actual output in tonnage may not be larger at all. So in the second line of our table we also show the approximate relative value of the dollars of former years compared with those of 1960. In the last line of the table we have multiplied GNP in its original or current dollar values with this series of "corrected" dollar values. This gives us GNP in "constant" prices, or in "real terms"—that is, with price variations washed out. These are the comparative totals we are looking for.*

* A word of warning is in order about these figures. All attempts to convert the GNP of one period into an "equivalent" GNP of another period are made approximate, at best, because the different components of GNP often display different price movements. The "corrected" figures are useful and roughly indicative, but they should not be thought of as precise translations across the years.

GROSS NATIONAL PRODUCT IN CURRENT AND CONSTANT
PRICES SELECTED YEARS

	1880	*1900*	*1920*	*1940*	*1960*
Gross National Product measured in the prices at which it was actually bought[a] (billions)	$9.18	$17.3	$88.9	$100.6	$504.4
Approximate value of past dollars in terms of 1960[b]	3.27	3.89	1.53	2.24	1.00
Gross National Product measured in dollars of 1960 purchasing power (billions)	30.0	67.3	136.0	225.4	504.4

[a] *Historical Statistics,* Series F104 and F1. Figures for 1880 and 1900 are nearest 5-year averages.
[b] Computed from *Historical Statistics,* Series F5.

Now we are beginning to see the sweep of advance. If we look at the last line of the table above *we can see that GNP in real terms more or less doubled every twenty years.* Here is the basis for the huge advance in living standards which will be the main subject of our inquiry in our next chapter.

While we are still interested in the producing, rather than the consuming side of the question, let us proceed one step more. If we take the last line of our previous table and compare it with the number of people who produced that Gross National Product, we see still another highly significant fact illustrated by our next table.

GNP AND EMPLOYED WORKERS

	1880	*1900*	*1920*	*1940*	*1960*	*% increase* *1880/1960*
GNP in 1960 dollars (billions)	30.0	67.3	136.0	225.4	504.4	1681
Employed workers[a] (millions)	10.5	29.1	42.4	47.5	66.7	635

[a] *Historical Statistics,* 1880–1920, D36; 1940, D5; 1960, *Economic Indicators.*

Now the full impact of industrial technology on output begins to emerge. Not only did our real GNP increase nearly 17-fold over the period, but *total output rose more than two-and-a-half times as fast as our working force.* And even this does not yet state the case fully. In 1880, the average work week was seventy hours. Today it is forty hours. Our output per person *per hour* has risen almost twice as fast as our over-all employment figures indicate.

What we have here is the historical reality of a process to which we were introduced in our last chapter—the extraordinary increase in productivity which stems from industrialization. On this productivity, it must now be obvious, hangs the vast difference which divides the industrial nations of the West from the unindustrialized nations of the South and East or, for that matter, of the pre-Industrial Revolution West, itself. Not all of the profoundly revolutionary effect of the continuing industrial revolution was a consequence of its huge leverage on productivity, but without that leverage the surrounding changes would never have taken place.

Economies of Large-Scale Production

Thus far we have treated the rise in productivity and output mainly on a national scale. Yet the dynamics of growth were no less startling—and perhaps even more significant—when followed at the level of the individual industrial plant itself. For no small part of the burst in output which began in the 1860's and 1870's in America was the result of a new technique of production, a technique which would develop into, and finally be called, *mass production*.

The technological aspects of mass production are in themselves a subject of fascinating interest. Allan Nevins describes an early Ford assembly-line process.

Just how were the main assembly lines and lines of component production and supply kept in harmony? For the chassis alone, from 1000 to 4000 pieces of each component had to be furnished every day at just the right point and right minute; a single failure, and the whole mechanism would come to a jarring standstill. . . . Superintendents had to know every hour just how many components were being produced and how many were in stock. Whenever danger of shortage appeared, the shortage chaser—a familiar figure in all automobile factories—flung himself into the breach. Counters and checkers reported to him. Verifying in person any ominous news, he mobilized the foreman concerned to repair deficiencies. Three times a day he made typed reports in manifold to the factory clearinghouse, at the same time chalking on blackboards in the clearing house office a statement of results in each factory-production department and each assembling department.[3]

Such systematizing in itself resulted in astonishing increases in productivity. With each operation analyzed and subdivided into its simplest components, with a steady stream of work passing before stationary men, with a relentless but manageable pace of work, the total time required to assemble a car dropped astonishingly. Within a single year the time required to assemble a motor fell from 600 minutes to 226 minutes; to build a chassis, from 12 hours and 28 minutes to one hour and 33 minutes. A stop-watch man was told to observe a three-minute assembly in which men assembled rods and piston, a simple operation. The job was divided into three jobs, and half the men turned out the same output as before.[4]

But what interests us in the context of our study are not the technical achievements of mass production as much as its economic results. Mass production is not only a method of increasing productivity; it is a way of vastly reducing cost. Even though the costly equipment needed for mass production increases the over-all expenses of production, it increases output even faster, so that cost *per item* drops considerably.

Imagine, for instance, a small plant which turns out 1,000 items a day with the labor of ten men and a small amount of equipment. Suppose each man is paid $10, each item before manufacture costs 10¢, and the daily amount of "overhead"—that is, the daily share of costs such as rent, plant maintenance, office salaries, and wear-and-tear on equipment—comes to $100. Then our total daily cost of production is $300 per day ($100 of payroll, $100 of raw material cost, and $100 of overhead). Divided among 1,000 items of output, our cost per item is 30¢.

Now imagine that our product lends itself to mass production techniques. Our payroll may then jump to $1,000 and with our much larger plant and equipment, our daily overhead to $5,000. Nevertheless, mass production may have boosted output as much as 100 times. Then our total daily cost of production will be $16,000 ($1,000 of payroll, $5,000 of overhead, and $10,000 of raw material

3 *Ford, the Times, the Man, the Company,* I, p. 507.
4 *Ibid.,* pp. 504, 506.

costs). Divided among our 100,000 items of output, our cost per item has fallen to 16¢. Despite a quintupling of over-all expense, our cost per unit has almost halved.

This is not a far-fetched example of what economists call *the economies of large-scale production*. A glance at the following table shows how mass production techniques did, in fact, boost output of Ford cars by more than one hundred times while reducing their cost by seven-eighths.

Date	Unit sales of Ford cars	Price of typical model
1907–8	6,398	$2,800 (Model K) touring
1908–9	10,607	850 (Model T) touring
1909–10	18,664	950 "
1910–11	34,528	780 "
1911–12	78,440	690 "
1912–13	168,304	600 "
1913–14	248,307	550 "
1914–15	221,805 (10 mos.)	490 "
1915–16	472,350	440 "
1916–17	730,041	360 "

Compiled from Nevins, *Ford, the Times, the Man, the Company*, pp. 644, 646–647.

Nor do the dynamics of the industrial process come to a halt with these formidable economies of large-scale production. With this technological achievement comes as well a new factor of primary importance for the market system itself. That factor is *size*.

It is not difficult to see why. Once a firm—by virtue of adroit management, improved product, advantages of location, or whatever other reason—steps out decisively in front of its competitors in size, *the economies of large-scale production operate to push it out still further in front*. Bigger size means lower cost. Lower cost means bigger profits. Bigger profits mean the ability to grow to still larger size. Thus the techniques of large-scale manufacture bring about a situation which threatens to alter the whole meaning of competition. From a mechanism which prevents any single firm from dominating the market, competition now becomes a force which may drive an ever-larger share of the market into the hands of the largest and most efficient producer.

The Great Entrepreneurs

We shall have much more to say about the economics of the drive to bigness. Yet, it may be helpful if we look once again at the actual historic scene in which this internal growth took place. For the processes of economic change described in this chapter did not occur in a vacuum. They were brought about by a social "type" and a business milieu which powerfully accelerated and abetted the process of industrial enlargement, much as the "New Men" had speeded along the initial industrializing process in England in the late eighteenth century.

The agents of change during the late nineteenth century in America were very much the descendants of their industrial forebears a century earlier. Like Arkwright and Watt, many of the greatest American entrepreneurs were men of humble origin endowed with an indomitable drive for business success. There was Carnegie in steel, Harriman in railroads, Rockefeller in oil, Frick in coke, Armour and Swift in meat packing, McCormick in agricultural machinery—to mention but a few. To be sure, the *typical* businessman was very different from these Horatio Alger stereotypes of the business hero. Economic historians, such as F. W. Taussig, looking back over the careers of the business leaders of the late nineteenth century, have discovered that the average entrepreneur was not a poor, industrious immigrant lad, but the son of well-circumstanced people often in business affairs themselves. Nor was the average businessman nearly so successful as a Carnegie or a Rockefeller.

Yet in nearly every line of business, at least *one* "captain of industry" appeared who dominated the field by his personality and ability. Though few achieved their supreme degree of pecuniary success, the number who climbed into the "millionaire class" was impressive. In 1880 it had been estimated that there were 100 millionaires in the country. By 1916 the number had grown to 40,000.

Interesting and significant differences distinguish the nineteenth century business leaders from those of a century earlier. The captains of industry were not typically men whose leadership rested on inventive or engineering skills. With the growth of large-scale production, the engineering functions became the province of salaried production experts, of second-echelon plant managers. What was required now was the master touch in guiding industrial strategy, in making or breaking alliances, choosing salients for advance, or overseeing the logistics of the whole operation. More and more the great entrepreneurs were concerned with the strategy of finance, of competition, of sales, rather than with the cold technics of production itself.

Then, too, we must make note of the entrepreneurial tactics and tone of the period. In a phrase which has stuck, Matthew Josephson once called the great men of business in this era "the robber barons." In many ways, they did indeed resemble the predatory lords of the medieval era. For example, in the 1860's a small group of California entrepreneurs under the guiding hand of Collis Huntington performed the astonishing feat of building a railroad across the hitherto impassible Rockies and Sierras. Aware that Huntington and his associates would thereby have a monopolistic control of all rail traffic to California, the Congress authorized the construction of three competing lines. But the legislators had not taken the measure of the wily pioneers. Before their own line was completed, they secretly bought the charter of one competitive line; and when the second proved somewhat harder to buy out, they simply built it out, recklessly flinging their lines into its territory until it, too, was forced to surrender. Thereafter it was no great trick to buy out the third, having first blocked it at a critical mountain pass. Only one competitive source of transportation remained: the Pacific Mail Steamship Company. Fortunately, this was owned by the obliging Jay Gould, a famous robber baron in his own right; and for the payment of a proper tribute, he agreed to eliminate San Francisco as a cargo port. There was now *no* way of bringing goods across the nation into Southern California except those which the Huntington group controlled. Counting the smaller lines and subsidiaries which passed into their grasp, *nineteen* rail systems, in all, came under their domain. It was not surprising that to the residents of California the resulting unified system was known as "the Octopus" and that its average freight rate was the highest in the nation.

And it was not just the railroad industry that used economic power to create a monopoly position. In whisky and in sugar, in tobacco and cattlefeed, in wire nails, steel hoops, electrical appliar.ces, tin plate, in matches and meat there was an Octopus similar to that which fastened itself on California. One commentator of the late 1890's pictured the American citizen born to the profit of the Milk Trust and dying to that of the Coffin Trust.

If the robber barons milked the public as consumers (and to an even greater extent bilked them as stockholders), they also had no compunctions about cutting each other down to size. In the struggle for financial control of the Albany and Susquehanna Railroad, for instance, James Fisk and J. P. Morgan found themselves in the uncomfortable position of each owning a terminal at the end of a single line. Like their feudal prototypes, they resolved the controversy by combat, mounting locomotives at each end and running them full tilt into each other—after which the losers still did not give up, but retired, ripping up the line and tearing down trestles as they went. In similar spirit the Huntington group that built the Central Pacific hired General David Colton to run a subsidiary enterprise for them, and the General wrote to his employers:

I have learned one thing. We have got *no true* friends outside of us five. We cannot depend upon a human soul outside of ourselves, and hence we must all be good-natured, stick together, and keep to our own counsels.

Whereupon he proceeded to swindle his true friends out of several millions.*

THE CHANGE IN MARKET STRUCTURE

It is impossible to consider the period of history in which we are concerned without taking into account the social type of the robber baron and the milieu in which he operated. Bold, aggressive,

---

* With all this buccaneering went, as well, another identifying mark of the times: conspicuous consumption. Frederick Townsend Martin, a repentent member of the gilded set, has written in his memoirs of parties at which cigarettes were wrapped in money for the pleasure of inhaling wealth; of a dog presented with a $15,000 diamond collar; of an infant resting in a $10,000 cradle attended by four doctors who posted regular bulletins on its (excellent) health; of the parade of fabulous chateaux stuffed with fabulous works of art on New York's Fifth Avenue; and of the collection of impecunious European royalty as sons-in-law of the rich.

acquisitive, competitive, the great entrepreneur was a natural agent
to speed along a process for which the technology of the day prepared the way. Under the joint impact of his personal drive for
aggrandizement and the self-feeding potentialities of the burgeoning
economies of large-scale production, a profound change in market
structure swept over the country. In industry after industry there
was visible a dramatic concentration of production into a few large
business units rather than numerous small ones.

By 1900, the number of textile mills, although still large, had
dwindled by a third from the 1880's; the number of manufacturers
of agricultural implements had fallen by 60 per cent over the same
period, and the number of leather manufacturers by three quarters.
In the locomotive industry, two companies ruled the roost in 1900,
contrasted with nineteen in 1860. The biscuit and cracker industry
changed from a scatter of small companies to a market in which one
producer had 90 per cent of the industry's capacity by the turn of
the century. Meanwhile in steel there was the colossal U.S. Steel
Corporation, which alone turned out over half the steel production of the nation. In oil, the Standard Oil Company tied up between 80 to 90 per cent of the nation's output. In tobacco, the
American Tobacco Company controlled 75 per cent of the output of
cigarettes and 25 per cent of cigars. Similar control rested with the
American Sugar Company, the American Smelting and Refining
Company, the United Shoe Machinery Company, and dozens more.

From an over-all view, the change was even more impressive. In
the early 1800's, according to the calculations of Myron W. Watkins,
no single plant controlled as much as 10 per cent of the output of a
manufacturing industry. By 1904, seventy-eight enterprises controlled over half the output of their industries, fifty-seven controlled 60 per cent or more, and twenty-eight controlled 80 per cent
or more. From industry to industry this degree of "concentration"
varied—from no significant concentration at all in printing and
publishing, for instance, to the highly concentrated market structure
of industries like copper or rubber. But there was no mistaking the
over-all change. In 1896, railroads excepted, there were not a dozen
$10,000,000 companies in the nation. By 1904, there were over 300
of them with a combined capitalization of over $7,000,000,000.
Together these giants controlled over two-fifths of the industrial

capital of the nation and affected four-fifths of its important industries.[5]

Clearly something akin to a major revolution in market structure had taken place. Let us examine more closely the course of events which led up to it.

The Change in Competition

The initial impact of the trend to big business was an unexpected one. Rather than diminishing the degree of competitiveness of the market structure, it extended and intensified it. In the largely agricultural, handicraft, and small factory economy of the early nineteenth century, "the" market consisted mainly of small, localized markets, each insulated from the next by the high cost of transportation and each supplied by local producers who had neither the means nor the motivation to invade the market on anything resembling a national scale.

The rise of mass production radically changed this fragmented market structure and, with it, the type of competition within the market. As canals and railroads opened the country and as new manufacturing techniques vastly increased output, the parochial quality of the market system changed. More and more, one unified and interconnected market bound together the entire nation, and the petty semi-monopolies of local suppliers were invaded by products from large factories in distant cities.

Quickly, a second development followed. As the new production techniques gained momentum, aggressive businessmen typically not only built, but overbuilt. "As confident entrepreneurs raced to take advantage of every ephemeral rise in prices, of every advance in tariff schedules, of every new market opened by the railroads and puffed up immigration," write Thomas Cochran and William Miller in a history of these industrializing times, "they recklessly expanded and mechanized their plants, each seeking the greatest share of the new melon."[6]

The result was a phenomenal burst in output but, simultaneously,

---

[5] *Cf.* J. S. Bain, "Industrial Concentration and Anti-Trust Policy," in *The Growth of the American Economy*, 2nd ed., Harold Williamson, ed. (Englewood Cliffs, N.J.: Prentice-Hall, Inc., 1951), p. 619.

[6] *The Age of Enterprise* (New York: Harper Torchbooks, revised ed., 1961), p. 139.

a serious change in the nature of competition. Competition now became not only more extensive, but more *expensive*. As the size of the plant and the complexity of equipment grew, so did the "fixed charges" of a business enterprise—the interest on borrowed capital, the depreciation of capital assets, the cost of administrative staff, the rent of land, and "overhead," generally. These costs tended to remain fairly constant, regardless of whether sales were good or bad. Unlike the payment of wages to a working force, which dropped when men were fired, there was no easy way to cut down the steady drain of payments for these fixed expenditures. The result was that the bigger the business, the more vulnerable was its economic health when competition cut into its sales.

The ebullience of the age—plus the steady growth of a technology that *required* massive investments—made competition increasingly drastic. As growing giant businesses locked horns, railroad against railroad, steel mill against steel mill, each sought to assure the coverage of its fixed expenses by gaining for itself as much of the market as it could. The outcome was the steady growth of cutthroat competition among massive producers, replacing the more restricted, local competition of the small business, small market world. On the railroads, for example, constant rate-wars were fought in the 1870's. In the oil fields, the coal fields, among the steel and copper producers, similar price-wars repeatedly broke out as producers sought to capture the markets they needed to achieve a profitable level of production. All this was unquestionably favorable to the consumer, as indeed competitive situations always are, but it threatened literal bankruptcy for the competing enterprises themselves—bankruptcy on a multi-million dollar scale.

The Limitation of Competition

In these circumstances, it is not difficult to understand the next phase of economic development. The giants decided not to compete.

But how were they to avoid competition? Since common law made it illegal to sign a contract binding a competitor to fixed prices or production schedules, there seemed no alternative but voluntary cooperation: trade associations, "gentleman's agreements," or "pools," informal treaties to divide the market. By the 1880's there were a cordage pool and a whiskey pool, a coal pool, a salt pool, and endless rail pools, all calculated to relieve the individual producers from the mutually suicidal game of all-out competition. But to little avail. The division of the market worked well during good times; but when bad times approached, the pools broke down. As sales fell, the temptation to cut prices was irresistible, and thus began the old, ruinous game of competition all over again.

The robber baron ethics of the day contributed to the difficulties. "A starving man will usually get bread if it is to be had," said James J. Hill, a great railway magnate, "and a starving railway will not maintain rates."[7] Typically, at a meeting of rail heads called to agree upon a common freight schedule, the president of one road slipped out, during a brief recess, to wire the new rates to his road, so that it might be the first to undercut them. (By chance, his wire was intercepted, so that when the group next met it was forced to recognize that even among thieves there is not always honor.)

During the 1880's, a more effective device for control became available. In 1879, Samuel Dodd, lawyer for the new Standard Oil Company, had a brilliant idea for regulating the murderous competition that regularly wracked the oil industry. He devised the idea of a trust. Stockholders of companies that wished to join in the Standard Oil Trust were asked to surrender their actual shares to the board of directors of the new trust. Thereby they would give up working control over their companies, but in return they would get "trust certificates" which entitled them to the same share in the profits as their shares earned. In this way, the Standard Oil directors wielded control over all the associated companies, while the former stockholders shared fully in the profits.

In time, as we shall see, the trusts were declared to be illegal. But by then still more effective devices were discovered. One was the *merger*, the coming together of two corporations to form a new, bigger one. In manufacturing and mining, alone, there were forty-three mergers in 1895 (affecting $41 million dollars worth of corporate assets); twenty-six mergers in 1896, sixty-nine mergers in 1897; in 1898 there were 303—and *1,208 mergers combined some $2,263,000,000 corporate assets* in 1899.[8] Another great wave of mergers occurred in the 1920's. In all, from 1895 to 1929, some $20

---

[7] Cochran and Miller, *op. cit.*, p. 141.
[8] *Historical Statistics of the United States* (Washington, D.C.: U.S. Bureau of the Census), Series V, 30, 31.

billions of industrial corporate wealth were merged into larger units.

Another effective means of limiting competition was the *holding company*. In 1888, New Jersey passed a law permitting one corporation to buy stock in another; a few years later, it permitted a New Jersey corporation to do business anywhere. Thus the legal foundation was laid for a central corporation which could control subsidiary enterprises by the simple means of buying a controlling share of their stock. By 1911, when the Standard Oil combine was finally dissolved, Standard Oil of New Jersey had used this device to acquire direct control over seventy companies and indirect control over thirty more.

Yet we must not think that it was only the movement toward trustification and merger which brought about the emergence of the giant firm with its ability to limit—or eliminate—competition. Equally, perhaps more, important was simply the process of internal growth. Ford and General Motors, General Electric and A.T.&T., DuPont and Carnegie Steel (later the core of U.S. Steel) grew essentially because their market was expanding and they were quick, able, efficient, and aggressive enough to grow faster than any of their competitors. All of them gobbled up some small businesses along the way, and most of them benefited from agreements not to compete. But their gradual emergence to a position of dominance within their industries was not, in the last analysis, attributable to these facts. It was the dynamism of their own business leadership, coupled with a production technique which made enormous size both possible and profitable.

The Threat of Economic Feudalism

Certainly, size became enormous. By the end of the nineteenth century, some business units were already considerably larger than the states in which they were located. Charles William Eliot pointed out in 1888 that a single railway with headquarters in Boston not only employed three times as many people as the entire government of the Commonwealth of Massachusetts, but enjoyed gross receipts nearly six times that of the state government which had created it. By comparison with the findings of the Pujo Committee of the U.S. Senate, not quite twenty-five years later, the railway was still small. The committee pointed out that the Morgan banking interests held 341 directorships in 112 corporations whose aggregate wealth exceeded by three times the value of *all* the real and personal property of New England. And not only was the process of trustification eating away at the competitive structure of the market, but the emergence of enormous financially controlled empires posed as well a political problem of ominous portent. As Woodrow Wilson declared: "If monopoly persists, monopoly will always sit at the helm of government. I do not expect to see monopoly restrain itself. If there are men in this country big enough to own the government of the United States, they are going to own it."[9]

Not surprisingly, from many quarters the trend to bigness was vehemently opposed. From the 1880's on, a series of state laws strove to undo the trusts which squeezed their citizens. Louisiana sued the Cottonseed Oil Trust; New York, the Sugar Trust; Ohio, the Oil Trust—but to little avail. When one state, like New York, clamped down on its trusts, other states, seeing the revenue available from a change in corporate headquarters, virtually invited the trust to set up business there. When the Supreme Court ruled that corporations, as "persons," could not be deprived of property without "due process of law," state regulation became almost totally useless.

It was soon clear that if something further were to be done, the federal government would have to do it. "Congress alone can deal with the trusts," said Senator Sherman in 1890, "and if we are unwilling or unable, there will soon be a trust for every production and a master to fix the price for every necessity of life."[10]

The result was the Sherman Antitrust Act, an act which, on its surface, was an effective remedy for the problem. "Every contract, combination . . . or conspiracy, in restraint of trade" was declared to be illegal. Violators were subject to heavy fines and jail sentences, and triple damages could be obtained by persons who proved economic injury because of unfair price rigging.

Indeed, under the Sherman Act a number of trusts were prosecuted; and in a famous action in 1911, the great Standard Oil Trust was ordered dissolved. Yet, despite the break-up of a few

9 Richard Hofstadter, *The Age of Reform* (New York: Alfred A. Knopf, Inc., 1955), p. 231.
10 Cochran and Miller, *op. cit.*, p. 171.

trusts, the act was singularly weak. For one thing, it was only gingerly applied; not until Franklin Roosevelt's time would the Antitrust Division of the Department of Justice have as much as a million dollars with which to investigate and control the affairs of a multi-billion dollar economy. In fact, during the first fifty years of its existence, only 252 criminal actions were instituted under the Sherman law. And then too, the prevailing judicial opinion of the 1890's and early 1900's was not much in sympathy with the act. The Supreme Court early dealt it a severe blow by finding, in the American Sugar Refining case, that manufacturing was not "commerce," and therefore the American Sugar Refining Company, which had bought controlling stock interests in its four largest competitors, was not to be considered as acting "in restraint of trade." It is not surprising that the concentration of business was hardly slowed in such a climate of opinion. As a humorist of the times put it: "What looks like a stone wall to a layman is a triumphal arch to a corporation lawyer."

These weaknesses led to further acts in 1914: primarily, the Clayton Antitrust Act, prohibiting specific kinds of price discrimination and the acquisition of stock in competing corporations; and the Federal Trade Commission, which sought to define and prevent "unfair" business practices. As we shall see later, these acts were not without their effect. Yet, undermining the entire anti-trust movement there remained one critical and vitiating fact. The purpose of anti-trust was essentially to restore competitive conditions to markets which were in danger of becoming "monopolized" by giant firms. Against this tendency, anti-trust legislation could pose a deterrent only insofar as the monopolization process resulted from the outright *combination* of erstwhile competitors. Against a much more fundamental tendency—the tendency of industrial technology to yield decisive advantages to large-scale producers— it could offer no remedy. While anti-trust effort concentrated its fire against collusion or amalgamation, it was powerless against the fact of spontaneous internal growth.

And therefore growth continued. Through most of the first quarter of the twentieth century, the biggest corporations not only grew, but grew *faster* than their smaller competitors. As Adolf Berle and Gardiner Means pointed out in a famous study in 1932, between 1909 and 1928 the 200 largest nonfinancial corporations increased their gross assets over 40 per cent more rapidly than all nonfinancial corporations.[11] Looking into the future, Berle and Means concluded:

Just what does this rapid growth of the big companies promise for the future? Let us project the trend of the growth of recent years. If the wealth of the large corporations and that of all corporations should each continue to increase for the next twenty years at its average annual rate for the twenty years from 1909 to 1929, 70 percent of all corporate activity would be carried on by two hundred corporations in 1950. If the more rapid rates of growth from 1924 to 1929 were maintained for the next twenty years 85 percent of corporate wealth would be held by two hundred huge units. . . . If the indicated growth of the large corporations and of the national wealth were to be effective from now until 1950, half of the national wealth would be under the control of big companies at the end of that period.[12]

The political and social consequences of such a trend as Berle and Means projected were truly incalculable. But the economic consequences were not. As the two authors wrote: "a society in which production is governed by blind economic forces is being replaced by one in which production is carried on under the ultimate control of a handful of individuals."[13] In the light of our historical study we can rephrase the conclusion very simply. If the trend to a new economic feudalism were left unchecked, it spelled the end of the market system.

The Structure of the Contemporary Market

Has the Berle and Means projection come true? The question brings to a climax our long survey of the changing market structure. We have been concerned with gathering up the various forces which created and shaped the market as a great system of economic control. Now we must see what the outcome of the process has been.

The first impression is not reassuring. Although we do not have statistics which are exactly comparable to those of Berle and Means, there can be little doubt of the overwhelming importance of the

11 *The Modern Corporation and Private Property* (New York: The Macmillan Company, 1932), p. 36.
12 *Ibid.*, pp. 40–41.
13 *Ibid.*, p. 46.

giant corporations in contemporary society. The table below, for instance, shows their predominance in a number of markets in 1955.

RELATIVE SHARE OF GIANT CORPORATIONS IN VARIOUS
SECTORS OF THE UNITED STATES ECONOMY
(*1955*)

Sector	All corporations		Corporations with assets of $250 million or more	
	Number	*Total assets* (*$ billion*)	Number	*Per cent of all corporation assets*
Manufacturing	124,200	$201.4	97	42
Mining[a]	9,700	13.3	(19)	(32)
Public Utilities	4,800	62.9	56	72
Transportation	21,900	43.5	30	61
Total	160,600	321.1	192	50

[a] Figures in parentheses show number and share of corporations with assets of $100 million or more.

Source: *The Corporation in Modern Society*, Edward S. Mason, ed. (Cambridge: Harvard University Press, 1959), p. 87. (The last row has been calculated from the above.)

The table speaks for itself. Note that the near-200 giant corporations above own one-half of all the assets of the entire group and that in the vital manufacturing sector fewer than 100 corporations own over 40 per cent of all the plant and equipment, cash and other wealth of their group.

Hence a first look at the American economy reveals clearly enough that the concentration of economic power is a dominant fact of economic life. Indeed, the table does not show the degree of concentration in many industries. In 1947, in the production of cars and trucks, farm machinery, tires, cigarettes, aluminum, liquor, meat, copper, tin cans, office machinery, and heavy electrical equipment, the top three companies in each field accounted for two-thirds or more of all the business done in their fields. In steel, chemicals, and dairy products, the top six firms accounted for two-thirds of the business.[14] In Professor Berle's words, this situation represents "a concentration of power over economics which makes the medieval

[14] Federal Trade Commission, *The Concentration of Production Facilities* (Washington, D.C.: Government Printing Office, 1949).

feudal system look like a Sunday School party. In sheer economic power this has gone beyond anything we have seen."[15]

But we must still look out over the rest of the economy. For giant business is not, after all, the only reality of the market structure. There are, today, some 4.6 million smaller businesses in the nation as well as 4.5 million farms. Do we see a drift toward concentration here?

Unquestionably, there are some signs of concentration even in the small business field. On the land, for instance, the total number of farmsteads has been steadily falling, and the importance of the very large farm has increased apace. In 1920, one per cent of all farms were larger than 1,000 acres, and these accounted for 23 per cent of all farm acreage. In 1954, 2.7 per cent of farms were larger than 1,000 acres, and these "giant" farms embraced over 45 per cent of all farm acreage.[16] Similarly in retailing, while the number of stores has steadily grown, so has the importance of the large retailing unit. In 1947 it was estimated that 400 retail companies and groups did 50 per cent of the over-the-counter sales of 1,500,000 retail establishments.[17]

Yet it would be unjustified to compare the degree of concentration in these fields, or in the service, or trade, or construction fields, generally, with that of the manufacturing sector. Rather, what we seem to find is a generally fragmented market structure for certain areas of the economy, existing side-by-side with a highly concentrated market structure in the key industrial (and financial) sectors. It is not unlikely that some further degree of concentration will take place in the small business fields as technological possibilities for the more efficient operation of larger units give impetus to the growth of progressive firms.* But surely, the key problem is in the industrial heart of the economy. Do the facts that we have seen mean that concentration has steadily worsened here since its beginnings in the late nineteenth century?

[15] *Economic Power and the Free Society* (New York: 1958), p. 14.

[16] *Statistical Abstract of the United States* (Washington, D.C.: Bureau of the Census, 1960), p. 621.

[17] Williamson, *op. cit.*, p. 767.

* This does not mean that the total *number* of firms (although probably not farms) will not grow. It is quite possible to have a larger number of business units even though a few very large ones are doing a growing share of the total business.

The Stabilization of Concentration

Surprisingly, this is not the conclusion to which the facts lead us. Although concentration is a massive reality in almost every field of industrial production today, it does not actually appear to be increasing. Instead, a comparison of concentration ratios, showing the proportion of each industrial market going to the four biggest companies in the industry, for 1901 and 1947, reveals some surprising facts. In some industries—tobacco, chemicals, stone, clay and glass, transportation equipment—there has been an increase in concentration. In others, no less important—food, textiles, pulp and paper, petroleum and coal products, rubber, machinery—concentration has *fallen* since 1901.[18] If we take the four largest companies in any industry in operation between 1947 and 1954 (the latest year for which figures are available) and if we compare the value of their total shipments to the value of all shipments in their industry, we find a similar mixed trend. In a few instances—such as the automobile industry, in which some early postwar competitors were shaken out—the concentration ratio has increased appreciably: in the case of autos, from 56 per cent in 1947 to 75 per cent in 1954. In the majority of industries, the movement was imperceptible and as likely to be upwards as downwards. In fact, among forty-three industries for which comparative statistics exist, twenty showed some tendency toward less concentration.[19]

Thus, despite the tremendous concentration of existing corporate power, the movement toward further concentration seems not to be evident.* As a well-known student of the problem, Professor M. A. Adelman of M.I.T., has concluded, since the completion of the last great merger wave of the 1920's, the level of concentration "has been a static condition, varying slightly from year to year, but increasing, if at all, at the pace of a glacial drift."[20]

[18] *Historical Statistics of the United States, Colonial Times to 1957*, Series V, 57, 58.

[19] *Statistical Abstract of the United States*, 1960, pp. 792–793.

* A fact which is confirmed again by the most recent study of the problem. This shows the share of total industrial corporate assets belonging to the top 100 firms as virtually unchanged from 1935 to 1958 (*American Economic Review*, December 1961, p. 989).

[20] "The Measure of Industrial Concentration,", *Review of Economics and Statistics*, November 1951, p. 295.

Causes for the Stabilization

What has produced this stabilization of concentration in our day? Two main reasons suggest themselves.

The first was *the restraining effect of anti-trust legislation.* At the point at which we left our historical narrative, we had seen only the ineffectiveness of the anti-trust legislation. But beginning in the 1930's, under Franklin Roosevelt, the idea of a truly strong enforcement of the various anti-trust acts began to gain favor. A vigorous campaign to block the drift towards greater concentration resulted in a number of suits brought against major corporations for restraint of trade. No less important was a change in the prevailing judicial view which now construed less narrowly the powers of the Constitution to impose social controls over business enterprise. In more recent years, the stringency of Justice Department rulings on permissible mergers has made the marriage of competitive firms increasingly difficult.

Expert opinion differs as to the effectiveness of the actual prosecutions under the different acts, but there is general agreement that the announced determination of the government brought about its results in an indirect manner. The knowledge that expansion beyond a certain share of the market would bring long and expensive court proceedings and bad "public relations" acted as a curb on the ambitions of large firms to grow beyond a certain size. As Thurman Arnold, a severe critic (and an effective administrator) of the anti-trust program put it: "The antitrust laws were based on a popular conception that great corporations *could* be made respectable. Following that ideal, great corporations *did* become respectable."[21]

Yet our first suggested reason seems to raise more questions than it answers. Surely "respectability" was hardly the object of the nineteenth century robber barons. The very fact that considerations such as these could work their effect alerts us to a second major cause for the slowing-up of concentration. We shall find it in *a basic change in the character of business management.*

We have already noticed a certain change in the character of the great entrepreneur, from the production oriented industrialist of the early nineteenth century to the sales and strategy oriented "captain of industry" of the late nineteenth. Yet throughout the first

---

[21] *The Folklore of Capitalism* (New Haven: Yale University Press, 1937), p. 221.

century of vigorous corporate expansion, one characteristic marked both types of business leaders. Both were the direct owners of their enterprises. The men who ran the corporations were themselves the men who had put up the capital, or who owned large blocks of stock in the enterprises themselves. The Carnegie Steel Company, the Standard Oil Company, the Ford Motor Company were all extensions of the personalities of Carnegie, Rockefeller, and Ford. This personal direction of affairs was the case with the overwhelming majority of the other major enterprises of the day.

But with the steady growth in size of these enterprises, a curious process of de-personalization began to set in. To run a huge industrial combine required an ever larger number of professional skills, and these skills in turn commanded an ever higher strategic price. Systematizing accounts, dealing with the emergent labor unions, organizing the first research—all aspects of a business which the old-fashioned entrepreneur himself carried out with the aid of a few clerks or partners—now became major "departmental" tasks within a concern. A certain *bureaucratization of private enterprise* set in unnoticed at the very time when entrepreneurs were beginning to raise alarmed cries about the incipient bureaucratic structure of government.*

A second factor in the changing character of management was the rapid rise, from the late nineteenth century on, of the corporation as the preferred form of business organization. A marvelously flexible and adaptable legal instrumentality, the corporation possessed numerous advantages for the enterpriser. Unlike the personal proprietorship or partnership, the corporation existed quite independently of its owners, survived their deaths, and could enter into binding contracts in "its" own name. Furthermore, by limiting the liability of its owners to the value of the stock they had bought, it protected a capitalist against limitless loss.

At the same time, the corporate instrument brought about a definitive change in the nature of ownership itself. As the original founders of businesses died, their stock was often inherited by heirs who did not have business ability and who receded into the background. In addition, the widening dispersion of stock among numer-

---

* We might note here a plausible (but unproved) supplementary reason for the leveling off of concentration. This is the possibility that corporate enterprises had reached the point at which further growth would bring not economies, but *dis*economies, of operation, owing to excessive overhead, red tape, and the like.

ous smaller investors slowly made it unnecessary for any group to own a *majority* of the stock to exercise control—that is, to direct the actual affairs of the company. In 1928, for example, the board of directors of U.S. Steel (which included two of the largest stockholders) held in all only 1.4 per cent of the company's stock. In that year, the biggest stockholder of American Telephone and Telegraph held but seven-tenths of one per cent of the company's total stock and the twenty biggest share owners of the Pennsylvania Rail Road held less than 3 per cent of that company's total stock.[22]

The result was that the directors of the corporation who controlled its policies were no longer even remotely the "owners" of the company. At the same time, the actual "owners"—the thousands or even millions of stockholders who were the legal owners of the corporation's shares—could certainly not exercise effective control over "their" enterprises.* The upshot was that corporate managements tended to become self-perpetuating groups, nominating their own successors and directing their corporate affairs as they thought best.

Best for whom? For the presumed legal owners, the stockholders? Or for the immediate interests of the management group itself? Or for the more nebulous interests of "the community"?

There were no obvious answers to these questions; but with the bureaucratization of management and the separation of ownership and control, one consequence did emerge very clearly. The uninhibited acquisitive drive of the highly personal corporate leadership of the late nineteenth century began to give way to a much more complex and considered set of business motivations. Making money—maximizing profits—was, of course, still a first rule of business life, since no corporation could long survive without profits. But it was no longer the only, or even always the overriding, rule of business life. More and more managers looked upon themselves as balancing many private "interests" in the general interest of the longevity of the enterprise itself. Their task was now to conduct the *government* of enterprises which had to function in a money-making world, rather than to run those enterprises as vehicles for personal money-making in the nineteenth-century manner.

Thus, the evolution of a more statesmanlike attitude in business

22 Berle and Means, *op. cit.*, pp. 47, 86.

* Today the dispersion of ownership has increased to the point at which probably 15,000,000 people own at least some stock. There are over 2,000,000 stockholders of A.T.&T., and over 100,000 stockholders in another 50-odd companies.

affairs brought a significant change in business tactics. But the change cannot be ascribed solely to a new outlook on the part of big businessmen. Behind that new outlook was *a change in the market environment.*

For if the great entrepreneurs or the robber barons of the last century had been blatantly acquisitive, no small part of their attitude could be laid to the intense competitive pressures of their times. In the days of cutthroat competition, the business chief had no alternative but to run his business in the unremitting pursuit of profits. In similar fashion, the ability of later corporation managers to take a longer view toward profits, to eschew the cruder money-making tactics and values of the past, and to adopt policies of social responsibility was itself testimony to an economic society in which all-out competitive, money-making behavior was no longer *essential.* The growth of a new "professional" management was a cause for the diminution of the motive of aggrandizement so characteristic of the nineteenth century, but it was also the result of a new market situation in which the old acquisitive traits were no longer so necessary to survival.

Oligopoly and Market Behavior

We call this new kind of market situation *oligopoly,* meaning a market shared by a few sellers. Note that it is not *monopoly,* which is a market entirely served by one seller. Neither is it "pure competition," such as we envisaged when we first looked into the theory of a market society.*

What is the essential difference? We will recall from Chapter 3 that the competitive process is the outcome of two quite separate struggles. The first of these is the struggle *across* the market—each buyer seeking to obtain goods or factors as cheaply as possible, and each seller trying to dispose of his output or his services as dearly as possible. This opposition of interests still prevails in an oligopolistic market.

The second ingredient of pure competition is the struggle on *each side* of the market, as sellers strive to outdo each other, and buyers

---

* In proper economic terminology, an oligopolistic market refers only to the market structure on the *sellers* side. In a market with a few large buyers we speak of oligopsony. A similar distinction exists between monopoly (a single seller) and monopsony (a single buyer).

do the same. It is this indispensable attribute of the fully competitive situation which lacks in an oligopolistic market.

There is a way of sharpening still further this distinction. In a competitive market, in which large numbers of sellers and buyers vie with one another, no single seller or buyer is in a position to affect the market price by his own actions. Regardless of how much he sells or buys, he is too small a participant in the market to alter its price. That price will change only when a large number of sellers or buyers increase or decrease their offerings. In a purely competitive situation, the price controls the marketers.

But in an oligopolistic situation this enforced subservience to the going price is replaced by a degree of control *over* the price. It is not, of course, total control, for there is still the opposition of interests we mentioned above. The oligopolist must still reckon with the counterforce of demand. But he has no "classical" restraints on his behavior as a supplier.

Because the oligopolist is one of only a *few* firms, he has no crowd of competitors at his elbow. Hence, rather than being forced to participate in a continuing contest among suppliers, he and his few fellow-sellers can *set* their prices as they deem best. Often an oligopolistic market is dominated by one very large firm which serves as "price leader," raising or lowering its prices as general economic conditions warrant, and being followed up or down by everyone else in the field. U.S. Steel in the steel industry, General Motors in the auto field, Corn Products Refining in the cornstarch industry have more or less consistently "led" their industries in this fashion. By and large, these prices are considerably higher than the prices which a pure competitive market would enforce. General Motors, for instance, "targets" its prices to attain a 15 to 20 per cent return after taxes, *calculating its costs on the assumption that it will use only 60 to 70 per cent of its total plant capacity.* U.S. Steel sets its prices high enough so that it can earn a small profit *even if it operates only two days out of five.* In fact "target pricing" has come to be the established procedure for leading manufacturing firms.[23]

Prices set by leading firms, rather than by the interplay of com-

[23] *Study of Administered Prices in the Steel Industry* and *Study of Administered Prices in the Automobile Industry,* Senate Report 1387, 85th Cong., 2d sess.; see also R. F. Lazillotti, "Pricing Objectives of Large Companies," *American Economic Review,* December 1958, pp. 921–940.

petition among many firms, are called *administered prices*. This does not mean that in each of these industries firms do not vie with one another. On the contrary, if you ask a General Motors or a U.S. Steel executive, he will tell you of vigorous competition. He may show you that Ford had edged out General Motors in such-and-such a line, or that Bethlehem Steel has captured some of U.S. Steel's business. The point, however, is *that the competition among oligopolists typically utilizes every means except one: price cutting.* The tactics of lowering price to secure a rival's business is not regarded as "fair play," although once in a while it breaks out, just as it did in the days of cutthroat competition of the 1880's.* But what was common practice then is rare now. Competition among oligopolists today means winning business away from another by advertising, customer service, or product design—but not by "chiseling"on price. Everyone recognizes that it is to his advantage not to disturb the market. There have been few instances in steel, or oil, or automobiles, or chemicals, or cigarettes when out-and-out price "warfare" has taken the place of nonprice "competition."

The Challenge to the Market System

Until now we have occupied ourselves with tracing the historic evolution and inquiring into the theoretical meaning of oligopoly. Now we must turn to a last and most important question: what are the consequences of this new market structure for the American economy? Or putting the question even more broadly: what are its consequences for the operation of a market economy?

We will remember that a distinguishing feature of that economy was the *power of control which was vested in the consumer.* There were two aspects to this power. First, a market society enabled consumers to have the ultimate decision as to the allocation of the factors of production. *Their* desires arranged the productive pattern of society, not the desires of society's rulers, its keepers of traditions, or

* On occasion, the administered prices in an oligopoly are maintained by out-and-out collusive agreement, which is strictly illegal. This was the case most recently when General Electric, Westinghouse, and a number of smaller manufacturers were discovered in 1959 to be rigging prices and sharing the market for heavy electrical equipment. A number of top executives in the main concerns were sent to jail, heavy fines were imposed, and the purchasers of the equipment sued for triple damages. More frequently, however, oligopolistic prices are maintained simply by tacit consent.

its producers. Second, the market society assured the consumer that he would be able to buy the output of society at the lowest price compatible with a continued flow of production. While producers might wish to make exorbitant profits from consumers, they would be prevented from doing so by the pressure of competition from other producers.

Now we have just seen the rise of a market structure which seems very far removed from this ideal blueprint of an economy. But how far is it actually removed? To what extent is our oligopolistic structure, in fact, bringing about a new ultimate principle of economic control—no longer the ideal sovereignty of the consumer, but a sovereignty of virtually all-powerful corporate producers?

It is not easy to give a simple answer to this profoundly important question.

In a general sense, the consumer certainly still rules the allocation of factors in the economy. If he does not choose to buy the goods produced by giant concerns, those concerns have no choice but to curtail the production of those goods. For example, in the mid-1950's the Ford Motor Company poured nearly a quarter of a billion dollars into the production of a new car, the Edsel. The car was rejected by consumers, and after a few years its production was quietly discontinued. Familiar, too, is the effect of a swing in consumer tastes. From the mid-1950's on, imports of foreign sports and small cars rose steadily—from 57,000 vehicles in 1955 to 668,000 in 1959. With the exception of AmericanMotors, the major car manufacturers insisted that the trend to compacts was only a fad and that Americans "wanted" bigger cars. But there was no brooking the contrary opinion of consumers themselves. Eventually, all the major manufacturers were *forced* into the production of small cars.

What then is the difference between this state of affairs and that of the "ideal" market system? One major difference lies in the fact that the great corporations today do not merely "fill" the wants of consumers. They themselves help to *create* these wants by massive efforts to interest the public in buying the products they manufacture. In 1960, for example, business will spend nearly as much on advertising its products—an estimated $12 billions—as our total expenditures for public elementary and secondary education. By way of contrast, in 1867 we spent only $50 million on advertising; and in

1900, only $542 million. So it is that while consumers still move about the factors of productions to satisfy their "wants," these wants are themselves influenced by the producers. In contrast to the ideal market where producers hasten at the beck of an imperious consumer demand, in the new market, consumers are to some extent themselves at the beck of an imperious producer demand.

We might note, for instance, that no sooner was the first small Ford placed on the market than the company announced a "luxury" small car, and this example was quickly followed by other producers. It may very well be that consumers prefer a large spectrum of sizes and shapes of automobiles. But it is difficult to square the original image of serving the consumers' uninfluenced wants with the process by which new models are designed and touted. We shall have a further word to say about this at the conclusion of our chapter.

The Pressure on Prices

The second main attribute of the ideal market was that consumer's interests were satisfied as cheaply as possible because prices were forced down to the average cost of producing goods. Is this still true?

We have already seen that prices in oligopolistic industries are considerably higher than they would be under competitive conditions. Yet they are not wholly without controls. If the competitive price struggle is conspicuously lacking within oligopolistic industries, there are other pressures which enforce a certain degree of price discipline.

One of these pressures has been called by Professor Galbraith "countervailing power."[24] By this, Galbraith means that in an oligopolistic world the opposition of interests across the market provides some compensation for the absence of a contest of interests on each side of the market. Today, powerful corporate sellers often face equally powerful corporate *buyers* across the market. The giant raw materials producer who faces little or no competition within his industry must sell to the giant chemical or other processing plant; the giant steel mill to the giant auto firm; the giant canner to the giant supermarket chain. Not least important, the large firm no longer

[24] Cf. John K. Galbraith, *American Capitalism, The Concept of Countervailing Power* (Boston: Houghton Mifflin Co., 1952), pp. 115 ff.

bargains with the individual employee, but with large and powerful unions. This kind of neutralization of economic power does not hold true in every market nor in every situation, but, Dr. Galbraith contends, it is true in enough markets and in enough situations to constitute a powerful restraining force on the unhindered exercise of oligopolistic power.

A second restraining force is the competition among different *products*. Even if all steel prices are kept at "administered" levels, steel as a whole must compete with aluminum. Nor does the competition end here. What we find, indeed, is an immense chain of interproduct competition—steel against aluminum, aluminum against glass, glass against plastics, plastics against wood, wood against concrete, concrete against steel. And this competition is without doubt effective. Note that automobile engines are now made of cast aluminum as well as of steel; that buildings are now sheathed in glass as well as brick or concrete; that cooking utensils are made of glass as well as of aluminum; that drinking "glasses" are often made of plastic.

Thus prices are not *wholly* free from control. But that does not mean that they are therefore adequately controlled. Oligopoly does not mean arbitrarily high prices, but it does mean a price structure which is considerably far removed from that which a more competitive system might enjoy. "What few will question," writes Gardiner Means in a study of steel pricing, "is that the after-tax target rates of 16 and 20 per cent and the actual earnings in excess of these targets are well above a competitive rate of return. Prices set to achieve these targets must involve substantial premiums over costs, taxes and a legitimate rate of return. To this extent, the public interest is not served. . . ."[25]

The Unresolved Problem of Economic Power

How shall we summarize this complicated situation with its pluses and minuses?

Without doubt, many of the aspects of a system of giant oligopoly are disquieting departures from the rationale of a market economy as the *servant* of the consumer. Yet it would be erroneous to con-

[25] *Pricing Power and the Public Interest* (New York: Harper & Brothers, 1962), p. 268.

clude that the emergence of these new attributes are nothing but a threat to the market system. On the contrary, in part at least, they can also be seen as new functional mechanisms for the *support* of that system.

Take first the phenomenon of advertising and the manipulation of consumers' wants. This seems at first glance a direct assault upon a prime principle of the market system—the sovereignty of consumers' wants. But is not advertising also testimony to the changing character of consumers' wants? In the nineteenth century, those wants were essentially focused on the basic requirements of simple existence: food, clothing, shelter. In the rich nation of the mid-twentieth century, however, these basic wants have been largely satisfied. Consumer demand is no longer driven to essentials, but hesitates before a whole range of possible luxuries and semi-luxuries.

Thus the fact that producers can manipulate and create these wants testifies to the much more important fact that *the wants themselves are now amorphous and vague and susceptible to influence.* Curiously, then, we can view the rise of advertising as an attempt to introduce an orderliness and intensity of demand into a society where purely spontaneous demand would no longer firmly indicate which patterns of economic activity producers should follow.

In similar vein, we cannot conclude that the price-setting power of oligopolistic firms has no economic function. For the achievement of a certain market stability, which is the purpose of administered pricing, is not without its benefits to the economy. For one thing, a return to the uninhibited price competition of the nineteenth century might very well lead to a resumption of cutthroat tactics from which would emerge not a nicely balanced competitive market, but an array of triumphant monopolies.

And then, too, it has often been pointed out that the most "ideally" competitive industries, such as agriculture, are typically those which offer the worst wages and which display the least progressive economic characteristics. On the other hand, in those industries were oligopoly has permitted larger than competitive profits to accrue, we tend to find not only higher wages and more "social conscience," but the most forward-looking (and expensive) commitment to research and expansion. As Dr. Galbraith has written in a wry commentary on this situation: "The showpieces [of the economy] are, with rare exceptions, the industries which are dominated by a handful of large firms. The foreign visitor, brought to the United States . . . visits the same firms as do attorneys of the Department of Justice in their search for monopoly."[26]

Thus the changing market structure has its uses as well as its abuses. We must see in it not only a departure from the market system, but also an attempt to find an accommodation within that system for a powerful new technology which impels all organizations toward large-scale operations.* We must understand that if oligopoly undermines the market system in some regards, it strengthens it in others.

Beyond this mixed economic judgment, there are, however, other considerations. In the end, the strictly economic consequences of oligopoly may be less important than its social and political consequences. The deliberate endless titillation of the consumer is not a pretty spectacle for those who see in man something more than a voracious consumer of goods. Neither is the emergence within a democratic society of a fortress of well-nigh impregnable economic power a wholly reassuring political sight. As Professor Berle has said, "Some of these corporations can be thought of only in somewhat the way we have heretofore thought of nations."[27] Unlike nations, however, their power has not been rationalized in law, fully tested in practice, or well defined in philosophy. Unquestionably, the political and social influence of the great corporations poses problems with which capitalism will have to contend for many years to come.

[26] *Op. cit.*, p. 96.

* We should note that the situation is not peculiar to America. In every industrial market society, a similar concentration of production has occurred. In England, for instance, Drs. Leak and Maizels have concluded that in 1935 a quarter of the labor force in any major industry typically works for the top three firms. Studies of concentration in France, Italy, Japan, Canada, Holland and Scandanavia reveal that in most cases it has proceeded further than in the United States.

[27] *Op. cit.*, p. 15.

6

The Evolution of Guided Capitalism

In our last chapter we concentrated on important aspects of the developing market economy, the swift rise in productivity, the impact of mass production, the thickening of the texture of the market. Now we must bring ourselves abreast of a second and no less important theme. This is the over-all performance of our economy from the point of view of the well-being which it has produced. This, too, is a problem into which we must gain some theoretical insight in order to grasp fully the meaning of what has happened. But as before, we had best begin with a view of history.

America in 1929

We in America today are nearer to the final triumph over poverty than ever before in the history of any land. The poorhouse is vanishing from among us. We have not yet reached the goal, but, given a chance . . . we shall soon with the help of God be in sight of the day when poverty will be banished from this nation.[1]

By 1929, the American economy had indeed shown the most extraordinary progress. Its population had grown from 76 million in 1900 to over 121 million, while ten years had been added to the expectation of life at birth for whites and thirteen for nonwhites. To hold and feed and sustain its growing numbers, the nation had built up two new cities to a million each, five to over half a million, nearly 1,500 from rural to urban classification; $75 billion worth of homes, $9 billion worth of new farm structures; over $30 billion worth of new industrial equipment. Meanwhile, there were jobs for 48 million people—all save 3.2 per cent of the labor force in 1929. Furthermore, these job holders had seen average weekly hours of work in manufacturing drop from nearly 60 in 1900 to 44. Average hourly earnings rose from twenty cents in 1909 to fifty-six cents, while consumer prices lagged sufficiently behind to allow a rise in real wages of some 10 to 20 per cent. It was not surprising, then, that an atmosphere of optimism gripped America in 1929 and that President Hoover's official words only reflected an informal sentiment throughout the nation.

Certainly few Americans suspected that a major economic calamity might be just around the corner. On the contrary, most people were concerned with quite another prospect of the American economy, and a highly attractive one. This was the great stock market boom—a boom which by 1929 had pulled perhaps 10,000,000 people into "the market," where they had the pleasure of watching their money painlessly and effortlessly grow. As Frederick Lewis Allen, the social historian of the twenties, described it in *Only Yesterday:*

The rich man's chauffeur drove with his ears laid back to catch the news of an impending move in Bethlehem Steel; he held fifty shares himself on a twenty point margin. The window cleaner at the broker's office paused to watch the ticker, for he was thinking of converting his laboriously accumulated savings into a few shares of Simmons. Edwin Lefevre (an articulate reporter on the market at this time who could claim considerable personal experience) told of a broker's valet who made nearly a quarter of a million in the market, of a trained nurse who cleaned up

[1] Herbert Hoover, November 8, 1928.

thirty thousand following the tips given her by her grateful patients; and of a Wyoming cattleman, thirty miles from the nearest railroad, who bought or sold a thousand shares a day.[2]

It was, of course, admittedly speculative, and yet the risks seemed eminently justified. Someone who had put $1,000 each year, from 1921 on, into a group of representative stocks would have found himself worth over $6,000 in 1925, almost $9,000 in 1926, well over $11,000 in 1927, and an incredible $20,000 in 1928. And that was just the beginning: during June and July of 1929 *The New York Times* Industrial Stock Averages went up nearly as much as they had during the entire year of 1928, which had been, in its time, a year of unprecedented rise. By August 1929, the three-months' summer spurt had already outdistanced the entire 1928 rise. In those three months alone, an investor who had bought 100 shares of Westinghouse would have almost doubled his money; even a buyer of staid A.T.&T. would have been richer by a third. It seemed that everyone had but to beg or borrow money to buy shares in order to get rich.

What pricked the bubble? No one knows exactly what final event was to blame. But when the boom did break, it was as if an enormous dam had suddenly crumbled. All the frenzy that had stretched out over two years in sending stocks up was concentrated in a few incredible weeks beating them down. On Tuesday, October 29, 1929 an avalanche of selling crushed the exchanges. On occasion there were *no* offers to buy stock at all—just to sell it. Goldman Sachs, a much sought-after investment trust, lost almost half its quoted value on this single day. By the end of the trading session (the ticker, lagging behind, stretched out the agony two-and-a-half hours longer than the actual market transactions) 16,410,000 shares of stock had been dumped. In a single day, the rise in values of the entire preceding year had been wiped out. A few weeks later, 30 billion dollars of "wealth" had vanished in thin air. Millions who had counted their paper gains and thought themselves well off discovered they were poor.

The great crash is in itself a fascinating chapter in the "madness of crowds." At first it seemed unconnected with anything bigger. In fact, the early weeks after the crash were regularly marked with ex-

2 Bantam ed., 1946, p. 349.

pressions of confidence: the general cliché of the day was that things were "fundamentally sound." Yet things were *not* fundamentally sound. The terrifying Crash ushered in the much more terrifying Depression.

The Great Depression

As Frederick Lewis Allen has written:

It was an oddly invisible phenomenon, this Great Depression. If one observed closely, one might note that there were fewer people on the streets than in former years, that there were many untenanted shops, that beggars and panhandlers were much in evidence; one might see breadlines here and there, and "Hoovervilles" in vacant lots at the edge of town (groups of tar-paper shacks inhabited by homeless people); railroad trains were shorter, with fewer Pullmans; and there were many factory chimneys out of which no smoke was coming. But otherwise there was little to see. Great numbers of people were sitting home, trying to keep warm.[3]

However invisible to the casual observer, the Depression was far from being a mere figment of the imagination. To begin with, Gross National Product fell precipitously from $104 billion in 1929 to $56 billion in 1933. Almost one dollar's worth of final output out of every two disappeared. As a result, unemployment soared. In 1929, the unemployed had numbered 1.5 million. By 1933 the number rose eightfold until *one person out of every four in the entire national labor force was without a job.* In the nation as a whole, residential construction fell by 90 per cent: there were virtually no houses built. Nine million savings accounts were lost as banks closed their doors. Eighty-five thousand businesses failed. In Pennsylvania in 1932 it was reported by the State Department of Labor that wages had fallen to five cents an hour in sawmills, six cents in brick and tile manufacturing, 7.5 cents in general contracting. In Tennessee, women in mills were paid as little as $2.39 for a fifty-hour week. In Kentucky, miners ate the weeds that cows ate; in West Virginia, people began to rob stores for food. In California, a child starved to death and was discovered to have been living on refuse. [4]

[3] *The Big Change* (New York: Harper & Brothers, 1952), p. 248.
[4] Arthur Schlesinger, Jr., *The Crisis of the Old Order* (Boston: Houghton Mifflin Company, 1957), pp. 249–250.

The Causes of the Depression: Speculation

How did this tragedy come about?

An immediate, precipitating cause was, of course, the speculative fever which had engulfed the economy by 1929. The mania was not just confined to Wall Street. Throughout the nation, a get-rich-quick philosophy had destroyed normal business and banking caution. Foreign bonds of the most dubious validity were eagerly (and sometimes ruthlessly) pushed by the banks into investors' hands or, worse folly, put into their own portfolios.* In addition, huge pyramided structures of investment trusts and holding companies erected a house of cards atop the operating base of enterprise. For instance the Georgia Power Company was controlled by the Seaboard Public Service Corporation, which was controlled by the National Public Service Corporation, which was controlled by the Middle West Utilities Company, which was controlled by Insull Utility Investments, Inc., which was controlled by the Corporation Securities Company of Chicago (which was controlled, in turn, by Insull Utility Investments, which presumably *it* controlled). Of these companies, only one—Georgia Power—actually produced electricity. The rest produced only profits and speculative opportunities. And the Insull empire was only one of *twelve* holding companies that owned 75 per cent of all the utility operating plants in the country.

All these manipulative activities helped to pave the way for the Depression. When the stock market finally crashed, it brought down with it an immense flimsy structure of credit. Individual investors who had borrowed to the hilt to buy securities had their stock sold out from under them to meet their indebtedness to brokers. Banks and financial institutions, loaded with dubious foreign bonds, were suddenly insolvent. Later, when the Depression really began, the funds of the utility operating companies which could have been used to provide employment were milked upstairs to rescue or to delay the collapse of the financial superstructure.

---

* Many of these deals were unsavory to the point of malfeasance. The son of the President of Peru, for instance, was paid $450,000 by the securities affiliate of the National City Bank for his services in connection with a $50,000,000 bond issue which the bank's affiliate then floated for Peru. The President's son's "services" consisted almost entirely of an agreement not to block the deal. Eventually, of course, the bonds went into default. (John K. Galbraith, *The Great Crash, 1929*. Boston: Houghton Mifflin Company, 1955, p. 186.)

Weakness on the Farm

In the vulnerability of an economy bound up with a rickety and speculative financial superstructure we have located one reason for the Great Depression—or, more specifically, one reason why the Wall Street Crash pulled down with it so much business activity. But we have far from exhausted the explanations for the Depression itself. For the Crash, after all, might have been no worse than many previous speculative disasters. Why was it protracted into a chronic and deep-rooted ailment?

The question turns our attention away from the spectacular misfortunes of 1929 to a consideration of the state of the economy as a whole in the years preceding the collapse. We have already characterized the first quarter of the twentieth century as a time of unprecedented expansion. Could it be, however, that behind the overall figures of rising output and incomes there were concealed pockets of trouble?

Even during the 1920's, economists would have agreed that one such worrisome sector existed. This was the farm sector. All through the 1920's, the farmer was the "sick man" of the American economy. Each year saw more farmers going into tenantry, until by 1929 four out of ten farmers in the nation were no longer independent operators. Each year the farmer seemed to fall further behind the city dweller in terms of relative well-being. In 1910 the income per worker on the farm had been not quite 40 per cent of the nonfarm worker; by 1930, it was just under 30 per cent.[5]

Part of this trouble on the farm, without question, stemmed from the difficult heritage of the past. Beset now by drought, now by the exploitation of powerful railroad and storage combines, now by his own penchant for land speculation, the farmer was proverbially an ailing member of the economy. In addition, the American farmers had been traditionally careless of the earth, indifferent to the technology of agriculture. Looking at the average individual farmer, one would have said that he was poor because he was unproductive. Between 1910 and 1920, for instance, while nonfarm output per worker rose by nearly 20 per cent, output per farm worker actually fell.

[5] E. A. J. Johnson and Herman E. Krooss, *The American Economy* (Englewood Cliffs, N.J.: Prentice-Hall, Inc., 1960), p. 351.

Between 1920 and 1930, farm productivity improved somewhat, but not nearly so fast as productivity off the farm. For the great majority of the nation's agricultural producers the trouble appeared to be that they could not grow or raise enough to make a decent living.

If we had looked at farming as a whole, however, a very different answer would have suggested itself. Suppose that farm productivity *had* kept pace with that of the nation. Would farm income as a whole have risen? The answer is disconcerting. The *demand* for farm products was quite unlike that for manufactured products generally. In the manufacturing sector, when productivity rose and costs accordingly fell, the cheaper prices of manufactured goods attracted vast new markets, as with the Ford car. Not so with farm products, however. When food prices fell, people did not tend to increase their actual consumption very greatly. Increases in over-all farm output resulted in much lower prices but not in larger cash receipts for the farmer. Faced with what is called an *inelastic demand*, a demand which does not respond in proportion to price changes, a flood of output only left the farm sector *worse* off than before.

That is very much what happened during the 1920's. From 1915 to 1920, the farmer prospered because World War I greatly increased the demand for his product. Prices for farm output rose, and his cash receipts rose as well; in fact, they more than doubled. But when European farms resumed their output following the war, the American farmers' crops simply glutted the market. Although prices fell precipitously (40 per cent in the single year 1920–1921), the purchases of farm products did not respond in anything like equal measure. As a result, the cash receipts of the farmer toppled almost as fast as prices. Meanwhile, his taxes were up by some 70 per cent, and his mortgage payments and his cost of living in general had approximately doubled.

There is a lesson here in theory as well as history. Had farmers constituted an oligopolistic market, the decline in farm income might have been limited. A few producers, facing an inelastic demand for their products, can see the sense in mutually curtailing output. Rather than flooding a market which does not want their product, they can agree, tacitly or otherwise, to hold back production to some amount which the market will absorb at a reasonable price. But the individual farmer is about as far from an oligopolist as one can imagine. When the price for his crop falls, it gains the individual farmer nothing to decrease his output. On the contrary, in his highly competitive situation, the best that he can do is to rush to sell as much as he can before things get worse—thereby unwittingly *making* things worse.

At its core, the trouble with the farm sector was that the market mechanism in this particular case did not yield a satisfactory result.* That might not have been so serious, had it not been for another development: while agriculture remained static and stagnant, the manufacturing sector was growing by leaps and bounds. Yet its growth was undermined because a fifth of the nation—the agricultural sector—was unable to match the growing volume of production with a growing volume of purchasing power. As the farmers' buying power lagged, it pulled down the demand for tractors, cars, gasoline and electric motors, and manufactured consumers goods, generally. Weakness on the farm was thus symptomatic of a weakness throughout the economy, a failure of purchasing power across the whole lower stratum of the nation to keep up with the tempo of national industrial production.

Weakness in the Factory

Most economists of the 1920's, as we have said, would have agreed that there was a source of potential trouble on the farm. Had we suggested that there might be another potential breeding ground for trouble in the factory or the mine, however, few would have given their assent. Most people's eyes, during the 1920's, were fixed on only one aspect of the industrial sector—production—and here there was surely little reason for complaint.

Yet had scrutiny penetrated a bit deeper, very serious signs might well have been spotted in this presumably most buoyant section of

* In theory, we will remember, there was a cure for situations in which the producers of one commodity were undercompensated relative to other pursuits: producers would leave the undercompensated field for more lucrative occupations. Indeed, the American farmer tried this cure. It has been estimated that 20 farmers left the soil to seek city work for every urban worker who came to the land. Unfortunately, the cure did not work fast enough. While the agricultural sector steadily diminished in relative size, it could not shrink its absolute numbers significantly. From 1910 to 1930 approximately 10 million farmers remained "locked" on the farm, perhaps half of them barely contributing to national output beyond their own meager livelihoods.

the economy. For while production was steadily rising, *employment* was not. In manufacturing, for example, physical output in 1929 was up 49 per cent over 1920, whilst employment was precisely unchanged. In mining, output was up 43 per cent, while employment had shrunk some 12 per cent. In transportation and in the utility industry again output was higher—slightly in transportation, spectacularly in utility's electrical output—and again employment had actually declined.

Over-all employment had not, of course, declined. It was significantly up in construction, in trade, and finance, in the service industries, and in government. But note that all these employment-absorbing industries were characterized by one common denominator: they were all singularly devoid of technological advance. Or to put it the other way around, all the employment-static or declining industries were singularly characterized by rapid technological advance. Pressing against the over-all upward tendency of the economy was an undertow of *technological displacement*.

Heretofore in our frequent consideration of technology, we have never stopped to inquire what its effects might be on employment. Rather, we have implicitly assumed those effects to be positive, as we dwelt on the capacity of industrial technology to increase output. Yet it is not difficult to see that technology need not always be favorable for employment. When a new invention creates a new industry, such as the automobile, it is clear that its employment-creating effect can be enormous. Yet, even in such an instance there is an undertow, albeit a small one, as the growing automobile industry crowds out the old carriage industry. When we turn to inventions which do not create new *demands*, but which merely make an established industry more productive, it is clear that the initial impact of technical change can generate serious unemployment.

How are such technologically displaced workers re-employed? We will return to this question later in our chapter. At this juncture, we want to examine still further the effect of rapid technological change in the "displacing industries," themselves, during the 1920's. Here we see an interesting fact. As production soared and employment sagged, the output per man-hour rose rapidly; in fact, between 1920 and 1929 it increased over 30 per cent in transportation, over

40 per cent in mining, and over 60 per cent in manufacturing.* This
much larger flow of production per hour meant that wages could
have been raised substantially or prices cut sharply. But this is not
what we find to have been the case. Only on the unionized railroads
did wage rates rise (by about 5 per cent). In mining, hourly earnings fell by nearly 20 per cent, and in manufacturing they remained
steady. Since the hours of work per week were also declining, the
average annual earnings of employees in these industries were far
from keeping pace with the rise in their productivity. In mining,
average yearly earnings fell from $1,700 to $1,481. In transportation
and manufacturing, yearly earnings fell from 1920 through 1922
and did not regain 1920 levels until 1928 and 1929.

Thus the gains from higher productivity were not passed along to
the industrial worker in terms of higher wages. Were they passed
along via lower prices? Yes, to some extent. The over-all cost of
living between 1920 and 1929 fell by about 15 per cent. Part of this
reduction, as we have seen, was due to falling food prices. Nonfood
goods fell sharply in price from 1920 postwar peaks to 1921; thereafter they, too, declined by about 15 per cent up to 1929, but the
fall was not enough to distribute all the gains from industrial technology. How do we know this? Because the *profits* of large manufacturing corporations soared between 1920 and 1929. From 1916
through 1925, profits for these companies had averaged around
$730-odd million a year; from 1926 through 1929, they averaged
$1,400 million. Indeed, in the year 1929, profits were triple those
of 1920.[6]

The Maldistribution of Income

Now we can generalize from what we have just discovered about
the trend of wages and profits, to state one further reason for the
sudden weakness which overcame the economy, beginning in 1929.
Income was distributed in such a way as to make the system vulnerable to economic shocks.

This does *not* mean that somehow the American economy was
failing to generate "enough" purchasing power to buy its own out-

* These productivity indexes cannot be computed from our previous output
and employment figures, since weekly hours changed. For the original figures, see
Historical Statistics of the United States, Series W.

[6] *Historical Statistics of the United States,* V 236.

put. An economy always creates enough potential buying power to purchase what it has produced, for behind the price tag of each item of output there is always an equivalent sum of income. We have only to look at any corporation income statement to see that all its costs of production have been matched by payments to someone: in part to workers as wages; in part to office help as salaries; in part to executives; in part to other enterprises as payments for raw materials, for rent, for services; in part to shareholders as dividends; in part to "itself" as depreciation accruals and retained profits. There can never be an insufficient creation of aggregate purchasing power, because *every cost is someone's income.*

There can, however, be a very serious *maldistribution* of the income payments arising from production. For not all the proceeds arising from production may be placed in the hands of people who will *exercise* their purchasing power. Incomes paid out to the lower-paid strata of the labor force do, indeed, return to the stream of purchasing power, for the working man tends to spend his wages quickly. But incomes which take the form of profits, or depreciation accruals, or as very high individual compensations may not quickly turn over as purchasing power. Profits or high incomes may be saved. They may eventually return to the great stream of purchasing demand, but income which is saved does not "automatically" return via the route of consumption expenditure. Instead, it must find a different route—the route of investment, of capital-building.

In our next pages we shall be dealing with this central problem. Now, it is enough for us to see how a shift of income distribution to potential savers creates the *possibility* for short-circuit in the economic flow. Returning to the economy in 1929, we can now see as well what was perhaps the deepest-seated reason for its vulnerability: the fact that its income payments were not going in sufficient volume to those who would surely spend them. We have already understood why farmers and working men, who were indeed possessed of a "limitless" desire to consume, were pinched in their *ability* to buy. Now we must complete the picture by seeing how the failure to distribute the gains of productivity to the lower-income groups swelled the incomes of those who were potential nonspenders.

What we see here is an extraordinary, and steadily worsening, concentration of incomes. By 1929, the 15,000 families or individuals at the apex of the national pyramid, with incomes of $100,000 or more each, probably received as much income as 5 to 6 million

PERCENTAGE SHARES OF TOTAL INCOME RECEIVED BY THE
TOP 1 PER CENT AND TOP 5 PER CENT OF THE
TOTAL POPULATION*

	Top 1 per cent	*Top 5 per cent*
1919	12.2	24.3
1923	13.1	27.1
1929	18.9	33.5

* The table shows the "disposable income variant": i.e., income after payment of taxes and receipt of capital gains.
Source: *Historical Statistics of the United States,* G135–6.

families at the bottom of the pyramid. There was more involved than just a matter of moral equity. It meant that the prosperity of the Twenties—and for the majority of the nation it *was* a prosperity of hitherto unequalled extent—in fact covered over an economic situation of grave potentialities. For *if* the nation's on-going momentum should be checked, in this lopsided distribution of purchasing power lay a serious problem. So long as the high profits and salaries and dividends continued to be returned to the income stream, all was well. But what if they should not be?

Deeper Reasons: The Business Cycle

Why should they not be returned? Why should not the circular flow of production and income go on indefinitely?

The questions once again call to our attention an aspect of the process of economic advance which we have not previously noted. The path of industrial advance, whose main trajectory we have already traced, did not take place in a regular and uninterrupted fashion. Rather, it manifested itself in a curiously uneven path—in periods of more-rapid-than-average advance and periods of slower-than-average advance, which we can trace well back into the nineteenth century.

Note from the chart (p. 152) how uneven is the line of the path of total output. We can trace this unevenness not alone in figures for production, such as we see above, but in the rise and fall of prices and in expansions and contractions of employment.* We call this irregular wave-like course *the business cycle.*

* This graph shows the swings of gross output *after* regular and predictable seasonal fluctuations (like the seasonal increase of retail sales at Christmastime) have been eliminated.

GROWTH OF GROSS NATIONAL PRODUCT

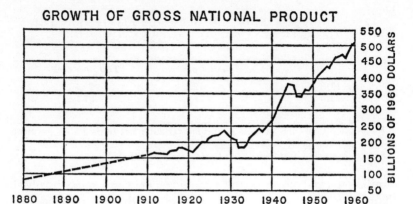

Source: *Economic Growth in the United States* (New York: Committee for Economic Development, 1961).

The business cycle is, in fact, an over-simplification. If we examine business statistics carefully, we can see a number of minor fluctuations as well as larger and bolder ones. Careful students of these fluctuations have discerned at least two basic rhythms of cycles. There is a short cycle which typically measures some two or three years from peak to peak (or from trough to trough). There is a longer cycle, lasting from seven to ten years, from peak to peak or trough to trough. (There is also some evidence of a "long swing" of twenty years from top to top.) Even this by no means exhausts the cycles that can be found by studying the data of production in various industries. For example, we can discern a fairly regular housing cycle with a seventeen-year duration, a textile industry cycle of about two years, a hog production cycle of three to five years, and a number of others. But usually, when we talk of "the" business cycle, we refer to the big seven- or eight-year swings.

The Critical Role of Capital Formation

What causes these cycles? If we think of them as *variations in the rate of growth,* we already know part of the answer. Since growth is caused by capital formation, these swings in growth must be caused by *swings in the rate of capital formation.* Behind the profile of prosperity and recession lies the critical variable element of expenditure for capital goods. When "times" are good, they are good because we are adding rapidly to our inventories, our stock of machines and equipment, our plant and housing, our public works. When times are bad, we are no longer building up as rapidly our stock of capital goods, private and public.

Why are capital expenditures so unstable?

The reason lies partly in the very nature of capital goods—in their durability, their long economic life. Unlike consumer goods, which tend to be quickly used up—*consumed*—capital goods endure. Their replacement tends to be more irregular than the cycle of consumer replacement. At least *some* consumption activity must always be maintained to sustain life itself, but for a considerable period a society can live off its old capital goods and can defer the day of renewing them.*

More important is the fact that *additional* capital goods—the net investment which constitutes the core of economic growth—are similarly subject to a much more irregular pattern of demand than additional consumer goods. Add to a man's income, and you are reasonably certain that he will add to his own consumption. Economists speak of a *propensity to consume,* a dependable tendency to translate higher incomes into at least some additional consumption.

The propensity to invest is a much more uncertain phenomenon. In contrast to consumer goods, capital goods are not bought for personal use. Nobody consumes a lathe or a blast furnace. These goods are bought because they are expected to yield a *profit* when put to use. Thus we commonly hear it said that a new store, a new machine, or an additional stock of inventory must "pay for itself," and so it must. The additional output that new capital investment makes possible must find a market. *If for any reason a profit is not anticipated, the new investment will not be made.*

The *expectation of profit* (which may be greater or less than profits actually being realized at the moment) plays a crucial role in

---

* Obviously there is not an absolutely clear-cut division between all consumer goods and all capital goods. Some consumer goods, like a TV set or a car, are durable, like capital goods, and are called "consumer durables." As we would expect, their purchases are also postponable, and therefore consumer durable sales also exhibit strong cyclical swings. If the exact placement of some goods is occasionally difficult, there is little confusion between the broad categories. A steel plant, a railroad, a hydroelectric dam are very clearly differentiated from food, clothing, or the movies.

the rate of capital formation. But why—and this is obviously the key question—should a profit not be anticipated?

There are many possible answers. One of them may be that a speculative collapse, such as the Great Crash, destroys "confidence" or impairs financial integrity and leads to a period of retrenchment while financial affairs are put in order. Another reason may be that costs shoot up and monetary troubles impede the boom: the banks may become loaned up and money for new capital projects may suddenly become "tight" and dear. Still another reason may be that consumption expenditures are sluggish, owing perhaps to a maldistribution of income, as in the late 1920's, thereby discouraging plant expansion. Or the rate of population growth or of family formation may decline, bringing a slowdown in the demand for housing. Or the boom may simply die a "natural death"—that is, the wave of technological advance on which it rode may peter out, the great investments needed to build up a tremendous industry may be completed, and no second wave of equal capital-attracting magnitude may immediately rise to take its place.

The Effects of Falling Investment

Many of these reasons, as we have seen, served to bring capital formation to a halt in the Great Depression. The Crash itself, with its terrible blow to confidence and to the solvency of banks and holding companies, the weakness of the agricultural sector, the drag of technological displacement, and the maldistribution of income, all combined to bring about a virtual cessation of economic growth. The figures below tell their own grim story.

GROSS PRIVATE DOMESTIC INVESTMENT
(billions of current dollars)

	Residential nonfarm construction	*Other construction*	*Producers' durable equipment*	*Change in inventories*
1929	3.6	5.1	5.9	+1.7
1932	.6	1.2	1.6	−2.6

The Great Depression can be characterized essentially as a tremendous and long-lasting collapse in the rate of capital formation. In housing, in manufacturing plant and equipment, in commercial building, in the accumulation of inventories, a paralysis afflicted the economy. Between 1929 and 1933 investment goods output shrank by *88 per cent* in real terms. Although the capital goods industries employed only one-tenth of the total labor force in 1929, by 1933 one-third of total unemployment had been caused by the shrinkage of these critical industries.

The effect on the economy was much greater than even these figures indicate. For it must now be clear that *the process of capital-creation is the route by which savings return to the income flow*. In part, these savings may be directly invested in business expansion by individuals who purchase new stock issues or by corporations who plow back their savings—their profits—into new plant and equipment.* Part of the savings may find their way into new capital goods via the financial intermediaries of the economy—the savings and commercial banks, the insurance companies, the pension funds that accumulate savings from individuals and lend them to capital-requiring industries. Whatever the path, however, what is all-important is that savings, that part of income which does not enter the consumption-goods stream of purchasing power, can re-enter the income stream only by the investment process.

The point is so centrally important that it warrants special emphasis. *Only if all savings are invested, directly or by financial intermediaries, will all the costs of production, in fact, become re-generated as new buying power.* When savings are not invested—when, for whatever reason, business firms or individual householders do not add to their stock of capital assets—part of the income arising from the process of production will *not* be translated into the salaries and wages and rents and profits needed to buy back the output of the economy.

The trouble does not end even there. When savings are not returned to active purchasing power because of a failure of capital formation to take place, the total amount of purchasing in the economy begins to fall: a steel worker, let us say, is laid off, or the profits of a construction company fall. This contraction in the circular flow of spending now begins to feed upon itself. Just as most

---

* When savings are invested in *existing* shares of the stock market, they do not automatically re-enter the income stream. Assets only change hands of ownership. A buoyant stock market may, however, tempt companies to float *new* stock on the market and thereby finance new capital projects.

people tend to increase their consumption when their income rises, so they almost surely reduce their consumption when income falls. The steel worker pares down his family budget to the bone; the owners of the construction company reduce their scale of living. *This, in turn, creates a further fall in incomes and employment.* A kind of snowball effect is created or, to use the proper economic term, a *multiplier effect.*

As capital expenditures fell during the early 1930's, they pulled down consumption expenditures with them and because of the multiplier effect, by an even larger amount than the fall in investment. From 1929 to 1933, consumption declined from $79 billion to $49 billion, nearly twice as large a drop as the absolute fall in investment. The fall of consumption, in turn, pulled down still further the flow of capital expenditures.*

To be sure, the process works the other way around, as well. When capital expenditures again begin to mount, consumption expenditures typically climb by an even larger amount. For example, President Truman pointed out in a radio address in 1949 that $1 billion of new public expenditures, which gave initial income to some 315,000 people, also added to the incomes of some 700,000 more. In expansion as well as in contraction, there is a typical *cumulative* pattern to economic activity, as success breeds further success, and failure further failure.

Investment in a Market Economy

We are almost ready to renew our historical narrative, but there remains one last connection to be grasped. That is the connection between capital formation as a technical phenomenon and the savings–investment process in a market society.

We will remember that we originally dealt with the capital-building process in our model of the peasant economy shifting its efforts into spades and machine tools. What we saw there was the technical mechanism—the economic engineering, if you will—by which it is *possible* for a society to increase its per capita output. In this chapter, we have dealt with another aspect of that same process. In the preceding pages we were interested in the means by which a

---

* Note that the *percentage* fall in investment is greater than that of consumption, but that the *absolute* fall in consumption is much larger than that of investment.

monetized, profit-oriented economy brings about (or fails to bring about) the underlying shifts in its allocation of labor and resources. In other words, *the complex process by which savings are converted into capital expenditure is the means by which a market society performs the operations of economic growth.*

Is there any assurance that the market society will dependably perform this indispensable task? The very existence of the business cycle answers the question for us: there is not. On the contrary, the whole history of capitalism, as a market society, is marked by periods of rapid, sometimes too rapid, growth, when profitable investment expectations inaugurated a cumulative expansive movement, and periods of slack growth, when the necessary link of expected profit failed to connect the savings process into capital construction.

Yet when we look back upon the history of capitalism, it is clear that we see something besides a mere upward and downward fluctuation of total output. Turning back to our chart of Gross National Product, for instance, we can see that there has been, over and above the cyclical swings, a steady climb of *growth.* To what can we attribute the fact that, despite its recurrent failures, capital formation nonetheless seems always to have regained its momentum—and, indeed, to have surpassed its previous peaks?

One reason lies in the tendency of a slumping economy eventually to "bottom out." As the snowball process of shrinkage continues, little by little the savings of the economy are squeezed out. When income drops to a very low figure, it is impossible to save on a major scale. As savings gradually decline, so also does the gap between incomes received and incomes spent. Eventually—albeit on a much lower level—the economy regains its unbroken flow of purchasing power.

Thereafter the stage is set for a resumption in capital-building. Confidence begins to mend. Excess inventories are worked off. Costs decline, and money is again available at cheap rates from the banks and insurance companies. And once even a small amount of net investment activity is generated, the multiplier mechanism boosts its effect on consumption, and this in turn generates more profitable investment expectations.

Yet this is not the central cause of the resurgence in capital formation. At the heart of the growth process lies a more powerful inducement for capital formation. This is the impelling force of *new technology.* An important new invention will usually make capital formation profitable even in the blackest depression. During the Great Depression itself, for instance, the production of rayon and acetate yarns, then a radically new product, jumped by 75 per cent, even though textile output as a whole declined.

If we widen our vision to include the whole history of similar inventions, it is clear that it has been demand-creating technology, on a gargantuan scale, which has offered the main incentive for capital-building. We began Chapter 5 with a brief account of one such invention, the automobile. Think now of the truly stupendous investment opportunities opened by the invention and perfection of the railroad, the steamship, the electric light and the electric motor, the telephone and radio, the airplane, the refrigerator and the washing machine, the movies, plastics, atomic energy. Once again the vital force of technological discovery enters the economic picture, this time not only as the bearer of the technical means for economic growth, but as the source of the spark of profit by which growth must be fired in a market society.

Our somewhat extended excursion into the theory of economic fluctuations thus comes to an end. Now we can understand the Great Depression not only as an historical phenomenon, but as an instance of a more endemic problem of a market society. We have seen how that society paved the way for the Great Depression by its malfunctions in the 1920's. We also have an understanding of how, in previous periods of economic failure, the momentum for renewed advance was achieved. Now let us follow for a short space the struggles of the American economy in the 1930's, as it sought to escape from the deepest and most destructive depression it had ever known.

THE NEW DEAL

"This nation asks for action, and action now . . . We must act and act quickly."

The words are from the inaugural address of the incoming President—Franklin Delano Roosevelt. It is hard today to reconstruct the urgency, the sense of desperation against which the words were addressed on March 4, 1933. A few hours before the actual inauguration ceremony, every bank in America had locked its doors. The monetary system was at the point of collapse. Nearly thirteen million Americans were without work. A veterans' march on Washington, 15,000 strong, in the previous year had been dispersed with tear gas, tanks, and bayonets. On the farms, mortgage-lifting parties, at which a noose was tactfully displayed, served as powerful deterrents to any representatives of insurance companies or banks who might be thinking of foreclosure. Meanwhile, a parade of business leaders before the Senate Finance Committee had produced a depressing sense of impotence. Said the president of a great railroad: "The only way to beat the depression is to hit the bottom and then slowly build up." "I have no solution," said the president of one of New York's biggest banks. "I have no remedy in mind," testified the president of U.S. Steel. "Above all we must balance the budget," urged a long string of experts.[7] The crisis was a deep and genuine one; it is doubtful if the United States has ever stood closer to economic collapse and social violence.

The new President's response was immediate and vigorous: in the three months after Roosevelt's inauguration, writes Arthur Schlesinger, "Congress and the country were subjected to a presidential barrage of ideas and programs unlike anything known to American history." This was the famous Hundred Days of the New Deal—the days in which, half by design, half by accident, the foundation was laid for a new pattern of government relationship to the private economy, a pattern which was to spell a major change in the organization of American capitalism.

We begin to trace its general outline in the main measures of the Hundred Days. In all, some fifteen major bills were passed: the Emergency Banking Act, which reopened the banks under what amounted to government supervision; the establishment of the Civilian Conservation Crops to absorb at least some of the young unemployed; the Federal Emergency Relief Act to supplement the exhausted relief facilities of states and cities; the Emergency Farm Mortgage Act which loaned four times as much to farmers in seven months as all federal loans in the previous four years; the Tennessee Valley Authority Act, setting up TVA, a wholly new venture into government enterprise; the Glass-Steagall Banking Act divorcing

[7] See Arthur Schlesinger, Jr., *op. cit.*, pp. 457–458.

commercial banks from their stock-and-bond floating activities and guaranteeing bank deposits; the first of the Securities Acts aimed at curbing stock speculation and reckless corporate pyramiding.

The Hundred Days only inaugurated the New Deal; it did not by any means complete it. Social Security, housing legislation, the National Recovery Act, the dissolution of public utility holding companies, the establishment of a Federal Housing Authority were yet to be passed. So was the Wagner Labor Act, which would result in a jump in trade union membership from 3.5 million in 1930 to 9 million in 1940. Indeed, it would not be until 1938 that the New Deal would be "completed" with the passage of the Fair Labor Standard Acts, establishing minimum wages and maximum hours for interstate commerce and banning child employment.

It would take us beyond the boundaries of our survey of general economic history to investigate the content of each of these important pieces of legislation, but we can gain an over-all view of the New Deal by summarizing its achievements against the backdrop of the problems and issues of economic history that we have already encountered. Then we can see that the New Deal is important as marking a genuine change in the development of the market economy itself. With its advent we begin to trace the evolution of a new kind of capitalism which, in significant ways, is different from that which we have heretofore studied. We must understand the nature of this evolution if we are to bring our survey of general economic history to its contemporary terminus in our own society.

The Market Problem

One general problem which confronted the New Deal we have noted earlier in the present chapter. This was the severe misfunction of the market mechanism in agriculture.

The problem, we will remember, arose in large part from the nature of the inelastic demand for farm products and the highly competitive, "atomistic" structure of the agricultural market itself. How did the New Deal seek to cope with this situation? It could not alter the inelasticity of demand, for this arose from the nature of the consumers' desire for food; but it could change the condition of supply which hurled itself, self-destructively, against an unyielding demand. Hence, one of the earliest pieces of New Deal legislation—the Agricultural Adjustment Act—sought to establish machinery whereby farmers, as a group could accomplish what they could not as competitive individuals: to wit—curtail their output.

The curtailment was sought by offering payments to farmers who agreed to cut back their acreage or in other ways to hold down their output. In the first year of the act, there was no time to cut back acreage, so that every fourth row of growing cotton had to be plowed under, and 6,000,000 live pigs were slaughtered. In a nation still hungry and ill-clad, such a spectacle of waste aroused sardonic and bitter comment. And yet, if the program reflected an appalling inability of a society to handle its distribution problem, its attack on overproduction was not without results. In both 1934 and 1935 more than thirty million acres were taken out of production in return for government payments of $1.1 billion. Farm prices rose as a result. Wheat, which had slumped to 38¢ a bushel in 1932, rose to $1.02 in 1936. Cotton doubled in price, hogs tripled, and the net income of the American farmer climbed from the fearful low of $2.5 billion in 1932 to $5 billion in 1936.

We need not here retrace the many later developments in the agricultural programs of the New Deal and its successors. Suffice it rather to make the point that the *central idea* of the A.A.A. has remained. Farmers' incomes are no longer permitted to reflect the extreme fluctuations characteristic of an inelastic market, but are cushioned by government payments earned by adhering to some form of crop limitation. The uncontrolled competitive struggle to market crops has given way to a continuing effort to achieve a balance between supply and demand by limiting supply itself.

Results and Implications of the Program

Has the idea worked well? It might have, but for one thing. Belatedly, technology caught up with American agriculture. Starting in the years before World War II and continuing thereafter with accelerating effect, productivity on the farm began to soar—in fact, it rose faster than productivity in industry. Despite the limitation of acreage, the output of crops increased steadily: between 1940 and 1960, for instance, the amount of cropland remained fairly constant, but the yield per acre increased by *40 per cent*. The result was a flood of output, huge quantities of which had to be purchased and stored by the government under its support programs. By early 1962, the Commodity Credit Corporation, the government's purchasing and storage agency, owned some $9 billion worth of agricultural commodities.

At best, in other words, the attempt to solve the farm problem has been but a partial success. It has not, for instance, succeeded in much improving the economic status of the 2,000,000 least productive small farmers, for these farmers are not able to raise enough crops to benefit substantially from crop supports. Nor has it succeeded in bringing about a sufficient reduction in farm output, so that the normal interplay of supply and demand would lift crop prices above their support levels and relieve the government of its purchase obligations.

Yet the attempt to improve the farm picture must not be brushed aside as ineffective. Without doubt, agriculture, as an income-producing activity, has benefited substantially—especially for the two million successful farmers who produce 90 per cent of our marketed farm product. Between 1940 and 1956 the farm operator families enjoying the use of electricity increased from 33 to 94 per cent, telephones increased from 25 to 52 per cent, mechanical refrigerators from 15 to 90 per cent. In the West, Midwest and Northeast, the independent farm operator is today, more than ever before, at a close parity to the urban middle class in terms of living standards.

Our primary interest, however, is not to assess the relative success or failure of the farm programs from early New Deal days to the present. It is, rather, to note that all of the programs spell a fundamental change in the role of the government in a market society. *The essence of that change is that the government now seeks to alter the structure of certain markets to allow the competitive process to produce socially acceptable results.*

It was not only in the agricultural sector that the government tried to ameliorate the functioning of the competitive process. In the industrial sector, as well, a new policy of active intervention sought to bring about a better working of the economic mechanism.

In industry as in agriculture, during the first years of acute economic distress, intervention mainly took the form of an attempt to limit supply. Under the provisions of the National Industrial Recovery Act (NIRA) passed in 1933, business was permitted to make sweeping price-and-production agreements (in return for wage agreements designed to better the incomes of the poorest paid). In other words, recovery was aimed at by legalizing the partial oligopolization of business.

The NIRA was greeted with great enthusiasm, and nearly 800 industrial "codes" were elaborated under it. But as the demoralized markets of the early 1930's regained some degree of orderliness, a new source of complaint arose. Smaller producers within many industries claimed that the codes favored the large producer. By the time the experiment was declared unconstitutional by the Supreme Court in 1935, it had already become apparent that the problem was not too much competition, but too little.

There arose a radical shift in policy signalled by the vigorous prosecution of the anti-trust laws, a development we traced in Chapter 5. Although the angle of attack had changed completely, the objective was much the same: *to make the market work.*

To what extent can the government make markets work? The answer, as we have seen, is far from certain. Against the powerful forces of oligopoly on the one hand, and the self-defeating competition of "atomistic" industries on the other, the market shaping powers of government may well prove to be inadequate. But in the formulation of the aim itself is evidence of a profoundly important change in the philosophy of the market society. No longer does *laissez-faire* constitute the ideal relationship between government and economy. Slowly there has arisen the conception of active public intervention to insure the orderly operation of the system.

Countering the Depression

The market system had broken down in a much more important way than was revealed in the farm glut or even in the manufacturing sector. Its real collapse in the 1930's was in its inability to solve the basic production problem itself—in its inability to put together human beings, capital, and land, in order to produce a satisfactory level of output for the nation.

It is curious that the Roosevelt administration had little clear idea of how to remedy this situation when it first took office. Neither, as we have seen, did the business community. Indeed, for nearly everyone, economists included, the only "remedy" for the Depression was thought to be a balanced budget for the government.

Yet there were emergencies to be faced that could not be deferred, even if they unbalanced the budget. Many of the unemployed were literally at the brink of starvation, and the resources of private, state, and local charity were in most instances exhausted. President Roosevelt, unlike his predecessor, did not believe that the receipt of federal relief would "demoralize" the unemployed any more than the receipt of federal loans from the Reconstruction Finance Corporation had "demoralized" business. By May of the inaugural year, a relief organization had been established; and a year later, nearly one out of every seven Americans was receiving relief. In nine states, one out of five families—in one state one out of three families—was dependent on public support. Not that relief did much more than keep these unfortunate families from starvation. The average grant per family was less than $25 per month.

The immediate aims of relief were humanitarian. Shortly, however, they were followed by thoughts of the *useful* possibilities of relief expenditures. Soon the great bulk of relief spending was being paid for public works of various sorts: schools, roads, parks, hospitals, slum clearance—and even federal art, theater, and writing projects.

As the public-works program grew, however, the finances of the federal government took a turn for the worse, until, by the mid-1930's, it was clear that something like a chronic deficit of $2 to $3 billion a year had been achieved. Each year the government spent more than it took in—not only for relief, but for conservation, farm subsidies, veterans' bonuses, public housing, aid to the states. To meet its bills it borrowed the necessary money from the public through the sale of government bonds to private individuals, to corporations, and to the commercial banks. Obviously, as the total amount of bonds outstanding grew each year, so did the total debt of the nation. In 1929, the national debt totaled $16.9 billion. By 1935 it had risen to $28.7 billion, and each year it steadily rose: to $36 billion in 1937, to $40 billion in 1939, to $42 billion in 1940.

The Economy Fails to Respond

At first the heavy spending of the federal government was greeted with wary acceptance by the business and banking communities as a necessary temporary expedient. Before long, however, even within the administration itself, the mounting deficit was regarded with considerable misgivings. The recurrent excesses of government expenditure over receipts was apologized for as "pump priming"—as an injection of government fuel which would, so to speak, start up the stalled motor of private expenditures. A few billions of government spending, it was hoped, would set into motion an upward spiral of spending and job expansion.

But the upward spiral did not materialize. After 1933, helped by government spending, *consumption* expenditures began to rise, but private capital expenditures lagged behind. Although they, too, improved after 1933, by 1938 they were still 40 per cent below 1929.

Why did private investment fail to rise? Partly, the answer lies in the fact that government deficits, themselves, frightened business. Coupled with the reform legislation of the New Deal, the new element of large-scale economic activity on the part of government caused business to lose its former "confidence." The businessman felt uncomfortable and ill-at-ease in a changing economic and political climate and was in no mood to plan boldly ahead for the future. The general outlook stressed caution rather than promise; cycles rather than growth; safety rather than gain. And then behind the psychological factors real forces were also at work. A much slower rate of population growth in the 1930's depressed the important housing market. Even more serious, no major industry-creating technological breakthrough, comparable to the railway or the automobile, held out sufficient promise of profitable growth to tempt private capital into a major capital-building boom of its own.

Thus, for many reasons the new federal expenditures did not prime the pump. Private investment did not spontaneously rise to take over its traditional propulsive function, now "temporarily" carried out by the government. With this reality came a further widening in the conception of the government's role within the market society. Government now began to be envisioned not only as a regulator of markets, but as a *permanent* stabilizing and growth-promoting agency for the market economy as a whole.

Compensatory Government Spending

The idea was slow in taking form and did not, in fact, receive its full-dress exposition until the middle 1930's.* As is often the case

---

* The most influential book setting forth the concept—albeit, in highly technical terms—was John Maynard Keynes' *General Theory of Employment, Interest and Money* published in 1936. Few books have roused such controversy or left so permanent a mark.

with new ideas, it seemed at first complicated and difficult, and even among professional economists its basic concepts were the subject of murky discussion for a number of years. Yet in retrospect, it appears as a very simple argument.

The key to prosperity or depression, it had become increasingly evident, lay in the *total volume of expenditure* which a market society laid out for its goods and services. When that volume was high, employment and incomes were high; when it declined, output and employment declined as well. And what determined the volume of expenditure? As we have seen, the stream of consumption spending tended to be a passive factor, rising when individuals' incomes rose and diminishing when they fell. The volatile item, as both history and theory made clear, was the stream of capital expenditure.*

From this starting point it is not difficult to take the next step. If lagging private capital expenditures were responsible for lagging employment and output, why could not the government step in to make up whatever deficiencies arose from private expenditure? There had always been, after all, a fairly regular flow of public expenditure, much of it for capital-creating purposes, such as roads or schools. Why could not this flow of public spending be deliberately enlarged when the occasion demanded, to maintain the needed total volume of expenditure? True, this required the government to borrow and spend and thereby increase its debt. But did not much private capital spending also result in corporate debts? And why could not the debt, itself, be handled as corporate debts which were never "paid off" in the aggregate but refunded, with new bond issues being sold to take the place of those coming due? †

To the economists of the Roosevelt administration, the answers to these questions seemed plain enough. The government not only could but should use its spending powers as an economic instrumentality for securing full employment. By this, they did not have

---

* Integrally connected with the expansion or contraction in total expenditure is the expansion or contraction in the volume of *money*. This process, a source of bewilderment to some senior bankers as well as to most college freshmen, can be mentioned only in passing in this account which seeks to concentrate on the "real" forces at work. The reader is warned however, that the role played by money is extremely important, although not to the extent that it vitiates the main lines of our exposition.

† It is worth noting that total corporate indebtedness has declined only in depression years. In normal times, it grows each year as corporations borrow funds for capital expenditure purposes. Total corporate debt in 1959 was $281 billion, compared with a $243 billion federal debt.

in mind a "radical" revision of capitalism. Rather, they envisaged the evolution of a new form of *guided* capitalism—of a market society in which the all-important levels of employment and output would no longer be left to the vagaries of the market but would be protected against decline and stimulated toward growth by public action.

This is not how matters appeared to many members of the nation, however, and especially to the business community. They saw government spending as inherently "wasteful," and the mounting debt as evidence that we would spend ourselves into "bankruptcy." Beneath these arguments there lurked a deeper suspicion, a suspicion that government spending, whatever the protestations to the contrary, was the entering wedge for socialism or worse.

The controversy raged through 1940. In a sense, it was an empty debate. At its peak, the annual deficit never touched $4 billion, and federal government purchases never contributed more than 6 per cent to Gross National Product. But if the fears of the conservatives were hardly realized, neither were the hopes of the liberals. For in the prevailing atmosphere of distrust, the remedy of government could never be more than half-heartedly applied. It was a holding operation and not an operation of growth. By 1939, although conditions had improved considerably over the levels of 1932, there were still 9.5 million people—17 per cent of the labor force—without work.

The Impact of the War

In the end, it was not theory that settled the history of compensatory government spending, but history that settled the theory. With the outbreak of World War II came a tremendous forced expansion in government outlays. Year by year, spending for war purposes rose, until in 1944 federal expenditures totaled just over $100 billion, and with this unprecedented rise in expenditure came an equally swift rise in GNP. By 1945, our Gross National Product had risen by 70 per cent in real terms over 1939, and unemployment had dwindled to the vanishing point. The "demonstration" that public spending could indeed impel the economy forward—indeed, could lift it beyond all previously imagined bounds—was unmistakable. So was the fact that a government could easily carry an enormously much larger debt—a debt which now towered over $250 billion—provided that its Gross National Product was also much larger.

And then, with the war had come a marked change in attitude both toward the government and to the economy in general. After four years of unprecedented effort, the American people looked to massive government action with a more accustomed eye; so, too, after four years of record output, they looked back upon the days of mass unemployment with a new feeling of shame. Perhaps most important of all, they looked ahead to the postwar period with considerable trepidation. Virtually every economist, contemplating the huge cutback in spending consequent upon a termination of hostilities, feared the rise of a vast new army of the unemployed. Even the most conservative opinion was uneasy at the political possibilities of such a return to the 1930's.

The upshot of the change in attitude was the passage of the Employment Act of 1946, one of the truly historic pieces of economic legislation. The act recognized (although in carefully circumspect terms) that it was "the continuing policy and responsibility of the Federal Government . . . to promote maximum employment, production, and purchasing power." It was, as we shall see, one thing to write such an act and another thing to implement it; but, without question, the Employment Act marked the end of an era. The idea that the best thing the government could do to promote recovery was to do nothing, the belief that a balanced budget was in all cases the goal for government fiscal policy, and beyond that, the trust in the blind forces of the market as inherently conducive to prosperity—all these once firmly held ideas of the past had been abandoned. The debate within capitalism was no longer whether or not government should undertake the responsibility for the overall functioning of the market system, but only over the specific means by which that end might be best achieved.

The Aftermath of the War: Inflation

The war ended in 1945; within a year, federal spending dropped by $40 billion, and the nation waited tensely for the expected fall in employment, incomes, and prices.

Instead, it found itself confronting the least anticipated of all eventualities: a rousing inflationary boom. It is true that unemployment doubled, rising to two million, but this was still less than 4 per cent of the labor force. Meanwhile, employment showed a steady rise: 54 million jobs in 1945; 57 million in 1946; 60 million in 1947; 63 million in 1950. Industrial production, after a brief postwar dip, was booming: by 1953 it would surpass its wartime peak with no sign of more than momentary turndown. Most striking of all was what happened to prices. Year by year, the cost of living rose: up a third between 1945 and 1948, up another 10 per cent between 1948 and 1952, up still another 7 per cent from then to 1957. In all, the purchasing power of the dollar declined by more than a third in the first twelve postwar years.

What was the cause of this totally unforeseen turn of events? There was no one single cause, but several. To begin with, the end of the war found America in a situation of "classic" inflationary potential: too much money and too little goods. The too little goods was, of course, the result of four years of wartime shortage; the too much money was the result of having added $150 billion to liquid savings during those same years of high incomes and consumer scarcity. With the end of the war, Americans lost no time in entering upon a mammoth spending spree.* Meanwhile, the nation's supply of money itself, in the form of bank deposits, was also high, owing to wartime financing. Banks and other credit institutions were all too happy to supply loans to consumers or corporations. Thus an enormous pressure of pent-up demand, financed out of past savings and current incomes, exerted its pressure on the price level.

A second reason for the inflationary boom was that spending was high in the nonconsumer areas. Government expenditures ceased falling in 1947 and sparked by rising state and local needs, began to increase again, augmented in 1950, when the Korean War added its fillip to federal expenditures. High exports and Marshall aid to Europe provided another stimulus. Perhaps more significant was that private capital expenditures proved themselves unexpectedly strong. Encouraged by the avalanche of consumer buying, by a host of new inventions and even industries stemming from the war, by a new impetus toward research and development, the

---

* In fact, it was this surprising and quite unexpected surge of consumption which was the main reason why the gloomy postwar economic forecasts were not fulfilled.

longest and steadiest period of capital accumulation in American history added its expenditures to the flow of purchasing power.

And then there was a third cause of the inflationary trend. In "pattern-setting" areas of industry, such as automobiles or steel, powerful unions succeeded in winning sharp wage increases. That, in itself, was not so unusual; but in these years of "easy money," there was nothing to prevent corporations from passing along the increases in terms of higher prices. What made matters still worse was that the wage increases (particularly in the mid-1950's) were often in excess of productivity increases, while the corporation price boosts (especially in the critical case of steel) were in excess of the wage boosts.[8] Easy money, strong labor unions, and oligopolistic industry all combined to create inflationary pressure points at strategic locations of the economy.

The Instruments of Policy

It was a very different situation from that which the advocates of compensatory government spending had envisioned in the late 1930's. All through the 1950's it was the problem of inflation which occupied the authorities—and without much more success than had attended their efforts to curb mass unemployment twenty years earlier. Yet the confrontation with the problem of inflation was not without results; for out of the debate which it created, there emerged for the first time a general consensus on the nature of the mechanisms the government was entitled to use in seeking to affect the over-all operation of the system.

They were three:

The first were *monetary controls,* mainly centered in the Federal Reserve banking system. By easing or tightening the reserve requirements which all banks had to maintain behind their deposits, the Federal Reserve was able to encourage or discourage lending, the source of much economic activity. In addition, by buying or selling government bonds, the Federal Reserve was able to make the whole banking system relatively flushed with funds, when these were needed, or relatively short of funds when money seemed in excess supply.

The second were *tax adjustments.* The pressure of consumer

8 See Gardiner Means, *Pricing Power and the Public Interest, op. cit.,* pp. 113 ff.

buying during the postwar boom served as a reminder of the fact that the largest fraction of the volume of total expenditure was always consumption spending. By raising or lowering taxes, particularly income taxes, the government could quickly increase or diminish this broad flow of purchasing power.

The third was *the federal budget*. By the 1950's, the great debate over the virtues of a balanced government budget had virtually come to an end. Among academic groups and in a widening circle of business leaders, the budget was recognized as a tool for regulating total national expenditure. In inflationary times, a budget surplus would serve to "mop up" part of the inflationary purchasing flow. In depressed times, a budget deficit (covered by borrowing) was a mechanism for generating a desired increase in that flow.

The idea of monetary controls was not new, but the general consensus on the use of taxes and budgets as deliberate instruments of economic policy to counter boom and recession *was* new. But again, it was not the force of theoretical argument which had won this historic agreement. Rather, it was the fact of historic change which had placed theory in a new light. For what commended the new means of influence over the market system were essentially profound changes in the structure of that system. Let us see what those changes were.

The Redistribution of Income

In our concentration on the functional problems of the economy in its years of depression, war, and inflation, we have omitted one extraordinary development. This was a marked movement away from the extreme inequalities of reward which so vividly marked the capitalism of the past.

In part, this was brought about by deliberately bolstering the economic position of lower income groups, through the support of trade unions, through the enactment of minimum wage floors, and through the passage of welfare legislation. The change was not entirely due to public policy, however. The occupational shifts which we noted at the commencement of our previous chapter played a powerful role, as workers shifted out of low-paid agricultural and unskilled labor into the semi-skilled and skilled categories of the factory.

However varied the causes, the results were striking:

PER CENT INCREASE IN AVERAGE INCOME
(1950 dollars)

	1956–36 to 1958
All groups	78
Lowest fifth	101
Second fifth	116
Third fifth	107
Fourth fifth	91
Highest fifth	57
Top 5 per cent	36

Source: *Statistical Abstract of the United States,* 1960, p. 319.

Note that the lowest and second fifths benefited almost twice as much as the highest fifth and more than three times as much as the top 5 per cent. While the bottom was coming up, the top was coming down—owing almost entirely to the pressure of much higher tax rates. Beginning with the New Deal and accelerating steeply during the war, a new attitude to—and enforcement of—income taxes bore down heavily on the affluence of the upper income groups. The table below gives us some idea of the change.

PER CENT SHARES OF TOTAL INCOME RECEIVED BY TOP
1 PER CENT AND TOP 5 PER CENT OF
TOTAL POPULATION

	1929	1940	1945	1957
Top 1%	18.92	9.89	7.71	n.a.
Top 5%	30.0	24.0	21.3	20.2

Source: *Historical Statistics of the United States,* G135, 105.

What had happened was quite extraordinary. The share of income going to the top one per cent had been cut by over 60 per cent. That going to the top 5 per cent had been cut by a third.

To be sure, we must exercise a certain caution in viewing these figures. They do not show large flows of income which are legally exempted from tax, such as tax-exempt interest, stock option rights, expense accounts and the like. We do not know the extent to which such new tax-induced ways of "smuggling" income reduce the reliability of the figures, but it may be by a fairly substantial amount.*

Nonetheless, with all these cautions, it is undeniable that the years following the New Deal ushered in a remarkable over-all redistribution of income. If we look back from a recent date to 1929, the change is truly startling.

INCOME DISTRIBUTION IN 1929 AND 1958

Income levels 1958	Per cent of all households with this actual income in 1958	Per cent of all households with equivalent of this income in 1929
Less than $2000	14	21
2000 — 3000	10	21
3000 — 4000	12	18
4000 — 5000	13	11
5000 — 10000	38	21
10000 +	13	8

Source: 1929, from *America's Capacity to Consume,* Brookings, 1934; p. 54. 1958, Survey of Current Business, April 1959, p. 14.

But now it is time to return to our main theme. For what we have here is not only a mass escalation in the income stratification of the nation—a development noteworthy in itself from the point of view of welfare. We see, as well, the development of a "middle-income" society *in which income taxation provides a powerful mechanism of economic influence.*

One last table should make the point. (See top of p. 174.)

The upward shift in the economic center of gravity of the nation has brought about a situation in which, for the first time, a change in income taxes can directly affect mass purchasing activity.

To a certain extent, let us note, this form of influence over the nation's expenditure works automatically. Because income taxes are graduated—that is, take a larger slice of income as the size of income increases—tax collections tend to rise *faster* (and to fall

* In addition, we must note that there is little if any evidence that the ownership of *wealth*—bank accounts, stocks and bonds, and the like—has changed much despite the change in incomes. Wealth in the United States is still highly concentrated in the topmost groups of the population; for instance, it is estimated that the top one per cent of all "spending units" own at least 65 per cent of all corporate stock and that the wealthiest one-tenth of one per cent owns 35 per cent of it. See Butters, *et al., Effects of Taxation: Investment of Individuals,* Cambridge, 1960, p. 25. Cf., also, Lampman, *Changes in the Share of Wealth Held by Top Wealth Holders,* 1922–56, NBER Paper 71, 1960.

IMPACT OF INDIVIDUAL INCOME TAXES

	Number of taxable returns (millions)	Total income tax paid ($ billions)	Total income tax as % of total consumption	Income tax liability of median family income ($)
1929	2.5	1.0	1	17
1940	7.4	1.4	2	101*
1957	46.8	34.4	12	622

Source: *Historical Statistics,* Series Y, 293, 299, 303, 307.
* (1941)

faster) than rises or falls in GNP. Hence there is an automatic release of additional purchasing power as business slackens and incomes decline; while as business booms and incomes swell, there is an automatic tightening of the reins.*

The Growth of the Government Sector

The redistribution of income provides us with an understanding of the rationale behind one of the new instruments of economic manipulation. An insight into the second of our new instruments is provided if we examine another structural alteration in the economy: the change in the relative size of the government contribution to Gross National Product.

The table below gives us the magnitude of the change.

GROWTH OF THE PUBLIC SECTOR
(*current dollars*)

Year	GNP (billions)	Gov't. purchases of goods and services (billions)		All gov't. purchases as per cent of GNP
		Federal	State & Local	
1929	104.4	1.3	7.2	8.1
1940	100.6	6.2	7.9	14.0
1960	504.4	52.9	47.2	19.8

Source: *Historical Statistics,* Series F, 67, 81, 86; *Economic Indicators* (Washington, D.C.: Government Printing Office, 1962).

* We should note that income taxes also affect *business* income in much the same way as they affect personal income.

It is clear from the table that a major shift has taken place. Whereas in 1929 less than one dollar in ten of national production owed its origin to government purchasing, today about one dollar in five of all goods and services produced is sold to some branch of the government.

Here, too, lies a source of the new concensus on the mechanisms of influence. Today the government is in a position of such commanding economic strength that it cannot *avoid* influencing the trend of total expenditure, even by relatively modest changes in its budgetary balance. For example, a 10 per cent fall in government receipts and a 10 per cent rise in expenditures will add to total GNP expenditures an amount equal to one-and-a-half times all manufacturing investment; in 1929, a similar change in the budget position would have contributed new purchasing power equal to only one-tenth of all manufacturing investment.

We should notice as well, that this form of control also has its "automatic" features. As incomes in the nation fall, government payments such as unemployment insurance or crop payments, rise; while, at the same time, its tax collections decline. And, of course, the budget can also be deliberately unbalanced by expanding or accelerating programs such as road construction and the like.

Remaining Problems

Does the existence of these automatic stabilizers and the general consensus on the mechanisms of influence mean that economic fluctuations such as the Great Depression cannot recur?

It is certainly unlikely in the extreme that the terrible experience of the early 1930's will be repeated. Many of its causes, as we noted, were rooted in particular excesses of the times, and these, to a very large extent, have been corrected. The flimsiness of the banking structure, the severe maldistribution of income—and perhaps most important of all, the barrier of inadequate economic understanding —have all been removed or much improved.*

---

* No small part of our present strengthened, defensive economic "posture" can be credited to the growing comprehension of the economics of compensatory government action on the part of the business community. The graduates of the colleges and business schools who now play an important role in the direction of corporate affairs are not likely to be panicked by government action to counteract a slump as were their fathers in the 1930's.

But this general reassurance should not lead us to the easy assumption that therefore economic fluctuations of considerable severity and unemployment of uncomfortable magnitude are not still possibilities. The basic cause of instability in the market system remains; and so long as anticipated profit is the critical link between savings and investment, it will continue to remain. Irregular bursts of capital formation, recurrent downward revisions of profit anticipations are virtually inseparable from an economic system in which the process of technical change and its conversion into real capital are left to the unguided impulses of individual business firms.

To be sure, we now possess powerful instruments of economic compensation against the *cumulative effects* of these shocks—protections we have never enjoyed (or understood) before. But the mere existence of these instruments does not guarantee that they will, in fact, be used. The political problems of adjusting taxes quickly, for instance, are well known—especially when the economic indications point to the need for a *rise* in taxes. Lingering fears of an unbalanced budget may delay or even prevent the use of compensatory government expenditure. Finally, let us remember that nearly half our present total government expenditure (and 85 per cent of our *federal* expenditure) goes for defense purposes. The effective use of a compensatory mechanism in a truly *peacetime* economy might be much more difficult than in an economy where a large defense sector offers a politically acceptable area for public spending.

There is, in addition, at least one weakness of the 1920's which we have *not* corrected. This is the trend toward technological displacement—a trend which in our day has assumed new and possibly menacing dimensions with the advent of the technology of automation. For example, between 1953 and 1960, manufacturing output rose by 17 per cent, while manufacturing employment on the production line *dropped* 5 per cent. During the same period, automobile output rose 26 per cent, while auto employment in the factories fell 16 per cent. Similarly, between 1950 and 1959, textile mill output rose by 14 per cent, while textile mill production workers decreased by over 25 per cent.[9] Thus an undercurrent of technological displacement has eaten into our job supply, and all the more seriously as a bulge in young job seekers has begun to swell our labor force.

[9] *Business in Brief,* Chase Manhattan Bank, March–April 1961; for textiles, *Statistical Abstract,* 1960, pp. 209, 781.

How does a market economy adjust to such a challenge?

We have already dealt with one response: the creation of new industries. There are other responses, no less important, to which we must now pay heed. One of these is to utilize the enormous gains in productivity to enjoy a much larger amount of *voluntary* unemployment. That is, we may absorb the work-displacing effect of technology by working less. As one writer has put it: "If the sixty-hour workweek still prevailed, only forty million workers would be needed to produce the 1961 national product and some 27 million workers would be unemployed."[10]

A second manner in which we absorb the long-term unemployment effects of technological progress is by shifting ever more of our labor force into "nonproduction" employment: trade and transportation, retail and service industries, government. We exchange material production for what might be called social production—for the network of nongoods-producing activities which is one of the hallmarks of a highly developed and prosperous economy. Today we employ fewer people in the United States in the actual production of goods—in agriculture, mining, manufacturing, and construction—than in the service sector of the economy: in trade, finance, retailing, and the like.[11]

No doubt these great compensatory shifts into new industries, into leisure and social production will continue, but the rate at which they manifest themselves must adjust itself to what seems to be an *accelerating* tempo of labor-displacing technological change. The growth of automation, with its possibilities for labor-displacing inventions in office work as well as in the factory, poses a major problem for our new instruments of economic policy and one with which they are not specifically designed to cope. What is needed to prevent pockets of technological unemployment from sapping the strength of the economy is not so much the broad corrective of increased aggregate expenditure as specific shifts of labor from distressed areas and industries to expansive industries and areas. To accomplish this end, the existing implements of economic correction may not be applicable.

[10] Gerard Piel, *Science in the Cause of Man* (New York: Alfred A. Knopf, 1961), p. 284.

[11] See Alvin H. Hansen, *Economic Issues of the 1960's* (New York: McGraw-Hill Book Company, Inc., 1960), p. 70.

A Final Prospect

It is well to remind ourselves, as we close this chapter of our economic history, that we have not yet solved the basic production problem of society with sufficient dependability to write off the danger of unemployment and recession. The problems of using our economic tools courageously, of adapting them to the needs of a genuinely peacetime economy, of coping with the undertow of technological displacement are far from solved.

Nor have we, for all our gains in income distribution, yet achieved a solution to the basic distribution problem of which we can be wholly proud. Negro families in America today, for example, average but half the income of white families, largely because job discrimination throws them into the bottom of the income heap. Of 16 million elderly people in the United States, some 2.5 million are without Social Security and live as wards of their communities on tiny incomes. The median income of all rural families in the South is only fractionally over $2,000, and again, for Negroes, half of that.

It is important to remind ourselves of these failures. And yet, the magnitude of the over-all achievement must not be underrated on this account. For the first time in history, something approaching a society of "average" well-being has been won. If the sweep of economic history which has given us this society is maintained, the future may well see the advent of the first society in which the economic problem, for all intents and purposes, is solved. By 1980, if our trend of growth of the last thirty years is maintained, average family incomes will have risen to at least $8,000, allowing for a population increase and calculating in terms of today's prices. By the year 2000, we should be able to expect average factory earnings to approximate $10,000. This assumes of course that we will continue to display a vigorous rate of economic growth and that neither depression nor war will bring expansion to a halt. No one would be wise in taking such projections as indicating anything but a general forecast of *potentialities*. But the fact is that the potentialities are there.

Will the American economy realize the promise before it?

As economists, we cannot answer the question with assurance. A knowledge of economic history and economic theory enables us to think about these problems with greater clarity and in a longer perspective than otherwise, but it would be idle to pretend that answers are vouchsafed to us. A host of mutually dependent factors—not all of them economic by any means—will determine the ultimate answer: the rate and kind of technological change, the skill and leadership of government, the degree of market flexibility of massive business and labor organizations, the subtle sociological influences stemming from affluence itself. Finally, we must realize that much of what the future will bring will not be decided by America. Our economy exists today in the midst of a revolutionary setting of history which, from many directions, is exerting powerful and unaccustomed pressures on our society. The future of American capitalism is inextricably tied up with the future of a world in ferment and upheaval. Thus it is appropriate that we turn now, in the next chapter of our survey of economic evolution, to the main events of economic history in the world about us.

7

The Drift of Modern Economic History

In our last chapters we have followed the broad development of American capitalism down to present times. Now, as we turn back from America to the continents of the East, West, and South an extraordinary fact strikes us immediately. When we left the European scene, in the early 1800's, capitalism was fast becoming the dominant form of economic society. England, as we saw, was the very cradle of industrial capitalism itself; France was rousing herself to follow in England's footsteps; elsewhere on the continent, if capitalism was not already established, it was clearly waiting in the wings for the last remnants of feudalism to disappear. Had we looked abroad from America at any time in the nineteenth century, our expectations would have been fully justified. By then all of Europe was unquestionably capitalist in orientation. And not only Europe—by the end of the nineteenth century, capitalism had reached out to touch most of the other continents of the world. In Asia and Africa, the main European nations had established colonies or spheres of influence which projected the imprint of capitalism into societies, many of which had barely awakened from an age-long slumber of ancient ways. In South America, as well, capitalism was clearly the main fertilizing influence. Even in reactionary Russia—the last of the great European powers to abolish the legal fetters of feudalism— by the early 1900's, capitalism had succeeded in creating a small but active nucleus from which further growth seemed assured.

Yet what do we find today? To our astonishment, the seemingly unopposed evolution of the world into a capitalist market system has not taken place. In Europe, its original birthplace, capitalism continues to be the dominant economic system; and, yet we find that socialist parties either hold power or constitute the main opposition in England, France, Belgium, Netherlands, Italy, Sweden, Norway, Denmark, Germany, and Austria. In Russia, the nucleus of capitalism has been entirely swept away by a communist society. In the huge continents of the East and South—in Asia and Africa and South America—we find that the original organizing impetus of capitalism has given way, in many of the most important nations, to a noncapitalist framework of economic organization. China is more communist than communist Russia. India proclaims herself a socialist state. So do Indonesia, Burma, Ceylon, Egypt, Ghana, Guinea. Only in South America do we find socialism absent from the official ideologies of political economy, and even there, the example of Cuba and the rumblings elsewhere hardly make it possible to anticipate the kind of capitalist society which we would have expected fifty years ago.

What happened outside America to abort the seemingly assured development of capitalism? A full answer to such a question would require much more than a book in itself, but we can begin to grasp the main picture of evolutionary trends if we follow, first, the factors which caused capitalism in Europe to take on a form different from that in America. From Europe it is not so long a jump, geographically or historically, to Russia; and from Russia we can turn with increased understanding to the so-called "underdeveloped" world.

European Capitalism: Feudal Heritage and National Rivalry

What are the reasons behind the turn of events in Europe? They must be sought, to begin with, not in the economic tendencies of European capitalism but in the social and political background whence those tendencies emerged.

Certainly the social background was significantly different from that of America. In the New World, capitalism developed with a population which had, to a large degree, spiritually and physically shed the feudal encumbrances of the Old World; but in that Old World, many of the social outlooks and habitudes of the past lingered on. An awareness of class position—and more than that, an explicit recognition of class hostility—was as conspicuous by its presence in Europe as by its absence in America. In Vienna, in 1847, writes one social historian:

> At the top were the nobles who considered themselves the only group worth noticing. The human race starts with barons, said one of them. Then there were the big businessmen who wanted to buy their way into the human race; the little businessmen; the proud but poor intellectuals; the students who were still poorer and still prouder; and the workers who were poor and had always been very, very humble.[1]

The result was a totally different climate for the development of an economic society. In America, building on a new and vigorous foundation, capitalism was, from the beginning, a system of social consensus; in Europe, building on a feudal base, it was deeply tinged with class conflict. While capitalism in America managed without any effort to embrace the aspirations of its "lower orders," in Europe, already by the time of the revolutions of 1848, those lower orders had turned their backs on capitalism as a vehicle for their hopes and beliefs.

Second and no less important in explaining the divergence of American and European economic evolution was the profound difference between the political complexion of the two continents. In America, save only for the terrible crisis of the Civil War, a single national purpose fused the continent; in Europe, an historic division

[1] Priscilla Robertson, *Revolutions of 1848* (New York: Harper & Brothers, Torchbooks, 1960), p. 194.

of languages, customs, and mutually suspicious nationalities again and again prevented just such a fusion.

Accordingly, American capitalism came of age in an environment in which political unity permitted the unhindered growth of an enormous unobstructed market, while in Europe a jigsaw puzzle of national boundaries forced industrial growth to take place in cramped quarters and in an atmosphere of continued national rivalry. It is curious to note that whereas Europe was considered "wealthier" than America all through the nineteenth century, in point of fact, American productivity in many fields began to outstrip that of Europe from at least the 1850's, and perhaps much earlier. For instance, at the Paris Exposition of 1854, an American threshing machine was twice as productive as its nearest (English) rival and eleven times as productive as its least (Belgian) competitive model.[2]

These advantages of geographic space, richness of resources, and political unity were widened by subsequent developments in European industry. Not surprisingly, European producers, like those in America, sought to limit the destructive impact of industrial competition, and for this purpose they turned to *cartels*—contractual (rather than merely voluntary) agreements to share markets or fix prices. Unlike the case in America, however, this self-protective movement received the blessing, overt or tacit, of European governments. Although "anti-cartel" laws existed in many European countries, in fact, these laws were almost never enforced: by 1914 there were over 100 international cartels, representing the most varied industries, in which most European nations participated.*

Cartelization was undoubtedly good for the profit statements of the cartelized firms, but it was hardly conducive to growth—either for those firms or new ones. By establishing carefully delineated and protected "preserves," the cartel system rewarded unaggressive behavior rather than economic daring; and together with the ever-present problem of cramping national frontiers, it drove European producers into a typical high-cost, high profit-margin, low-volume pattern rather than into the American pattern of very large plants with very high efficiencies. The difference in economic scale is dra-

---

2 Cochran and Miller, *op. cit.*, p. 58.

* By 1939 an estimated 109 cartels also had American participation, since American companies were not prohibited by anti-trust laws from joining international restrictive agreements.

matically illustrated by steel. In 1885, Great Britain led the world in the production of steel; fourteen years later her entire output was less than that of the Carnegie Steel Company alone.

As a result, by the early twentieth century, European productivity lagged very seriously behind American. A study by Professor Taussig in 1918 showed that the daily output of coal per underground worker was 4.68 tons in the United States, as contrasted with 1.9 tons in Great Britain, 1.4 tons in Prussia, and 0.91 tons in France. In 1905, the output of bricks per person was 141,000 in the United States and 40,000 in Germany; pig iron production was 84.5 tons per worker in 1909, compared with only 39 tons in Great Britain in 1907.[3] As the twentieth century went on, United States production pulled steadily ahead.

The divergence was strikingly noticeable in per capita incomes. In 1911, for example, when per capita income in the United States was $368, the corresponding figure for Great Britain was $250, for Germany $178, for France $161, for Italy $108. By 1928, American per capita income was $541 (in unchanged dollar values), while that of the United Kingdom was only $293; of Germany, $199; of France, $188; and of Italy, $96.[4] While American per capita incomes had grown by nearly 46 per cent, English and French per capita incomes had increased only a third as rapidly, German incomes rose only about a quarter as fast, and Italian per capita incomes had actually declined.*

The Breakdown of International Trade

Still another consequence followed from the division of European industry and agriculture into national compartments. To a far greater extent than in America, it made the development of European capitalism subject to the expansion of *international trade*.

It is significant that we have been able to describe the main lines of American economic growth without even mentioning interna-

---

[3] From Heinrich E. Friedlaender and Jacob Oser, *Economic History of Modern Europe* (Englewood Cliffs, N.J.: Prentice-Hall, Inc., 1953), p. 224.

[4] *Ibid.*, p. 522.

* We must be wary of placing too much faith in the translation of one income—say £500—into its "equivalent"—$1400. Until we know the price levels, the living standards and customs of the nations we are comparing, we make such translations strictly at our own risk. But changes *within* a country, from year to year, are, of course, as meaningful in one currency as in another.

tional trade. American growth did depend, to a very important degree, on commodities and capital funds which it was able to obtain from other lands. In Colonial times, foreign trade was the very economic lifeline of the country; and even in 1850 it is estimated that 20 per cent of the goods we consumed were imported.[5] By 1880, however, this was reduced to 10 per cent, and thereafter the trend was steadily downward. Imports as a per cent of GNP were never above 5 per cent in the twentieth century, and latterly, scarcely half of that. Similarly, exports, although of critical importance for certain industries (and for agriculture), never bulked as a major fraction of our total output. Thus international trade, taken as a whole, never dominated our economic picture.

In Europe, however, quite the contrary was the case. Here the division of the continent into many national units made international trade a continuous and critical preoccupation of economic life. For instance, a study has shown that in 1913, when manufactured imports provided but 3.6 per cent of United States' consumption of manufactured goods, they provided 9 per cent of Germany's, 14 per cent of England's, 21 per cent of Sweden's.[6] Perhaps even more striking is the degree to which some nations in Europe depended on international trade for the foodstuffs on which they lived: in the five years preceding World War I, for instance, England produced less than 20 per cent of the wheat she consumed and barely over 55 per cent of the meat.[7] We find the same dependence on foreign trade in the export side of the picture. Whereas the United States in 1913 exported a mere fifteenth of its national product, France and Germany exported a fifth, and Britain nearly a quarter of theirs.

To a far greater degree than America, Europe lived by foreign trade. The significance here needs underscoring, particularly for Americans. For we do not often appreciate that trade (with its semantic emphasis on "exchange") is, in fact, inextricably associated with production and *productivity*.

Why productivity? Because trade enables us to concentrate our effort and resources on the production of those things for which they

[5] J. Frederic Dewhurst, *et al.*, *America's Needs and Resources* (New York: Twentieth Century Fund, 1947), p. 513.

[6] *Der Deutsche Aussenhandel* (Berlin: 1932), II, 23.

[7] Friedlaender and Oser, *op. cit.*, p. 206.

are best suited. We could, for instance, at very considerable cost grow coffee in the United States. To do so, however, would use our land, labor, and capital in highly inefficient ways, instead of putting them to use where their productivity is high—say, in the production of cars. The fact that we can *trade* cars for coffee gives us the best of both worlds: we can have our coffee without sacrificing our productivity by producing a coffee crop. Ideally, the same advantages accrue to the coffee producer who would be sacrificing his productivity were he to devote his resources to the production of cars.* Trade makes possible a *division of labor* from which *all* gain.

Here we clearly see the advantage possessed by the enormous unbroken American market over the fragmented national markets of Europe. In America, the division of labor was permitted to attain whatever degree of efficiency technology made possible; for, in the end, virtually all products entered into a single vast market where they could be exchanged against one another. In Europe, where the need for, and the potential benefits of, a far-reaching division of labor were no less pressing, a tangle of national barriers prevented the optimal specialization of effort from taking place.

What was visible in Europe was a struggle between the need for international trade as a primary means for advancing productivity and the retarding hand of national suspicions, rivalries and distrusts. A striking example was provided as recently as the early 1950's by the great cluster of European steel and coal industry near the German-Belgian-Luxembourg borders. Here, in a triangle, 250 miles on a side, was gathered 90 per cent of European steel-making capacity in a kind of European "Pittsburgh." But this natural geographic division of labor had to contend with political barriers which largely vitiated its physical productivity. Typically, German coal mines in the Ruhr sold their output to French steelmakers at prices 30 per cent higher than to German plants; while, in turn, French iron-ore producers charged far higher prices in Germany than at home. As a result, while American steel production soared 300 per cent between 1913 and 1950, the output of Europe's steel triangle rose but 3 per cent during the same period.

* As we shall later see, there are complications, with roots deep in history and politics, which prevent the full benefits of trade from manifesting themselves with many of the world's "coffee producers." The reasons for this will emerge in our discussion of the underdeveloped countries at the end of this chapter.

Our example, itself, poses a question, however. Prior to 1913, as we have seen, something like a great international division of labor did, in fact, characterize the European market, albeit to nothing like the extent seen in America. By 1913, we will remember, a very considerable flow of international trade was enhancing European productivity, despite the hindrances of cartels and national divisiveness. It was only the beginning of a truly free and unhampered international market, but at least it *was* a beginning.

What brought this promising achievement to an end? Initially, it was the shock of the first World War, with its violent sundering of European trade channels and its no less destructive aftermath of punitive reparations, war debts, and monetary troubles. In a sense, Europe never recovered from its World War I experience. The slow drift toward national economic separatism, at the expense of international economic cooperation, now accelerated fatefully. Tariffs and quotas multiplied to place new handicaps before the growth of international trade. Then, the Depression of 1929 came as the final blow. As the Depression spread "contagiously," nation after nation sought to quarantine itself by erecting still further barriers against economic contacts with other countries. Starting in 1929, an ever-tightening contraction of trade began to strangle economic life on the continent.* Between the late 1920's and the mid-1930's, manufactured imports (in constant prices) fell by a third in Germany, by nearly 40 per cent in Italy, by almost 50 per cent in France.[8] As international trade collapsed, so did Europe's chance for economic growth. For two long decades there followed a period of stagnation which earned for Europe the name of the "tired continent."

European Socialism

Against this background of economic malfunction it is easier to understand the growing insecurity which afflicted European capitalism. During the 1930's serious rumblings were already heard. In England, the Socialist Labour Party had clearly displaced the middle-class Liberals as the Opposition. In France, a mildly socialist

---

* It was not only European trade which declined, but *world* trade. For 53 grim months following January 1929, the volume of world trade was lower each month than the preceding.

[8] *Industrialization and Foreign Trade* (League of Nations, 1945), p. 160.

"Popular Front" government came to the fore, as it did in Austria. Even in Italy and Germany, the fascist dictators repeatedly declared their sympathy with "socialist" objectives—and whereas their declarations may have been no more than a sop to the masses, it was certainly indicative of the sentiments the masses wanted to hear.

What was the aim of European socialism?

We can sum it up in two words: *equality* and *planning*. By equality, socialism meant first, of course, greater economic equality—higher wages for the working class and more stringent taxation for the upper class. But the meaning of the word did not confine itself to economic privilege. It stood also for social and political equality, for an end to the privileges of hierarchical status which, as we have seen, were deeply entrenched in the European heritage. Thus European socialism was a movement closely associated with *political democracy*, a fact which earned for it the enmity of not only the Right, but of the Communist Left as well.*

Socialism was concerned with removing more than the existing injustices of the European capitalist order; it sought as well to remove the economic malfunction of that order by replacing it with a planned economy. This objective did not imply, as with the Communists, the total state control of all enterprise and agriculture. To most socialists, planning meant only that the strategic centers of production would be nationalized, while the remainder of the economy would be regulated by indirect controls, not too much unlike those we have seen developed in America, reinforced by appropriate actions taken by the nationalized sector itself.

By the end of World War II, socialist ideas were clearly in the ascendant throughout most of Europe. Even before the war was concluded, the Labour Party swept into office in England and rapidly nationalized the Bank of England, the coal and electricity industries, much of the transport and communications industry, and finally steel. As the first postwar governments were formed, it was evident that a socialist spectrum extended across Europe from Scandanavia through the Lowlands and France to Italy (where the communists came within an ace of gaining power). To many observers, it seemed as if capitalism in Europe had come to the end of its rope.

---

* Another very important difference between the Socialist and Communist movements was that the Socialists preached gradualism rather than revolution, and abhorred the use of violence.

Yet, European capitalism did not come to an end. Instead, beginning in the late 1940's and early 1950's, it embarked on what is unquestionably its period of strongest economic growth. How could this have come about?

The first reason was that the postwar Socialist governments were not revolutionary but reform administrations. Once in power, they quickly instituted a number of welfare and social planning measures, such as public health facilities, family benefits and allowances, improved social security and the like, but they did not engage in changes of a sweeping order. When many of the socialist governments, facing the exigencies of the postwar period, were voted out again, they bequeathed to the conservatives the framework of a welfare state *which the conservatives accepted.* Consequently, we find today that in most European states, welfare expenditures form a considerably higher proportion of government expenditures than they do in the United States. We get some idea of this if we compare *nondefense* government expenditure among Western nations.

GOVERNMENT NONDEFENSE PURCHASES OF GOODS AND SERVICES
AS A PROPORTION OF GNP

	Per cent
U.S. (1957)	9.7
West Germany (1953)	14.3
Belgium (1952)	11.0
United Kingdom (1953)	13.1
Sweden (1952)	13.6

Source: Francis Bator, *The Question of Government Spending* (New York: Harper & Brothers, 1960), Table 14, p. 157.

Hearkening back to one of the traditional weaknesses of European capitalism, we can say that this represents an attempt to create a social service state which will mend the historic antagonism of the lower classes.

The second reason was even more important. This was the rise of a movement *within* the conservative ranks to overcome a still more dangerous heritage of the past—the national division of markets.

This great step toward creating a full-scale continental market for European producers is called the European Community—or more usually, the Common Market.

To some extent, the Common Market was born out of the vital impetus given to European production by the Marshall Plan. Despite Marshall aid, it soon became apparent that Europe's upward climb would necessarily be limited if production were once again restrained by cartels and national protectionism. To forestall a return to the stagnation of the pre-war period, a few far-sighted and courageous statesmen, primary among them Jean Monnet and Robert Schuman, proposed a truly daring plan for the abolition of Europe's traditional economic barriers.

The plan as it took shape called for the creation of a *supra-national* (not merely an inter-national) organization to integrate the steel and coal production of France, Germany, Italy, Belgium, Luxembourg, and the Netherlands. The new Iron and Steel Community, was to have a High Authority with power to eliminate all customs duties on coal and steel products among members of the Community, to outlaw all discriminatory pricing and trade practices, to approve or disapprove all mergers, to order the dissolution of cartels, and to provide social and welfare services for all Community miners and steelworkers. The Authority was to be given direct power to inspect books, levy fines, and enforce its decrees—and still more remarkable, it was to be responsible not to any single member government but to a multi-national Parliament and a multi-national Court, both to be created as part of the Community. A Council of Ministers was to act as a *national* advisory and permissory body, but even here action could be taken by majority vote, so that no single nation (or even two nations) could block a decision desired by the Community as a whole.

By the fall of 1952, the Coal and Steel Community was a reality, and it lost no time going about its business. At mid-1954, customs duties and discriminatory pricing within the coal and steel "triangle" had been virtually eliminated, and roughly 40 per cent more coal and steel was being shipped across national boundaries than had been shipped prior to the establishment of the Community.

The success of the Coal and Steel Community led, in 1956, to the next two organizations: Euratom, a supranational atomic power agency, and the Common Market itself, an organization which was to do for commodities in general what the Coal and Steel Community had done for its products. Under the Common Market treaty, a definite schedule of tariff cuts was laid down, envisaging by 1969, at the latest, an entirely unimpeded continental market for Common Market members, with a single "external" tariff vis-à-vis the world. In addition, there were to be a single agricultural policy and, perhaps most imaginative, full freedom for the inter-member mobility of both capital and labor.

The Common Market is still in the process of achieving many of these goals, although it is well ahead of its timetable. Already, however, it has led to a remarkable increase in European production. By the early 1960's, industrial production has more than doubled, and agricultural output has risen by a third. Over the entire decade, western Europe's rate of growth has exceeded by 50 per cent that of the United States, and most important of all, for the first time the standard of living for the middle and working classes of Europe has begun to resemble that of America.

The Rise of Conservative Planning

It is not merely in these prosperous statistics that the European situation reminds us of the general course of affairs in the United States. Looking deeper, we can see a more profound resemblance. Abroad, as in America, the market system has had to turn toward what we might call "conservative planning" in order to survive.

In Europe, the direction of public intervention has perforce concerned itself with international trade more than is the case with the United States. The underlying problems and philosophy of conservative planning are much the same nonetheless. A need to keep the market process within bounds, to insure its continued smooth operation, to stabilize and, if need be, to stimulate its operation, has resulted in a strengthening of the role of government in both market societies. A growing agreement on the role of government as the active guardian of social welfare marks European as well as American capitalism, and a consensus on the use of monetary and tax and budgetary powers of adjustment again testifies to a common avenue of approach to the solution of common problems on both sides of the Atlantic.

This does not mean that the European situation is entirely comparable to America. Although the economy of Europe is today more dynamic, more hopeful, than perhaps ever in the past, its political problems have not yet been fully overcome. An undercurrent of political dissension continues to threaten the stability of many European countries, not only from the extreme Left but from the far Right, bringing about a certain tension in political life from which the United States has been mercifully spared. Then, too, the continued presence of a strong "socialist" movement, no matter how cooled its ardor or how watered-down its program, indicates that capitalism as an *ideology* is not yet without substantial opposition.

Thus European capitalism remains, to a certain extent, on political trial, despite its economic recovery. Yet, if history teaches us anything, it is that economic success tends to breed political success. If the trend of the past decade can be continued—and the purely economic auguries are reasonably favorable—there is surely reason to hope for a strengthening of the European social consensus and for a further healing of its historic political wounds.

NONMARKET ECONOMIES: THE SOVIET UNION

In the recovery of European capitalism through its development of a conservative planning structure, we have seen one aspect of the slow evolution of the modern economic history. Clearly, however, this is not the most significant change of the past half-century or so. For this we must look to the emergence of a *totally planned, nonmarket* society as the dominant economic pattern for at least a quarter of the globe. Here the guiding impetus of change has been the Soviet Union.

Early Soviet Planning

We cannot here recount in detail the history of Soviet socialism. Let us, rather, begin by noting the extraordinarily difficult problem that faced the revolutionary leaders who had secured the victory of "socialism" in Russia in 1917. In the first place, Russia was a semifeudal society in which capitalism was restricted to a small industrial and commercial sector. Second, both production and distribution were highly disorganized in the chaotic situation following the civil war. Finally, there was little guidance in the official literature of the Communist movement as to how a socialist society should be run. Marx's *Das Kapital,* the great seminal work of communism, was entirely devoted to a study of capitalism; and in those few essays in which Marx looked to the future, his gaze rarely traveled beyond the watershed of the revolutionary act itself. With the achievement of the revolution, Marx thought, a temporary regime known as "the dictatorship of the proletariat" would take over the transition from capitalism to socialism, and thereafter a "planned socialist economy" would emerge as the first step towards a still less specified "communism." In the latter state—the final terminus of economic evolution according to Marx—there were hints that the necessary but humdrum tasks of production and distribution would take place by the voluntary cooperation of all citizens and that society would turn its serious attention to matters of cultural and humanistic importance.

In reality, the Revolution presented Lenin, Trotsky, and the other leaders of the new Soviet Union with problems far more complex than this utopian long-term design. Shortly after the initial success of the Revolution, Lenin nationalized the banks, the major factories, the railways, and canals. In the meantime, the peasants, themselves, had taken over the large landed estates on which they had been tenants and had carved them up into individual holdings. The central authorities then attempted for several years to run the economy by requisitioning food from the farms and allocating it to factory workers, while controlling the flow of output from the factories themselves by a system of direct controls from above.

This initial attempt to run the economy was a disastrous failure. Under inept management (and often cavalier disregard of "bourgeois" concerns with factory management), industrial output declined precipitously—by 1920 it had fallen to *14 per cent* of prewar levels. As goods available to the peasants became scarcer, the peasants, themselves, were less and less willing to acquiesce in giving up food to the cities. The result was a wild inflation followed by a degeneration into an economy of semi-barter. For a while, toward the end of 1920, the system threatened to break down completely.

To forestall the impending collapse, in 1921 Lenin instituted a New Economic Policy—the so-called NEP. This was a return toward a market system and a partial reconstitution of actual capitalism.

Retail trade, for instance, was opened again to private ownership and operation. Small-scale industry also reverted to private direction. Most important, the farms were no longer requisitioned but operated as profit-making units. Only the "comanding heights" of industry and finance were retained in government hands.

There ensued for several years a bitter debate as to the course of action to follow next. While the basic aim of the Soviet government was still to industrialize and to socialize (i.e., to replace the private ownership of the means of production by state ownership), the question was how fast to move ahead—and, indeed, *how* to move ahead. The pace of industrialization hinged critically on one highly uncertain factor—the willingness of the large, private peasant sector to make food deliveries with which the city workers could be sustained in their tasks. To what extent, therefore, should the need for additional capital-goods be sacrificed in order to turn out the consumption goods which could be used as an inducement for peasant cooperation?

The Drive to Total Planning

The student of Russian history—or, for that matter, of economic history—will find the record of that debate an engrossing subject.[9] But the argument was never truly resolved. In 1927, Stalin moved into command, and the difficult question of how much to appease the unwilling peasant disappeared. Stalin simply made the ruthless decision to appease him not at all, but to *coerce* him by collectivizing his holdings.

The collectivization process solved in one swoop the problem of securing the essential transfer of food from the farm to the city, but it did so at frightful social (and economic) cost. Many peasants slaughtered their livestock rather than hand it over to the new collective farms; others waged outright war or practiced sabotage. In reprisal, the authorities acted with brutal force. An estimated five million "kulaks" (rich peasants) were executed or put in labor camps, while in the cities an equally relentless policy showed itself vis-à-vis labor. Workers were summarily ordered to the tasks required by the central authorities. The right to strike was forbidden,

9 See Alexander Erlich, *The Soviet Industrialization Debate: 1924–1928* (Cambridge, Mass.: Harvard University Press, 1960).

and the trade unions were reduced to impotence. Speed-ups were widely applied, and living conditions were allowed to deteriorate to very low levels.

The history of this period of forced industrialization is ugly and repellent, and it has left abiding scars on Russian society. It is well for us, nonetheless, to attempt to view it with some objectivity. If the extremes to which the Stalinist authorities went were extraordinary, often unpardonable, and perhaps self-defeating, we must bear in mind that industrialization on the grand scale has always been wrenching, always accompanied by economic sacrifice, and always carried out by the more or less authoritarian use of power. We have already seen what happened in the West at the time of the Industrial Revolution, with the forced emigration of the peasantry by enclosure and the heavy-handed exploitation of labor; and without "excusing" these acts, we have seen their function in paving the way for capital accumulation.

In much the same fashion, when the Soviet leaders deliberately held down consumption, regimented and transferred their labor forces into the new raw industrial centers, and ruthlessly collected the foodstuffs to feed their capital-building workers, they were, in fact, only enforcing the basic process of industrialization. What was new about the Soviet program was that totalitarian control over the citizenry enabled the planners to carry out this transformation at a much faster tempo than would have been possible had protests been permitted. Under Stalin's iron will, the planners did not scruple to exercise their industrializing power to the hilt.

Without seeking to justify the Russian effort, it is worth pondering one last question. Can rapid industrialization, with its inescapable price of low consumption, ever be a "popular" policy?* Will poor people willingly vote for an economic transformation which will not "pay out" for twenty or forty years? Does rapid and large scale industrialization *necessitate* a large degree of authoritorian political control? We will return to these problems when we turn to

---

* We might note in passing that universal male suffrage was not gained in England until the late 1860's and 1870's. Aneurin Bevan has written: "It is highly doubtful whether the achievements of the Industrial Revolution would have been permitted if the franchise had been universal. It is very doubtful because a great deal of the capital aggregations that we are at present enjoying are the results of the wages that our fathers went without." (From Gunnar Myrdal, *Rich Lands and Poor*, New York: Harper & Brothers, 1957, p. 46.)

underdevelopment, but we might well begin to think about them now.

The Planning Mechanism

A massive industrialization drive requires a determined effort to hold consumption to a minimum and to transfer resources to capital-building, an effort greatly facilitated, as we have seen, by the totalitarian political apparatus. But there is still another question to be considered. How are the freed resources to find their proper destination in an integrated and workable industrial sector?

Let us remind ourselves again of how this is done under a market economy. There, the signal of profitability serves as the lure for the allocation of resources and labor. Entrepreneurs, anticipating or following demand, risk private funds in the construction of the facilities which the future will require. Meanwhile, as these industrial salients grow, smaller satellite industries grow along with them to cater to their needs.

The flow of materials is thus regulated in every sector by the forces of private demand, making themselves known by the signal of rising or falling prices. At every moment there emanates from the growing industries a magnetic pull of demand on secondary industries, while, in turn, the growth salients themselves are guided, spurred, or slowed down by the pressure of demand from the ultimate buying public. And all the while, counterposed to these pulls of demand, are the obduracies of supply—the cost schedules of the producers themselves. In the cross fire of demand and supply exists a marvelously sensitive social instrument for the integration of the over-all economic effort of expansion.

And in the absence of a market? Clearly, the mechanism must be supplied by the direct orders of a central controlling and planning agency. *In a growing industrial economy, a planning agency must act as a substitute for the market.* Let us reflect for a moment what this entails.

To begin with, it means that the planning agency must provide a substitute for the forward-looking operations of the great entrepreneurs in a market economy. In place of a Carnegie or a Ford, building their plants in anticipation of, or response to, an insistent demand for their products, the planning body must itself set over-all goals and objectives for economic growth. Not the consumer but the planners' own judgment and desires determine the force of "demand."*

Establishing the over-all objectives is only the first and perhaps the easiest part of the planning mechanism. It is not enough to set broad goals and then assume that they will be fulfilled by themselves. We must remember that planning in a totalitarian economy is not superimposed on a market structure in which individuals take care of the "details" of production according to the incentives of price and profit. In a totally planned economy, each and every item which goes into the final plan must also be planned. Schedules of production are needed for steel, coal, coke, lumber, on down to nails and paper clips, for there is no "automatic" device by which these items will be forthcoming without a planning directive. Supplies of labor must also be planned; or if labor is free to move where it wishes, wage rates must be planned in order to draw labor where it is wanted.

Thus supplementing and completing the master objective of the over-all plan must be a whole hierarchy of sub-plans, the aggregate of which must bring about the necessary final result. And here is a genuine difficulty. For an error in planning, small in itself, if it affects a strategic link in the chain of production, can seriously distort—or even render impossible—the fulfillment of the total plan.

How is this infinitely complicated planning system carried out in the Soviet Union? It is begun by breaking down the over-all, long-term plan into shorter one-year plans. These one-year plans, specifying the output of major sectors of industry, are then transmitted to

* In the case of the Soviet Union, the planning authority has typically set its demand goals in terms of Five Year Plans. The first of these, from 1928 to 1932, had as its basic objective the intensification of industrialization in heavy industry, with special emphasis on electrification; the second took as its main goal the development of transportation and the beginning of agricultural planning; the third plan (1938–1942) was essentially occupied with producing the needs for a war economy; the fourth, from 1946 to 1950 was mainly a plan of reconstruction from wartime damage, with continuing emphasis on heavy industry; a fifth plan, 1951–1955, emphasized a steep increase in output with some stress being given (for the first time) to consumer goods. The present plan is by far the most ambitious. A Seven-Year Plan (1959–1965) aims to increase industrial output by 80 per cent, agricultural output by 70 per cent, and to bring significant increases in housing, a sector long neglected in the interests of industrialization, and in consumer goods, generally. In addition, the plan contemplates reducing the workweek to thirty-five hours by 1965.

various government ministries concerned with, for example, steel production, transportation, lumbering, and so forth. In turn, the Ministries refer the one-year plans further down the line to the heads of large industrial plants, to experts and advisers, and so on. At each stage, the over-all plan is thus unraveled into its subsidiary components, until finally the threads have been traced as far back as feasible along the productive process—typically, to the officials in charge of actual factory operations. The factory manager of, for instance, a coking operation is given a planned objective for the next year, specifying the output needed from his plant. He confers with his production engineers, considers the condition of his machinery, the availability of his labor force, and then transmits his requirements for meeting the objective back upward along the hierarchy. In this way, just as "demand" is transmitted downward along the chain of command, the exigencies of "supply" flow back upward, culminating ultimately in the top command of the planning authority (the Gosplan) itself.[10]

From this description of the tasks of planning, it is obvious that planning is an enormously complex task. Indeed, the very complexity of the task is such that more than one economist in the first days of chaos following the Russian Revolution, declared socialism to be "impossible."

We know that it is not impossible. In fact, by some criteria, a system of planning works more effectively than a market system, but that is a subject which we shall postpone for our final chapter. Here we are interested only in tracing the historic trajectory of the market system to its various destinations. At the moment, we shall only note the replacement of the market by a planning mechanism within the communist world, reserving until later the implications we can draw from this development.

THE UNDERDEVELOPED WORLD

With our brief account of the evolution of capitalism in Europe and socialism in Russia, we bring to an end our discussion of economic history in the West. We cannot write finis to our chapter,

[10] For an excellent nontechnical description, see Robert W. Campbell, *Soviet Economic Power* (Boston: Houghton Mifflin Company, 1960).

however, until we realize that in all our discussion of the trend of economic events in Europe and Russia—and in the United States, too—we have touched on the economic fate of only a minority of mankind.

Now we must direct our eyes eastward and southward to areas in which live the vast majority of humankind. During our account of the long sweep of Western advance, we have simply ignored their economic existence. Mere parochialism, however, was not the reason for our concentration on Western economic progress. Rather, it was that, taken in the large, *there was no economic progress in the rest of the world.* This is not to say that tides of fortune and misfortune did not mark these areas, that great cultural heights were not achieved, and that the political or social histories of these regions does not warrant interest and study. Yet the fact remains that the mounting tide of *economic* advance which has engaged our attention was a phenomenon limited to the West. It is no doubt something of an oversimplification, but it is basically true to claim that in Asia, Africa, South America, or the Near East, economic existence was not materially improved for the average inhabitant from the twelfth—and, in some cases, the second—to the beginning of the twentieth century. Indeed, for many of them it was worsened. A long graph of non-Western material well-being would depict irregular rises and falls but an almost total absence of cumulative betterment.

The near end of such a graph would show the standard of living of three-quarters of the human race who inhabit the so-called "underdeveloped' areas today. Most of this mass of humanity exists in conditions of poverty which are difficult for a Westerner to comprehend. When we sum up the plight of the underdeveloped nations by saying that a billion human beings have a standard of living of "less than $100 a year," and that another, more fortunate, billion people enjoy in a year one-quarter to one-half the income a typical American family spends in a single *month,* we give only a pale statistical meaning to a reality which we can scarcely grasp.*

* In Iran, for instance, in years of famine, the children of the poor examine the droppings of horses to extract morsels of undigested oats. In Calcutta, 250,000 people have no home whatsoever and live in the streets. In Hong Kong, large numbers of families of four or more live in one bed-space in a noisome dormitory. In Cali, Colombia, when the river rises, the city's sewers run through the homes of the poor. In Hyderbad, Pakistan, child labor employed in sealing the ends of bangles over a kerosene flame is paid eight cents—per *gross* of bangles.

The Background to Underdevelopment

Why are the underdeveloped nations so pitiably poor? Only a half-century ago it was common to attribute their backwardness to geographic or climatic causes. The underdeveloped nations were poor, it was thought, either because the climate was "too debilitating" or because "natural resources" were lacking. Sometimes it was just said that "the natives" were too "childlike" or racially too "inferior" to improve their lot.

Bad climates may have had adverse effects. Yet, many "hot" areas have shown a capacity for sustained economic growth (for example, the Queensland areas of Australia), while we have also come to recognize that a number of underdeveloped areas, such as Argentina and Korea, have completely temperate climates. So, too, we now regard the lack of resources in many areas more as a *symptom* of underdevelopment than a cause—which is to say that in many underdeveloped areas, resources have not yet been *looked for*. Libya, for instance, which used to be written off as a totally barren nation, has within the last few years been discovered to be a huge reservoir of oil. Little is heard today about native childishness or inherent inferiority. (Perhaps we remember how the wealthy classes similarly characterized the poor in Europe not too many centuries ago.) Climate and geography and cultural unpreparedness unquestionably constitute obstacles to rapid economic growth—and in some areas of the globe, very serious obstacles—but there are few economists who would look to these disadvantages as the main causes of economic backwardness.

Why then are these societies so poor?

The answer takes us back to an early chapter of our book. These are poor societies because they are *traditional* societies—that is, societies which have developed neither the mechanisms of command nor of the market by which they might launch into a sustained process of economic growth. Indeed, as we examine them further we will have the feeling that we are encountering in the present the anachronistic counterparts of the static societies of antiquity.

Why did they remain traditional societies? Why, for instance, did Byzantium, which was economically so advanced in contrast with the Crusaders' Europe, fall into decline? Why did China, with so many natural advantages, not develop into a dynamic economic society? There are no simple, or even fully satisfactory, answers. Perhaps the absence of economic progress elsewhere in the globe forces us to look upon our Western experience not as the paradigm and standard for historic development, but as a very special case in which various activating factors met in an environment peculiarly favorable for the emergence of a new economic style in history. The problem is one into which we cannot go more deeply in this book. At any rate, it is today an academic question. The dominant reality of our times is that the backward areas are now striving desperately to enter the mainstream of economic progress of the West. Let us examine further their chances for doing so.

The Conditions of Backwardness

Every people, to exist, must first feed itself; there is a rough sequence to the order of demands in human society. But to go beyond existence, it must achieve a certain level of efficiency in agriculture, so that its efforts can be turned in other directions. What is tragically characteristic of the underdeveloped areas is that this first corner of economic progress has not yet been turned.

Consider the situation in that all-important crop of the East, rice. The table below shows the difference between the productivity of rice fields in the main Asiatic countries and those of the United States and Australia.

RICE PRODUCTION
(100 kilograms per hectare)

U.S.	34.3
Australia	45.9
Burma	14.8
China (1954)	24.7
India	12.6
Indonesia	16.5
Thailand	14.3
Philippines	11.9

Source: Benjamin Higgins, *Economic Development* (New York: W. W. Norton & Co., Inc., 1959), p. 16.

What is true of rice can be duplicated in most other crops.* It is a disconcerting fact that the backward peasant nations which de-

* This table shows only the productive differentials of equal areas of land. When we consider that a single American farmer tends up to a hundred times as large an acreage as a peasant in an underdeveloped area, the difference in output per man would be much more striking.

pend desperately on their capacity to grow food cannot even compete in these main products with the advanced countries: U.S.
Louisiana rice undersells Philippine rice, California oranges are not
only better but cheaper than Indonesian oranges.

Why is agriculture so unproductive? One apparent reason is
that the typical unit of agricultural production in the underdeveloped lands is far too small to permit efficient farming. What
has been called "postage stamp cultivation" marks the pattern of
farming throughout most of Asia and a good deal of Africa and
South America. John Gunther, reporting the situation in India
twenty years ago, described the situation vividly:

> There is no primogeniture in India as a rule, and when the peasant dies
> his land is subdivided among all his sons with the result that most hold-
> ings are infinitesimally small. In one district in the Punjab, following
> fragmentation through generations, 584 owners cultivate no less than
> 16,000 fields; in another, 12,800 acres are split into actually 63,000 hold-
> ings. Three quarters of the holdings in India as a whole are under ten
> acres. In many parts of India the average holding is less than an acre.[11]

In part, this terrible situation is the result of divisive inheritance
practices which Gunther mentions. In part, it is due to landlord
systems in which peasants cannot legally own or accumulate their
own land; in part, to the pressure of too many people on too little
soil. There are many causes, with one result—agriculture suffers
from a devastatingly low productivity brought about by grotesque
man/land ratios.

These are, however, only the first links in a chain of causes for low
agricultural productivity. Another consequence of these tiny plots,
is an inability to apply sufficient capital to the land. Mechanical
binders and reapers, tractors and trucks are not only impossible to
use efficiently in such tiny spaces, but they are costly beyond the
reach of the subsistence farmer. Even fertilizer is too expensive:
in much of Asia, animal dung is used to provide "free" fuel rather
than returned to the soil to enrich it.

This paralyzing lack of capital is by no means confined to agriculture. It pervades the entire range of an underdeveloped economy.
The whole industrial landscape of a Western economy is missing: no

[11] *Inside Asia* (New York: Harper & Brothers, 1939), p. 385.

factories, no power lines, no machines, no paved roads meet the eye for mile upon mile as one travels through an underdeveloped continent. Indeed, to a pitiable extent, an underdeveloped land is one in which human and animal muscle power provide the energy with which production is carried on. In India in 1953, for instance, 65 per cent of the total amount of productive energy in the nation was the product of straining man and beast.[12] The amount of usable electrical power generated in all of India would not have sufficed to light up New York City.

Social Inertia

A lack of agricultural and industrial capital is not the only reason for low productivity. As we would expect in traditional societies, an endemic cause of low per capita output lies in prevailing social attitudes. Typically, the people of an underdeveloped economy have not *learned* the "economic" attitudes which make for rapid industrialization. Instead of technology-conscious farmers, they are tradition-bound peasants. Instead of disciplined workers, they are reluctant and untrained laborers. Instead of production-minded businessmen, they are trading-oriented merchants.

For example, Dr. Alvin Hansen reports from his observations in India:

Agricultural practices are controlled by custom and tradition. A villager is fearful of science. For many villagers insecticide is taboo because all life is sacred. A new and improved seed is suspect. To try it is a gamble. Fertilizers, for example, are indeed a risk . . . To adopt these untried methods might be to risk failure. And failure could mean starvation.[13]

In similar vein a UNESCO report tells us that

In the least developed areas, the worker's attitude toward labour may entirely lack time perspective, let alone the concept of productive investment. For example, the day labourer in a rural area on his way to work, who finds a fish in the net he placed in the river the night before, is observed to return home, his needs being met . . .[14]

[12] Daniel Wit & Alfred B. Clubok "Atomic Power Development in India" *Social Research,* Autumn 1958, p. 290.

[13] *Economic Issues of the 1960's* (New York: McGraw-Hill Book Company, Inc., 1960), pp. 157–158.

[14] *Report on the World Social Situation,* UNESCO, March 9, 1961, p. 79.

An equally crippling attitude is evinced by the upper classes, who look with scorn or disdain upon business or production-oriented careers. UNESCO also reports that of the many students from the underdeveloped lands studying in the United States—the majority of whom come from the more privileged classes—only 4 per cent were studying a problem fundamental to all their nations: agriculture.[15]

All these attitudes give rise to a *social inertia* which poses a tremendous hurdle to economic development. A suspicious peasantry, fearful of change which might jeopardize the slim margin which yields them life; a work force which does not respond to monetary incentive; a privileged class which is not interested in production— these are all part of the obdurate handicaps which an underdeveloped nation must overcome.

Further Problems: Population Growth

Many of these problems, as we anticipated, remind us of the pre-market economies of antiquity. In addition, there is one more obstacle facing the underdeveloped lands with which the economies of antiquity did *not* have to cope. This is the presence of a crushing rate of population increase which threatens to nullify the efforts of the underdeveloped areas to emerge from their backward condition.

A few figures are all that is needed to make the point. Let us begin with our southern neighbor, Mexico. Today Mexico has a population equal to that of New York, Pennsylvania, New Jersey, and Connecticut. Forty years from now, if Mexico's present rate of population increase continues, it will have as many people as the present population of these four states *plus* the rest of New England, *plus* the entire South Atlantic seaboard, *plus* the entire West Coast, *plus* Ohio, Indiana, Illinois, Michigan, and Wisconsin. Or take the Caribbean and Central American area. Today, that small part of the globe has a population of 66 million. In forty years, at present growth rates, its population will outnumber by 30 million the entire population of the United States today. By that year, South America, now 20 per cent less populous than we, will be 200 per cent larger than our present population. India will then very likely number a billion souls. China will probably number 1.6 billion.

We have already seen one result of the relentless proliferation of

15 *Ibid.*, p. 81.

people in the fragmentation of land holdings. But the problem goes beyond mere fragmentation. Eugene Black, president of the International Bank for Reconstruction and Development (the World Bank) tells us that in India a population equivalent to that of all Great Britain has been squeezed out of any landholding whatsoever—even though they still dwell in rural areas.[16] Consequently, population pressure generates massive and widespread rural poverty, pushing inhabitants from the countryside into the already overcrowded cities. Five hundred families a day move into Jakarta from the surrounding Javanese fields where population has reached the fantastic figure of 1,100 per square mile (compare American population density of 50.4 people per square mile).

Even these tragic repercussions of population growth are but side-effects. The main problem is that population growth adds more mouths almost as fast as the underdeveloped nations manage to add more food. They cancel out much economic progress by literally eating up the small surpluses which might serve as a springboard for faster future growth.

Ironically, this population "explosion" in the underdeveloped countries is a fairly recent phenomenon, attributable largely to the incursion of Western medicine and public health into the low-income areas. Prior to World War II, the poorer countries held their population growth in check because death rates were nearly as high as birth rates. With DDT and penicillin, death rates have plunged dramatically. In Ceylon, for example, the death rates dropped 40 per cent in one year following the adoption of malaria control and other health measures. As death rates dropped in the underdeveloped areas, birth rates, for many reasons, continued high, despite efforts to introduce birth control. In the backward lands, children are not only a source of prestige and of household labor for the peasant family, but also the only possible source of "social security" for old age. The childless older couple could very well starve: as parents or grandparents they are at least assured of a roof over their heads.

Is there a solution for this grim question? In the long run, the hope for a flattening out of the population curve no doubt lies in the changed patterns of life of an industrial society, with its later

---

[16] Eugene R. Black, *The Diplomacy of Economic Thought* (Cambridge, Mass.: Harvard University Press, 1960), p. 9.

marriages, its postponed children, its enhanced status of the female, and its general acceptance of birth control. With rising living standards, we can expect—or at least reasonably hope for—a dropping birth rate, at least compared with the present torrential rates. But this may take a long while to realize. In the interim, the Niagara of births will continue to pose the most serious of all handicaps to achieving that high standard of living which will be its only cure.

The Role of Imperialism

This gives us a brief introduction to underdevelopment as it exists today. Before we turn to the problem of how this condition can be remedied, we must inquire into one more question. Why did not the market society, with all its economic dynamism, spread into the backward areas?

In point of fact, the active economies of the European and American worlds did make contact with the underdeveloped regions beginning with the great exploratory and commercial voyages of the fifteenth and sixteenth centuries, but it was not until the nineteenth century that the contact became more systematic than mere adventure and plunder. Starting in the first half of that century and gaining momentum until the first World War, came that scramble for territory we call the Age of Imperialism.

What was this imperialism? It was, in retrospect, a compound of many things: militarism, jingoism, a search for markets and for sources of cheap raw materials to feed growing industrial economies. Insofar as the colonial areas were concerned, however, the first impact of imperialism was not solely that of exploitation. On the contrary, the incursion of Western empires into the backward areas brought some advantages. It injected the first heavy dose of industrial capital: rail lines, mines, plantation equipment. It brought law and order, often into areas in which the most despotic personal rule had previously been the order of the day. It introduced the ideas of the West, including, most importantly, the idea of freedom, which was eventually to rouse the backward nations into a successful effort to overthrow their foreign dependence.

Yet if imperialism brought these positive and stimulating influences, it also exerted a peculiarly deforming impulse to the underdeveloped—indeed, then, totally undeveloped—economies of the East and South. In the eyes of the imperialist nations, the colonies were viewed not as areas to be brought along in balanced development, but essentially as immense supply dumps to be attached to the mother countries' industrial economies. Malaya became a vast tin mine; Indonesia, a huge tea and rubber plantation; Arabia, an oil field. In other words, the direction of economic development was steadily pushed in the direction which most benefited the imperial owner and not the colonial peoples themselves.

The result today is that the typical underdeveloped nation has a badly lopsided economy, unable to supply itself with a wide variety of goods. It is thereby thrust into the international market with its one basic commodity. For instance in South America, we find that Venezuela is dependent on oil for 92 per cent of its exports; Colombia, on coffee for 77 per cent of its exports; Chile, on copper for 66 per cent of its foreign earnings; Bolivia, on tin for 62 per cent of its exports; Honduras, on bananas for 51 per cent of its foreign earnings. On the surface, this looks like a healthy specialization of trade. We shall shortly see why it is not.

Economic lopsidedness was one unhappy consequence of imperialism. No less important for the future course of development in the colonial areas was a second decisive influence of the West: its failure to achieve political and psychological relationships of mutual respect with its colonial peoples. In part, this was no doubt traceable to an often frankly exploitative economic attitude, in which the colonials were relegated to second-class jobs with third-class pay, while a handful of Western whites formed an insulated and highly paid managerial clique. But it ran deeper than that. A terrible color line, a callous indifference to colonial aspirations, a patronizing and sometimes contemptuous view of "the natives" runs all through the history of imperialism. It has left as a bitter heritage not only an identification of capitalism with its worst practices, but a political and social wariness toward the West which deeply affects the general orientation of the developing areas.

The Engineering of Development

Up to this point we have concentrated our attention on the conditions of, and the background to, underdevelopment. Now we must ask, how can an underdeveloped nation emerge from its poverty? How can it put itself on the road to growth?

From what we have already learned, we know the basic answer to this question. The prerequisite for economic progress for the under-developed countries today is not essentially different from what it was in Great Britain at the time of the Industrial Revolution, or what it was in Russia in 1917. To grow, an underdeveloped economy must build capital.

How is a starving country able to build capital? When 80 per cent of a country is scrabbling on the land for a bare subsistence, how can it divert its energies to building the dams and roads, the ditches and houses, the railroad embankments and the factories which, however, indispensable for progress tomorrow, cannot be eaten today? If our postage stamp farmers were to halt work on their tiny unproductive plots and go to work on a great project like, say, the Aswan Dam, who would feed them? Whence would come the necessary food to sustain these capital workers?

Here is our grim "model" of a peasant economy from Chapter 4 come to life, and we will remember from that model that when con-sumption could not be cut, growth could not ensue. Still, when we look again at the underdeveloped lands, the prospect is not quite so bleak as that. In the first place, these economies *do* have unemployed factors. In the second place we find that a large number of the peasants who till the fields are not feeding themselves. They are, also, in a sense, taking food from each others' mouths.

As we have seen, the crowding of peasants on the land in these areas, has resulted in a diminution of agricultural productivity far below that of the advanced countries. Hence the abundance of peasants working in the fields obscures the fact that *a smaller num-ber of peasants, working the same fields, could raise a total output just as large—and maybe even larger*. One observer has written: "An experiment carried out near Cairo by the American College seems to suggest that the present output, or something closely approaching it, could be produced by about half the present rural population of Egypt."[17] Here is an extreme case, but it can be found to apply, to some degree, to nearly every underdeveloped land. For

[17] From Ragnar Nurkse, *Problems of Capital Formation in the Underdeveloped Countries* (New York: Oxford University Press, 1958), p. 35, fn. 2.

a large fraction of the agricultural population, a portion of their little crop is won only at the expense of someone else.

Now we begin to see an answer to the dilemma of the under-developed societies. In nearly all of these societies, there exists a disguised and hidden surplus of labor which, if it were taken off the land, could be used to build capital. Most emphatically, this does not mean that the rural population should be literally moved, en masse, to the cities where there is already a hideous lump of indi-gestible unemployment. It means, rather, that the inefficient scale of agriculture conceals a reservoir of both labor and the food to feed that labor if it were elsewhere employed. By reducing the number of tillers of the soil, a work force can be made available for the building of roads and dams, while this "transfer" to capital building need not result in a diminution of agricultural output.*

This rationalization of agriculture is not the only requirement for growth. When agricultural productivity is enhanced by the crea-tion of larger farms (or by improved techniques on existing farms), *part of the ensuing larger crop must be saved.* In other words, the peasant who remains on the soil cannot enjoy his enhanced pro-ductivity by raising his standard of living and eating up all his larger crop. Instead, the gain in output per cultivator must be siphoned off the farm. It must be "saved" by the peasant cultivator and shared with his formerly unproductive cousins, nephews, sons, and daughters who are now at work on capital-building projects. We do not expect a hungry peasant to do this voluntarily. Rather, by taxation or exaction the government of an underdeveloped land must arrange for this indispensable transfer. Thus in the early stages of a *successful* development program there is apt to be no visible rise in the peasant's food *consumption,* although there must be a rise in his food *production.* What is apt to be visible is a more or less efficient—and sometimes harsh—mechanism for assuring that some portion of this newly added productivity is not consumed on the farm but is made available to support the capital-building worker.

* In sparsely settled lands we cannot apply the same strategy because there is no surplus population on the farm. Here we must *create* a surplus farming population by first raising agricultural productivity through better seeds, better technology, etc. This "created" labor surplus can then be put to work building capital.

What we have just outlined is not, let us repeat, a formula for immediate action. In many underdeveloped lands, as we have seen, the countryside already crawls with unemployment, and to create, overnight, a large and efficient farming operation would create an intolerable social situation. We should think of the process we have just outlined as a long-term blueprint which covers the course of development over many years. It shows us—as did our earlier model— that the process of development takes the form of a huge internal migration from agricultural pursuits where labor is wasted, to industrial and other pursuits where it can yield a net contribution to the nation's progress.

The Problem of Industrialization

Our model also showed us that capital-building is not just a matter of freeing hands and food. Peasant labor may construct roads, but it cannot, with its bare hands, build the trucks to run over them. It may throw up dams, but it cannot fashion the generators and power lines through which a dam can produce energy. In other words, what is needed to engineer the great ascent is not just a pool of labor. It is also a vast array of *industrial* equipment.*

How is this equipment obtained? In our model, by expanding the machine-tool—that is, the capital equipment building—subsector. But an underdeveloped economy does not have a capital equipment building sector. Consequently, *in the first stages of industrialization, before the nucleus of a self-contained industrial sector has been laid down, a backward nation must obtain its equipment from abroad.*

This it can do in one of three ways. (1) It can buy the equipment

---

* An allied problem of no less importance arises from the lack of technical training on which industrialization critically depends. At the lowest level, this is evidenced by appalling rates of illiteracy (80 and even 90 per cent) which make it impossible, for instance, to print instructions on a machine or a product and expect them to be followed. And at a more advanced level, the lack of expert training becomes an even more pinching bottleneck. United Nations economists have figured that Nigeria alone will need some 20,000 top-level administrators, executives, technicians, etc., over the next 10 years and twice as many subordinates. On a world-wide scale, this implies a need for at least 700,000 top-level personnel and 1,400,000 second-level assistants. Not one per cent of these skilled personnel exists today, and to "produce" them will be a task of staggering difficulty. Yet, without them it is often impossible to translate development plans into actuality.

from an industrialized nation by the normal process of *foreign trade.* Brazil, for example, can sell its coffee and use the foreign currency it receives to purchase abroad the tractors, lathes, and generating equipment it needs. (2) It can receive the industrial equipment by *foreign investment* when a corporation in an advanced nation chooses to build in a backward area. This is the route by which the United States got much of its capital from Britain during the nineteenth century, and it is the means by which the underdeveloped nations themselves received capital during their colonial days. (3) It may receive the foreign exchange needed to buy industrial equipment as a result of a grant or a loan from another nation or from a United Nations agency such as the World Bank. That is, it can buy industrial equipment with *foreign aid.*

Trade Problems

Of these three avenues of industrialization, the most important is foreign trade. In all, the underdeveloped nations earn from $30 to $40 billions a year from foreign trade. Not all of this, by any matter of means, however, is available for *new* industrial capital. A lion's share of export earnings, unfortunately, must go to pay for indispensable imports—replacements of old equipment, or even food.

In addition, another problem plagues the underdeveloped nations in foreign trade. We have seen how international trade is the means by which a great international division of labor can be achieved— that is, by which productivity can be enhanced in all trading countries, by enabling each to concentrate on those products in which it is most efficient.

With the underdeveloped nations, however, this international division of labor has worked badly. First, as we have seen, their structural difficulties have prevented them from developing their productivities even in their main occupational tasks. Second, most of them suffer from another problem. As sellers of raw commodities —and usually of only one raw commodity—typically, they face a highly inelastic demand for their goods. Like the American farmer, when they produce a bumper crop, prices tend to fall precipitously and demand does not rise proportionately. At the same time, the industrial materials they buy in exchange tend to be firm or to rise in price over the years. Thus the "terms of trade"—the actual *quid pro quo* of goods received against goods offered—tend to move against the poorer nations. They give more and more coffee for less and less machinery. In 1957 and 1958, when commodity prices took a particularly bad tumble, the poorer nations actually lost more in purchasing power than the total amount of all foreign aid they received. In effect, they subsidized the advanced nations!

That is why all the underdeveloped nations are seeking commodity stabilization agreements (not altogether dissimilar from the support programs which stabilize American farm incomes). Recently, there have been signs that the Western nations—belatedly—are recognizing the need for some such device if the underdeveloped nations are to be able to plan ahead with some degree of assurance of the size of their incomes.

Another hopeful possibility lies in the prospect of encouraging diversified exports from the underdeveloped nations—handicrafts, light manufactures, and others. The difficulty here is that these exports may compete vigorously with the domestic industry of the advanced nations; witness the problems of the American textile industry in the face of textile shipments from Hong Kong and Japan. No doubt, a source of additional earnings lies along this path, but it is unlikely to rise rapidly in the near future.

Limitations on Private Foreign Investment

A second main avenue of capital accumulation for the backward nations is foreign investment. Indeed, before the second World War this was *the* source of their industrial wealth. Today, however, it is a much diminished avenue of assistance. On the one hand, the former capital-exporting nations are no longer eager to invest private funds in areas over which they have lost control and in which they fear to lose any new investments they might make. In addition, most of the European nations are now busy investing their available capital at home. On the other hand, many of the poorer nations, for reasons that we have already discussed, view Western capitalism with an uneasy eye. They see in the arrival of the branch of a powerful corporation another form of the domination they have just escaped in the past. They scent "imperialism" even when the most equitable terms are suggested. Foreign investment is often hampered by restrictive legislation in the underdeveloped nations, even though it is badly needed. As a result, not much more than $2½ billion a year from all the advanced nations goes overseas as foreign investment in the underdeveloped world.

We must also recognize that foreign capital, particularly that going into the most backward nations, has not been particularly useful in building up an industrial nucleus for further development. Foreign capital tends to concentrate in the extractive industries, such as oil production, ore mining, or plantation agriculture. These investments often form small self-sufficient enclaves within the underdeveloped world and fail to stimulate the surrounding economy to growth. For instance, the Belgian Union Minière de Haut Katanga, a vast modern mining operation, existed for years in the primitive Congo without shedding any perceptible impetus toward general economic growth. At a later stage in economic development —perhaps at the stage now reached by some South American nations —foreign private capital may play a dynamic role in the industrializing process; but in the earliest stages, it tends to exert a relatively small developmental impact.

The Crucial Avenue of Aid

These considerations enable us to understand the special importance which attaches to the third channel of capital accumulation—foreign aid. Surprisingly, perhaps, in the light of the attention it attracts, foreign aid is not a very large figure. In all, international assistance, both from individual nations such as the United States and from the UN and its agencies, does not exceed $5 billion a year (*not* including international military aid). This is no more than 2 or 3 per cent of the total output of the underdeveloped world and only 10 to 15 per cent of its earnings from its export trade.

It is, however, *30 per cent* of the capital formation of the underdeveloped areas. Thus foreign aid makes possible the accumulation of industrial capital much faster than could be accomplished solely as a result of the backward lands' export efforts or their ability to attract foreign private capital. To be sure, an increase in foreign earnings or in private capital imports would have equally powerful effects on growth. But we have seen the difficulties in the way of rapidly increasing the receipts from these sources. In the near future, foreign aid represents the most effective channel for *quickly* raising the amount of industrial capital which the under-developed nations must obtain.

Foreign aid, particularly from UN sources, is also an extremely important source of *technical assistance* which enables the backward regions to overcome the handicaps imposed by their lack of skilled and trained personnel. For the near term, this may be even more important in promoting growth than the acquisition of the industrial capital itself. Largely because of this bottleneck of skills, it is estimated that the underdeveloped countries could not at best absorb much more than perhaps $8 billion a year in foreign aid during this decade.

The Economic Possibilities for Growth

Against all these handicaps, can the underdeveloped nations grow? Can the shackles of low productivity be cast off and the terrible conditions of poverty relegated to the past? Economic analysis tells us that they can. *In theory, to achieve a "take-off" into self-sustained development it is necessary only for capital formation to boost output a little faster than population growth.* A small surplus will then be generated. If this surplus is used to create capital, next year's output will be still higher. Accordingly, a larger surplus will result—and this in turn can be plowed back to create still more capital—and so on, in a steady cumulative process.

Have any of the underdeveloped nations reached the point of take-off? A very few may have: Mexico, Puerto Rico, possibly Brazil or Argentina. The vast majority have not.

Nevertheless, the outlook is by no means totally black. The pure economic analysis of development does not indicate insuperable obstacles. For many nations, an increase in their present rates of capital formation of 50 to 100 per cent—a difficult but by no means unthinkable goal—should bring them close to, or beyond, the point of cumulative growth. Indeed, economists at the United Nations calculate that there are perhaps twenty countries (whose populations aggregate to nearly half the underdeveloped world) where a great ten-year effort can bring economic development to the threshold of a self-sustaining climb.[18] In none of these countries will anything

18 See e.g., Paul G. Hoffman, "Bread upon the Water," in the 1962 *Encyclopaedia Britannica Yearbook*.

like a massive alleviation of poverty have been achieved. But the stage will be set for such an advance; the major roadblocks will have been removed; the possibility of a truly large-scale accumulation of capital will be at hand.

Social and Political Problems

Economic analysis makes it possible in theory to foresee a long slow developmental climb. But this is not yet the end of our analysis. For it is impossible to think of development only in terms of economics. As we have seen in the case of Western growth, *economic development is nothing less than the transformation of an entire society.* When we talk of building capital, we must not imagine that this entails only the addition of machines and equipment to a peasant society. It entails the conversion of a peasant society into an industrial one. It means a change in the whole tenor of life, in the expectations and motivations, the environment of daily existence itself.

We have already noted some of the changes which economic development imposes on a society. Illiterate peasants must be made into literate farmers. Dispirited urban slum-dwellers must be made into disciplined factory workers. Old and powerful social classes, who have for generations derived their wealth from feudal land tenure, must be deprived of their vested rights and oriented toward often despised business pursuits. Above all, the profligate generation of life, conceived in dark huts as the only solace available to a crushed humanity, must give way to a responsible and deliberate creation of children as the chosen heirs to a better future.

These changes will *in time* be facilitated by the realization of development itself. A growing industrial environment breeds industrial ways. The gradual realization of economic improvement brings about attitudes which will themselves accelerate economic growth. A slowly rising standard of living is likely to dampen the birth rate, in the underdeveloped areas, as it did in the West.

All these changes, as we have said, may take place in time. But time is what lacks. The changes must begin to take place now, today, so that the process of development can gain an initial momentum. The transition from a backwards, tradition-bound way of life to a modern and dynamic one cannot be allowed to mature at its own slow pace. Only an enormous effort can inaugurate—much less shorten—the transition from the past into the future.

Collectivism and Underdevelopment

These sobering considerations converge in one main direction. They alert us to the fact that *in the great transformation which is now commencing in the underdeveloped areas, the market mechanism is apt to play a much smaller role than in the comparable transformation of the West during the Industrial Revolution.*

We will recall how lengthy and arduous was the period of apprenticeship through which the West had to pass in order for the ideas and attitudes, the social institutions and legal prerequisites of the market system to be hammered out. When the Industrial Revolution came into being, it exploded on an historic situation in which market institutions, actions, customs had already become the dominant form of economic organization.

None of this is true in the underdeveloped nations today. Rather than having their transition to a market society behind them, many of those nations must leap overnight from essentially feudal relationships to commercialized and industrialized ones. Many of them are not even fully monetized economies. None of them have the network of institutions—and behind that, the network of "economic" motivations—on which a market society is built.

Hence it is not difficult to foresee that the guiding force of development is apt to be tilted in the direction of central planning. Regardless of the importance of private enterprise in carrying out the individual projects of development, the driving and organizing force of economic growth will be principally lodged with the government.

Even were the market relationships of free enterprise more fully developed, much of the initial needs of development are in any event unsuited to private enterprise. Schooling and health, administration and training, the provision of great public works like dams, irrigation systems, basic housing, etc. are not projects whose initiation can be left to the profit system. As Dr. Wilfred Malenbaum, an authority on Indian development efforts, has put it:

In India, as in other underdeveloped countries, government must not only provide this heavy dose of economic and social overhead investment but must also undertake many specific operations which in the United States, for example, belong distinctly within the scope of the private businessman. The reasons for this . . . stem from the thinness of the supply of entrepreneurs—even in India which is more blessed in this regard than are other poor countries. There is also the difficulty of raising enough funds privately for really big investments like steel mills. Of major importance, moreover, is the fact that there have been decades of relative inaction by the private business sector. . . . [The Indian businessman] is less sensitive to the new as a spur for improving the old. Be that as it may, government will need to fill a broad big business leadership role in India.[19]

Political Implications

But the outlook indicates more than a growth of economic command. Implicit also in the harsh demands of industrialization is the need for strong political leadership—not only to initiate and guide the course of development, but to *make it stick.* For it is not only wrong, but dangerously wrong, to picture economic development as a long, invigorating climb from achievement to achievement. On the contrary, it is better imagined as a gigantic social and political earthquake. As Eugene Black has pointed out, we delude ourselves with buoyant phrases such as "the revolution of rising expectations" when we describe the process—rather than the prospect—of development.[20] To many of the people involved in the bewildering transformations of development, the revolution is apt to be marked by a loss of traditional expectations, by a new awareness of deprivation, a new experience of frustration. For decades, perhaps generations, a developing nation must plow back its surplus into the ugly and unenjoyable shapes of lathes and drills, conveyor belts and factory smokestacks. Some change toward betterment is not ruled out, particularly in health, basic diet, and education; but beyond this first great step, material improvement in everyday living will not—cannot—materialize quickly.

As a consequence, many of the policies and programs required for development, rather than being eagerly accepted by all levels of society are apt to be resisted. Tax reform, land reform, the curtailment of luxury consumption are virtually certain to be opposed by the old order. In addition, as the long march begins, latent resent-

[19] Higgins, *op. cit.,* pp. 47–48.
[20] *Op. cit.,* p. 9.

ments of the poorer classes are likely to become mobilized; the underdog wakens to his lowly position. Even if his lot improves, he may well feel a new fury if his *relative* well-being is impaired. Writing of Mexico, one of the fastest developing nations, the anthropologist Oscar Lewis quotes the findings of a Mexican economist that "in 1955 one-hundredth of the gainfully employed population took 66 per cent of the national income, while the remaining 99 per cent received only 34 per cent; in 1940, the distribution had been exactly the reverse."[21] Lewis warns:

The political stability of Mexico is grim testimony to the great capacity for misery and suffering of the ordinary Mexican. But even the Mexican capacity for suffering has its limits, and unless ways are found to achieve a more equitable distribution of the growing national wealth and a greater equality of sacrifice during the difficult period of industrialization, we may expect social upheavals, sooner or later.[22]

These considerations enable us to understand how, along with a rise in economic standards can come a *rise* in social tensions* and this prospect, in turn, enables us to appreciate the fearful demands placed upon political leadership, which must provide the impetus, the inspiration—and, if necessary, the discipline—to keep the great ascent in motion.

In the politically immature and labile areas of the underdeveloped world, this exercise of leadership typically assumes the form of "strong man" government. In large part, this is only the perpetuation of age-old tendencies in these areas, but in the special environment of development, a new source of encouragement for dictatorial government arises from the exigencies of the economic process itself. Powerful, even ruthless, government may be needed, not only to begin the development process, but to cope with the strains of a *successful* development program.

It is not surprising, then, that the political map reveals the presence of authoritarian governments in many developing nations today. The communist areas aside, we find more or less authoritarian

21 "Mexico Since Cardenas," *Social Research* (Spring 1959), p. 26.
22 *The Children of Sanchez* (New York: Random House, 1961), p. xxxi.
* The strains of the early Industrial Revolution in England, with its widening chasm between proletariat and capitalist, are pertinent to a projection of the possible course of affairs in the developing nations.

rule in Egypt, Ghana, Guinea, Pakistan, Burma, Vietnam, South Korea, Indonesia, and the succession of South American junta governments. From country to country, the severity and ideological coloring of these governments varies. Yet in all of them we find that the problems of economic development provide the main rationale for the tightening of political control. At least in the arduous early stages of growth, some form of political command seems as integral to economic development as the accumulation of capital itself.

The Challenge to the West

Does this imply that the underdeveloped nations are apt to follow the route of communism?

It is certainly a possibility not to be lightly dismissed. For its political and social ugliness notwithstanding, communism offers a means of achieving the Great Transformation. There is no secret about this means. A communist nation, like a capitalist one, must take its workers from agriculture, must rationalize its agriculture, must import basic industrial equipment, and must relentlessly plough back its increments of output into more capital, more capital, ever more capital. The difference is that communism or total collectivism does the job with little of the "inefficiencies" of a free society. Where land is needed, it is simply taken; where workers are required, they are moved; where opposition is encountered, it is suppressed.

As was the case in Russia, all this is likely to be accomplished at a fearful social cost. In communist China, too, millions have been put to death for opposing the regime, and life for the remainder has been regimented and militarized to a chilling degree. Yet such an iron hand weighs less heavily on peoples who have never known any form of government other than despotism and who will submit to the yoke of communism if they see a chance of lifting the yoke of poverty from their grandchildren.

This last point is crucial. Until its famine disaster of 1959–1960, China was growing at a rate at least twice that of India.[23] Russia is growing two to three times as fast as the United States. Com-

[23] See e.g., A. Doak Barnett, *Communist Economic Strategy: The Rise of Mainland China* (Washington, D.C.: The National Planning Association, 1959), p. 11.

munism or total collectivism *is* a way out of underdevelopment, and to see it in any less serious—and in this regard, respectful— light is to underestimate its challenge.

Can the West match that challenge?

We do not yet know. Few if any of the underdeveloped countries *want* to go communist. Their leaders are not blind to the excesses of communism, still less to the burdens of becoming Soviet or Chinese satellites. They are aware that the scale of foreign aid which the Communists can offer is considerably less than our own; and they know that the West has vast resources of men, materials, and money which could be mobilized to speed the great transition and to alleviate its strains.

What they do not know is whether the West is prepared to offer assistance on the scale and for the length of time that would be required to bring these countries through the gauntlet of early development. Nor do they know whether the West is prepared to accept the realities of development as they will likely emerge, bring- ing to the fore economic structures and political ideologies different from, and sometimes unsympathetic to, both capitalism and de- mocracy.

Perhaps the West itself does not know the answers to these search- ing questions. It is difficult for us to confront the hard choices which development offers, difficult to swallow the growth of more or less collectivist economies and governments, difficult to abet a process whose initial outcome seems so inimical to our immediate interests.

It would be fatuous to pretend that somewhere, concealed in this picture, is an answer which will solve all problems happily. Rather, the likelihood is very great that the West, quite as much as the underdeveloped areas themselves, will have to make bitter choices and to follow unwelcome paths for many years. Yet, the fact that many alternatives are closed does not mean that none remain. There are degrees of command, political as well as economic, which result in a very different tenor of existence for those who must bear the burden of development and which offer very different possibilities for the future. Nothing could be more disastrous for the West than to overlook these differences and to brand all nonmarket economies or all nondemocratic governments as constituting a single undesir- able species. In the mold of economic development is being cast the shape of much of world civilization for the future. On the capacity of the West to overcome its stereotyped conception of other societies, on its capacity to discriminate between mere oppression and purposeful social direction, on its capacity to persevere in the encouragement of development despite inevitable disappointments and failures will depend much of the outcome of the central process of historic change in our time.

8

The Making of Economic Society

*W*ith this sombre look at the underdeveloped areas we bring
to a conclusion our overview of general economic history.
Throughout the pages behind us we have followed a
grandiose theme of economic development in the West, and now
at the terminus of our study, this same long process is about to be
commenced in the East and South. Thus, from our vantage point,
we can see the beginning of world-wide economic development
as a genuine watershed in human history. An active and dynamic
form of economic life, until recently the distinctive characteristic
of the industrial West, is about to be generalized over the face of
the globe. The process of diffusion will take generations—perhaps
even centuries—but it marks a profound, irreversible, and truly
historic alteration in the economic condition of man.

Yet, if the process of economic growth is henceforth to be carried
out on a global scale, it is also clear that there will be a significant
change in the auspices under which this process is likely to unfold.

As we have seen, it is command rather than the market system which is in the ascendant as the driving force in the underdeveloped regions. And when we combine the geographic extent of these regions with those in which communism has become firmly entrenched, it seems that command now bids fair to become *the* dominant means of organizing economic activity on this planet, as tradition was not very long ago.

But again there is a difference. During the centuries in which tradition held sway over most of the world, the economies run by the market system were the locus of progress and motion. Today and in the future, one cannot with assurance say the same. For a pre-eminent motive of the rising economies of command is to *displace* the market societies as the source of the world's economic vitality.

Does this mean that economic history now writes finis to the market system? Does it mean that the market, as a means of solving the economic problem, is about to be relegated to the museum of economic antiquities, or at best limited to the confines of North America and Western Europe? The question brings to a focus our continuing concern with the market system through history. Let us attempt in these last pages to give an appraisal of its prospects.

THE STAGES OF ECONOMIC DEVELOPMENT

We might well begin such an appraisal by taking a last survey of the array of economic systems which marks our times. It is, at first glance, an extraordinary assortment: we find, in these mid-years of the twentieth century, a spectrum of economic organization which represents virtually every stage in economic history from the earliest and most primitive. But at second look, a significant pattern can be seen within this seemingly disordered assemblage. The few remaining wholly traditional economies, such as those of the Near East or tribal Africa, have not yet begun to move into the mainstream of economic development. A much larger group of underdeveloped nations, in which institutions of economic command are now rising amid a still traditional environment, have just commenced their development efforts and are now coping with the initial problems preparatory to eventual all-out industrialization. Going yet further along we find the economies of iron command, such as China and to a lesser extent Russia; here we find national communities which are (or recently were) wrestling with the gigantic task of rapid massive industrialization. Finally, we pass to the market economies of the West, to encounter societies which have their developmental days behind them and are now concerned with the operation of high-consumption economic systems.

The categorization suggests a very important general conclusion. *The economic structures of nations today bear an integral relation with their stage of economic development.* Acts of foreign intervention aside, the choice of command or market systems is not just the outcome of political considerations, of ideologies and preferences. It is also, and perhaps primarily, the result of functional requirements which are very different at different levels of economic achievement.

The Inception of Growth

We have already noted this connection in our discussion of the underdeveloped areas. Now, however, we can place what we have learned into a wider frame of reference. For if we compare the trend of events in the underdeveloped economies with the "equivalent" stage of development in Western history, we see a significant point of resemblance between the two. The emergence of command in the development-minded countries today has a parallel in the mercantile era, when the Western nations also received a powerful impetus toward industrialization under the organizing influence of the "industry-minded" governments of that period.

Thereafter, to be sure, the resemblance ceases. In the West, following the first push of mercantilism, it was the market mechanism which provided the main directive force for growth; in the underdeveloped lands, as we have seen, this influence is likely to be preempted by political and economic command.

Three main reasons lie behind this divergence of paths. First, the underdeveloped areas today start from a lower level of preparedness than did the West in the seventeenth and eighteenth centuries. Not only have the actual institutions of the market not yet appeared in many backward lands, but the whole process of acculturation has failed to duplicate that of the West. In many ways—not all of them economic—the West was "ready" for economic development, as Chapter 3 sought to make clear. A similar readiness is not in evidence in the majority of the backward lands today, with the result that development, far from evincing itself as a spontaneous process, comes about as the result of enforced and imposed change.

Second, the West was able to mount its development effort in leisurely tempo. This is not to say that its rate of growth was slow or that strong pressures did not weigh upon many Western countries, arousing within them feelings of dissatisfaction with their progress. Yet the situation was unlike that of the backward areas today. Here immense pressures, both of population growth and of political impatience, create an overwhelming need and desire for speed. As a result, the process of growth is not allowed to mature quietly in the background of history, as it did for much of the West, but has been placed at the very center of political and social attention.

Finally, the underdeveloped countries, who suffer from so many handicaps in comparison with the developmental days of the West, enjoy one not inconsiderable advantage. Because they are in the rear guard rather than the vanguard of history, they know where they are going. In a manner denied to the West, they can see ahead of them the goal they seek to reach. They do not wish to reach this goal, however, by retreading the painful and laborious path marked out by the West. Rather, they intend to shortcut it, to move directly to their destination by utilizing the mechanisms of command to bring about the great alterations that must be made.

Can economic command significantly compress and accelerate the growth process? The remarkable performance of the Soviet Union is proof enough that it can. A number of market economies have grown for short periods of time as rapidly as the Russian economy, but none has grown so fast for so long a period of time. More important, no other economy in the twentieth century has leaped so dramatically from peasanthood to industrial leadership. In 1920 Russia was but a minor figure in the economic councils of the world. In the 1960's, it is second only—though still a far second—to the United States, but the gap between the two nations is being narrowed rapidly. Over the past ten years the annual rate of increase in Soviet output has been between 6 and 12 per cent—double or triple that of the United States. Unless the rate of Soviet growth slows down, which is possible but by no means inevitable, or unless the American rate of growth increases, total Soviet industrial production will be larger than total American production in about a generation.*

We know the key to rapid growth in a totally planned economy. It lies in its ability to generate very large savings by holding down consumption and to channel its freed resources into the most productive kinds of capital. A United States government study shows that in 1959 new Soviet industrial investment, measured in American prices of 1955, was $29.9 billion—almost 70 per cent more than the corresponding American industrial investment. Similarly, Soviet investing in agriculture caught up with American agricultural investment in 1954, and in 1959 doubled the American farm figure— $10.1 billion against $4.8 billion.[1]

By way of contrast, American investments in housing, transportation, and communication were almost double their Soviet counterparts. But this is just the point. Primarily, these were investments aimed at providing consumers' benefits, not a faster rate of industrial progress. What gives to a planned economy its advantage in promoting growth is precisely the fact that it can disregard the desires of consumers and direct its resources single-mindedly into those industries with the highest leverage for growth.

Economies in Mid-Development

Once the development process is well under way, however, the relative functional merits of the market and the command mechanisms begin to change. After planning has done its massive tasks— enforcing economic and social change, creating an industrial sector, rationalizing agriculture—another problem begins to assume ever more importance. This is the problem of efficiency, of dovetailing the innumerable productive efforts of society into a single coherent and smoothly functioning whole.

In the flush period of mid-development, the market mechanism easily outperforms the command apparatus as a means of carrying out this complex coordinating task. Every profit-seeking entrepre-

---

* Estimating Russian growth is extremely difficult, owing to inadequate or inaccurate statistics, official secrecy, etc. See, e.g., A. Nove, *Communist Economic Strategy*, National Planning Association, 1959, pp. 38–42.

[1] *Fortune*, October 1961, pp. 108–9; also *The New York Times*, April 16, 1961.

neur, every industrial salesman, every cost-conscious purchasing agent becomes in effect part of a gigantic and continuously alert planning system within the market economy. Command systems do not easily duplicate their efforts. Bottlenecks, unusable output, shortages, waste, and a cumbersome hierarchy of bureaucratic forms and officials typically interfere with the maximum efficiency of the planned economy in mid-growth.*

What we see here is not just a passing problem which can be easily ironed out. Rather, it expresses the fact that centralized economies of command do not naturally enjoy a congruence between private action and public necessity. Commenting on the extraordinarily low productivity of collective farms in Russia, one observer notes that plowing on these farms is done on a contract basis by Machine Tractor Stations. But since the Tractor Stations' performance is judged by the *area* they cover, they have little incentive to do careful work. (And since the collective farmers cannot turn to a competitive tractor business, they have no power to penalize an inefficient job.)[2] A Russian critic candidly cites a similar instance from industry: he notes that a wise factory manager aims at achieving 105 per cent of his plan, not 125 per cent, for in the latter case he will set an impossible target for himself in the following year.[3]

By way of contrast, the traditional strength of the Western market system has rested on its "natural" integration of private behavior and public requirement. As we have seen, this coordination was based on the predictable outcome of gain-seeking individuals in a competitive environment. In such an environment, an "invisible hand" led men to the very tasks that society desired, and the internal allocation problems of the economy seemingly solved themselves.

More than that, the classical market mechanism solved the economic problem with a minimum of social and political controls. Impelled by the drives inherent in a market society, the individual marketer fulfilled his public economic function without constant attention from the authorities. In contradistinction to his counterpart

---

* It is only fair to note, however, that the market system also generates some allocatory waste peculiar to its own mode of operation. Thus we have the typical clustering of gas stations at a single corner, the senseless proliferation of car models, the use of skilled talents to persuade buyers that similar goods are, in fact, "different," and above all, the terrible waste of unemployment.

2 Campbell, *op. cit.*, pp. 72–73.

3 A. Nove, "The Politics of Economic Rationality," *Social Research*, Summer 1958, p. 134.

in a centralized command society, who is often aware of being prodded, cajoled or even threatened to act in ways which do not appeal to his self-interest, the classical marketer obeyed the peremptory demands of the market as a voluntary exercise of his own economic "freedom."

Thus it is not surprising that we find many of the motivating principles of the market being introduced into command societies. For as these societies settle into more or less established routines, they too can utilize the pressure of want and the pull of pecuniary desire to facilitate the fulfillment of their basic plans. In Russia, for instance, direct labor allocation has been largely abandoned in favor of a free movement of workers guided by wage differentials. In the "entrepreneurial" posts, lucrative bonuses aim at encouraging managerial efficiency: a factory manager who overfulfills his quota by 10 per cent can earn up to 77 per cent of his base pay and can pass along substantial bonuses to members of his junior staff. Meanwhile, the planning system itself has been greatly decentralized, and we even find among some Soviet economists the cautious advocacy of a pricing system which would much more closely resemble that of the market than is now in use.[4]

Economic freedom, as we know it in the West, is not yet a reality, or even an official objective, in Soviet Russia. The right to strike, for example, is not recognized, and nothing like the fluid consumer-responsive market system is allowed to exert its influence on the general direction of economic development. But the introduction of a widespread incentive system argues strongly that some of the principles of the market society are apt to find their place in planned societies at the appropriate stage of economic development.*

[4] Campbell, *op. cit.*, pp. 110, 120–121, 135–136.

* A number of economists have worked out models for planned economies in which industrial managers would run their industries for "profit," just as in a market society, and would thus be subject to market controls. The profits of their industries would, of course, go to the state. In Yugoslavia, where a remarkable amalgam of central planning and supervised profit-seeking has been worked out, something resembling this theoretical scheme may be in the process of formation. For a discussion of "market socialism," see F. M. Taylor and O. Lange, *On the Economic Theory of Socialism*, ed. B. E. Lippincott (Minneapolis: University of Minnesota Press, 1938) or Joan Robinson, *Exercises in Economic Analysis* (New York: St. Martin's Press, 1961), Part V. For the Yugoslav experience, see Janez Stanovnik, "Planning Through the Market," *Foreign Affairs,* January 1962, pp. 252–263.

High Consumption Economies

Thus our survey of successive stages of development brings us to a consideration of Western economic society—that is, to the advanced economies which have progressed beyond the need for forced industrialization and now enter the stage of high consumption.

From our foregoing discussion, it is clear that the market mechanism finds its most natural application in this fortunate period of economic evolution. This is not to brush aside the grave problems which the market presents—problems we have investigated in previous chapters. Yet, insofar as the advanced Western societies have reached a stage in which the consumer is not only permitted but encouraged to impose his wants on the direction of economic activity, there is little doubt that the market mechanism fulfills the prevailing social purpose more effectively than any other.

Nonetheless, we should note that, even here, the market is not in every regard superior to planning. For one thing, it is an inefficient instrument for provisioning societies—even rich societies—with those goods and services for which no "price tag" exists, such as education or local government services or public health facilities.

A market society "buys" such public goods by allocating a certain amount of taxes for these purposes. Its citizens, however, tend to feel these taxes as an exaction, in contrast with the items they voluntarily buy. Typically, therefore, a market society underallocates resources to education, city government, public health or recreation, since it has no means of "bidding" funds into these areas, in competition with the powerful means of bidding them into autos or clothes or personal insurance. The result, as Professor Galbraith writes, is that "The line which divides our area of wealth from our area of poverty is roughly that which divides privately produced and marketed goods and services from publicly rendered services."[5]

A second and perhaps even deeper-seated failing of the market system is its application of a strictly economic calculus to the satisfaction of human wants and needs. The market is an assiduous servant of the wealthy consumer, but an indifferent servant of the poor one. Thus it presents us with the anomaly of a surplus of luxury housing existing side-by-side with a shortage of inexpensive housing, although the social need for the latter is incontestably greater than

[5] *The Affluent Society* (Boston: Houghton Mifflin Company, 1958), p. 251.

for the former. Or it pours energy and resources into the multiplication of luxuries for which the wealthier classes offer a market, while allowing more basic needs of the poor to go unheeded and unmet.

These shortcomings, together with those we have examined earlier, such as the problems of oligopoly and general economic instability, have a common attribute. They are all indicative of a central weakness of the market system—its inability to formulate public needs above those of the market place.

So long as the public need roughly coincides with the sum of the private interests to which the market automatically attends, this failing of the market system is a minor one. But in an advanced economic society, it tends to become ever more important. As primary wants become satisfied, the public aim turns toward stability and security, objectives not attainable without a degree of public control. As technological organization becomes more complex and massive, again a public need arises to contain the new agglomerations of economic power. So, too, as wealth increases, pressure for education, urban improvement, welfare and the like, comes to the fore, not only as an indication of the public conscience, but as a functioning requirement of a mature society. And finally, the public stimulus and management of continued growth take on increased political urgency as the passive acquiescence of a poor society is replaced by the purposeful aspirations of a well-to-do community.

We have already paid much attention to the rise of planning in the advanced market societies as a corrective force to deal with just such problems. Now we can go so far as to generalize the economic meaning of this trend. *Planning arises in the advanced market societies to offset their inherent goal-setting weaknesses, just as the market mechanism arises in advanced command societies to offset their inherent motivational weaknesses.* In other words, planning and market mechanisms, in those societies which have begun to enter the stage of high consumption, are not mutually incompatible. On the contrary, they powerfully supplement and support one another.

What seems to impend at the moment, then, is a *convergence of economic mechanisms* for the more advanced societies. In the planned economies the market is being introduced to facilitate the smoother achievement of established objectives, while in the market economies, a degree of planning is increasingly relied upon to give order, stability, and social direction to the outcome of private activity.

This does not imply that the two major systems today are about to become indistinguishable. The convergence of economic mechanisms may blur, but it is not likely to obliterate, the basic distinctions between them. Nor does the convergence of mechanisms in itself portend profound changes in the larger social structures of socialism and capitalism. Throughout this book we have sought to draw a careful line between the economic substructure and the political and social superstructure. The locus and use of power, the institutions of government, and most important, the actual experience of daily existence in both capitalism and socialism are conditioned by, but by no means wholly traceable to, their underlying economic systems.

Hence a gradual rapprochement of the economic mechanisms should not lead us to hasty conclusions about the rebirth of "capitalism" in the Soviet Union or the advent of "socialism" in the United States. Capitalism and socialism alike exist not as textbook models but as historic societies, each with its identity, its nationality, its traditions and beliefs. As always before, economic change will have to make its peace with social and political realities, and in this continuing mutual adjustment, the role of economic forces is far from a mechanical one. If anything, the use of economic mechanisms which are functionally apposite to the situation should increase the viability of *both* societies. Socialism and capitalism will then have to adjust their differences in ideology and national purpose shorn of the fond belief that the economic doom of the other is rapidly approaching.

The Changing Nature of the Economic Problem

Can we conclude our final appraisal of the market system in this tone of guarded optimism?

Unfortunately, our analysis is not yet complete. For the trajectory of economic development, which has provided us with the framework for our analysis, is itself still unfinished. The succession of stages of economic development does not promise to come to an end in the high consumption economies of the present. On the contrary, its momentum seems certain to carry it far beyond the present lineaments of society. The curve of scientific discovery continues to rise almost vertically beneath our feet. The tempo of technological improvement, the enormous additions to capital, and the resulting increase in wealth, all point to a future in which the economic environment will be as substantially altered from its present-day condition as that present-day condition is different from economies in a far lower stage of evolution.

In what way will this impending change affect the market system?

The answer brings us back to the opening pages of this book, for it involves the nature of the economic problem itself. We will remember that we first posed that problem as the need to mobilize and allocate human energies and to distribute the social product in a manner that would assure society of its continued existence. It was survival itself which we named as the basic challenge to the economic system—a choice amply justified by the ragged and hungry condition of mankind over most of history, and even today, over most of the globe.

But in the advanced economies of the future this problem will surely recede into the background, as it has already begun to do in the high consumption economies of the present. Although it can never be lost to sight, it will no longer be survival which claims the main attention of society. Nor will it any longer be growth—at least not in the paramount degree to which growth concerns the economies emerging from backwardness or even in the milder degree to which it continues to concern the advanced economies today. Rather, the central problem which is likely to confront the societies of tomorrow is nothing less than the creation of *a new relationship between the economic aspect of existence and human life in its totality.*

The Problem of Abundance

We find one aspect of this problem already close at hand. As the advanced societies do their job of linking science with life, of taking the edge off scarcity, there opens before them a great alternative. On the one hand, the opportunity arises to divert society's energies away from their eternal economic concerns to new areas of human fulfill-

ment—education, the arts and sciences, recreation and personal cultivation, the beautification of the environment. On the other hand,
the opportunity also presents itself to occupy the new area of human
freedom with the production and consumption of an ever larger volume of ever less-valued goods.

As we have already remarked, a market society does not cope easily
with this choice of social opportunities. Its established mechanism
continues to direct human energies into the accustomed economic
channels, despite the declining social importance of the activities
which fill these channels. Thus the danger exists that the market
system, in an environment of genuine abundance, may become an
instrument which liberates man from real want only to enslave him
to purposes for which it is increasingly difficult to find social and
moral justification.

This is perhaps an aesthetic rather than an economic problem.
But the issue goes deeper than one's social preferences. For at the
same time that the growing level of mass affluence points to a de-
valuation of much economic activity, so also does it point to a
weakening of the very motivational base on which a market economy
rests. As well-being grows, the traditional pressures fade; want and
need become less dependable guides for human behavior. We have
seen one consequence of this in the rise of advertising as a private
means of forming and directing consumers' "demands." Now we can
foresee that in a society of very great abundance, not only these culti-
vated desires but even the basic incentive to maximize income or
minimize expenditure may well lose the ability to direct human behavior. In that event, the market system would cease to wield its
necessary control over individual action, and society would have to
look to some other means of social control to insure the necessary
accomplishment of its basic tasks.

The Problem of Work

If the growth of affluence itself poses a subtle threat to the functional efficacy of the market mechanism, another danger is signalled
by the growth of technology.

For the cumulative impact of technology is radically altering the
basic relation on which all economics rests: the relation of man and
nature. This alteration is not only evident as an increasing material

sufficiency. It is noticeable as well in the changing definition of "work" itself.

Over most of the past, work has been an onerous imperative of existence. The need to work has been the universal prerequisite of social continuity—a prerequisite which crowded out much else of life. Even in the most advanced nations today, work continues to be an inescapable requirement for the majority, although its demands have been incomparably lightened over the years.

This importunate and exhausting predominance of work is certain to be markedly diminished in the not too distant future. It has been many times pointed out, for instance, that today we labor but 60 per cent of the time our ancestors did three generations ago, and that leisure has come to be a preoccupation which rivals that of work. If the present trend of technological advance is maintained (and there is every reason to believe that it will accelerate), this compression of labor time is certain to continue and very likely to increase. If Russia succeeds, as she has announced, in reducing her basic work week to 35 hours by 1965, we can be sure that the United States will reduce her own. By 1980—or by the year 2000—a work week of 30 hours, even of 20 hours, is by no means unimaginable.

In many ways, the implications of this trend present the market system with unprecedented problems. For in addition to its various cultural and institutional preconditions, the market system has always taken for granted one self-evident social phenomenon: a mass participation in the economic process. It was the tacit assumption—indeed, the obvious fact—that virtually every family was in some way directly engaged in the economic process which assured a general *dispersion of income* among all members of the community.

But in the highly automated world toward which technology appears to be moving us, this universal participation in the economic process can no longer be taken as an unchallengeable assumption. On the contrary, it is perfectly possible to assume that economic engagement will become the function of a minority rather than of the overwhelming majority, that work will become more of a privilege than a necessity. This view does not forecast a condition of social poverty: on the contrary, it is posited on the most enormous social abundance. But whether the market will then provide the mecha nism by which that abundance is distributed—or by which access to productive tasks is regulated—is, to say the least, a debatable question.

Beyond the Making of Economic Society

These problems lie some distance in the future—precisely how far depends on the rate at which the advanced societies of today realize the revolutionary potential which abundance and technology hold out for them. Yet the implications of a changing economic environment are clear enough. In the foreseeable economies of genuine abundance and technological mastery, the market mechanism appears to have a declining functional relevance. Both economic and social problems can be divined for which some form of planning, rather than the market, must provide the answer.

To most of us, this may appear as a disturbing conclusion. Yet its full meaning must be viewed in the light of the long perspective in which we have permitted ourselves to look ahead—a perspective which envisages societies at a stage of development wholly different from our own. Then we can see that the declining relevance of the market mechanism is itself symptomatic of a changing relevance of *all* economic control mechanisms. In an environment in which the work of society has been reduced to a small fraction of its present time and in which the social product is very large, the economic problem turns from accumulation—public or private—toward administration. It is man who must then govern things rather than things which must govern man.

It is with such a vista—at once hopeful and problematic—that we leave our historic survey of the market system. Looking not only backward to the past, but forward to the very limit of our historic visibility, we can see the market system itself as groping toward an ultimate transcendence of economics as a fetter on mankind. Over most of history scarcity has imposed its harsh demands on man, forcing him to acquiesce in repressive and cruel social arrangements in order that life might go on. Only recently, first under the market system, more latterly under the system of command, has man begun to work toward a world in which he would be free from want—free, at least, in the sense that the material requirements for a good life no longer lay beyond easy grasp.

Now there can be seen the prospect of a final stage of economic development—a stage in which the making of economic society, as a painful struggle, comes to an end. For the first time, an orderly and generous solution to the economic problem begins to approach within human capability. The great question will then be whether men will use their triumph over nature to achieve a much more difficult victory over themselves.

Index

Abundance, problem of, 232–33
Adelman, M. A., 128
Advertising, 135, 138–39
Agriculture:
  in antiquity, 21–22
  in underdeveloped lands, 201, 208–10
  in U.S., 127, 145–47, 160–63
Alberti, Leon Battista, 73
Allen, Frederick Lewis, 141–42, 143
Allocation:
  as economic problem, 7–8, 11
  growth and, 98–99
  market system and, 65, 229–30
  planned economy and, 196–98, 226–28
Antitrust, 123–24, 129, 163, 183n.
Aristotle, 26, 28, 29, 40
Arkwright, Richard, 78, 79, 80, 81, 85
Arnold, Thurman, 129
Automation, 176–79, 233–35
Automobile industry, growth of, 103–4
Aquinas, Thomas, 39

Beard, Miriam, 19, 53n.
Berle, Adolf, 124, 125, 126–27, 139
Big business (see also Oligopoly):
  change in management of, 129–32
  concentration in, 126–27
  growth of, 118, 121–25
  problems of, 135–39
Bourgeoisie, rise of, 48, 51, 57–58, 71
Boswell, James, 81
Boulton, Matthew, 77–78, 79, 80, 81
Budget, government, 159, 163–68, 171–72, 174–76 (see also Government)
Business cycles, 151–58, 176
Businessmen (see Entrepreneur)

Calvinism, 53–56
Capital:
  factor of production, 63–64
  goods, 89, 151–58
  lack in underdeveloped areas, 202–3
  and productivity, 89–90
  sector, 92–93
Capital formation, 92–96
  and business cycles, 151–58, 166, 176
  and government spending, 165–67
  and saving, 94–96, 155–58
  in underdeveloped areas, 208–14

Capitalism:
  early industrial, 81–88
  European, 180–92
  future of, 178–89, 230–31
  and growth, 99–100
  guided, 162–63, 166–68, 170–78
  rise of, 69–71
Capitalist (see Entrepreneurs)
Carlyle, Thomas, 79
Cartels, 183–84, 190
Catholic Church, 38–40, 53–56
Chrematistike, 29
Cicero, 26
Cities:
  in antiquity, 23–24
  in medieval era, 35, 47–49, 51
Clayton Antitrust Act, 124
Cochran, Thomas, 119, 121n., 183n.
Colbert, Jean Baptiste, 71
Collectivism:
  in underdeveloped areas, 216–20, 224–26
  in U.S.S.R., 194–95
Command:
  in antiquity, 24–25
  and growth, 98
  and industrialization, 195
  and solution of economic problem, 12–14, 230–36
  and underdeveloped areas, 216–19, 224–26
Common Market, 190–92
Communism (see also U.S.S.R.):
  primitive, 28
  and socialism, 188
  and underdeveloped areas, 219–20
Communist Manifesto, 100
Competition:
  in agriculture, 146–47, 160–63
  cutthroat, 119–20, 138
  in feudal era, 37–38
  limitation of, 120–22
  in oligopoly, 132–39
  "pure," 65–68
  regulation of, 160–63
  and size, 114, 119–22
Concentration:
  corporate, 125–28
  European, 139n., 183
  growth of, 118–25

More, Sir Thomas, 61–62
Multiplier, 155–58

National power, growth of, 50–52
Nevins, Allan, 103, 112–13, 114n.
New Deal, 158–67

Oeconomia, 29
Ohlin, Goran, 32n., 47n.
Oligopoly, 132–39, 146–47, 162–63
Output (*see also* Productivity):
  farm, 145–47, 161–62
  Gross National Product, 107–12
  Industrial Revolution and, 81–82, 87–88
  mass production and, 112–14

*P*easant:
  in antiquity, 22–23
  enclosures of, 60–63
  in feudalism, 32–33
  industry and, 83
  in underdeveloped areas, 202–4
Piel, Gerard, 177n.
Pirenne, Henri, 34, 39n., 41
Planning:
  "conservative," 189–92, 230–31
  European socialism and, 188
  growth of, in market societies, 229–36
  mechanism of, 196–98, 226
  in underdeveloped areas, 216–18
  in U.S., 170–78
  in U.S.S.R., 193–96, 226–28
Pliny, 22
Population problem, 201, 204–6
Power:
  in antiquity, 27
  corporate, 122–23, 125, 137–39
  countervailing, 136–37
  national, 50–51
Power, Eileen, 33n., 60–61
Prices:
  administered, 133–34, 170
  in competitive market, 65–69
  constant, 110–11
  mass production and, 112–14
  in oligopolistic market, 133–39
  as signals, 65–69
  "target," 133, 137
Production problem, 5–8
  in U.S., 163 ff., 178
Productivity:
  in agriculture, 21, 145–47, 161–62, 227
  and capital, 89–90
  European and American, 183–84
  and foreign trade, 185–86
  and Gross National Product, 111–12
  of labor, 89–90
  in manufacturing, 147–49

in underdeveloped countries, 201–10
Profit motive:
  in antiquity, 26–27
  in big business, 131–32
  in feudalism, 34–40
  in market societies, 43, 64–68, 233
  in planned societies, 226–29
Profits:
  and growth, 98–100, 153
  manufacturing, in 1929, 149
Propensity to consume, 153, 155–58
Protestant ethic, 53–56

*Q*uesnay, Francois, 75n.

*R*eform in early capitalism, 86–87
Religion and economic life, 28, 38–40, 53–56
Robber barons, 115–17, 121, 129–30
Rome, fall of, 30–31
Roosevelt, Franklin, 124, 129, 158, 159, 164, 166

*S*t. Gerald of Aurillac, 39
Saving:
  and Calvinist ethic, 55
  and government spending, 166–67
  in Industrial Revolution, 97
  and investment, 94–95, 155–56
  in underdeveloped countries, 209–10
Scarcity, 4–5, 235–36
Schlesinger, Arthur, Jr., 143n., 159
Self-interest, 64–68, 131–32, 226–29, 233
Serf, 32–33 (*see also* Peasant)
Sherman Antitrust Act, 123–24
Size (*see* Economies of large-scale production; Big business)
Slavery, 13, 22, 24–25, 32
Smith, Adam, 10, 18
Socialism:
  European, 187–89, 192
  future of, 226–31
  "market," 228n.
  and planning, 196–98
  in U.S.S.R., 192–96
Sombart, W., 55n., 56n., 73n.
Soviet Union (*see* U.S.S.R.)
Specialization of labor, 3–4, 90
Speculation, 141–42, 144, 154
Standard Oil Company, 118, 121, 122, 123, 130
Stock market, 141–42, 144, 155n.
Stockownership, 130–31
Surplus, 25–26

*T*ake-off," 214
Taussig, F. W., 115, 184

Acknowledgments

In this brief conclusion it is pleasant to have the opportunity to acknowledge my indebtedness to those who have been of particular assistance in this book. To reverse the usual order of things, I should like first to thank my wife who, as on previous occasions, has gone over the manuscript with a perceptive eye, and whose general support and presence have been indispensable. Goran Ohlin, of Columbia University, was kind enough to peruse the text from the viewpoint of an economic historian and offered an invaluable critique of both history and theory, for which I am much indebted to him. Peter L. Bernstein, of the New School for Social Research and Bernstein-Macauley, Inc., provided a searching and detailed criticism based on his teaching and professional experience; it is in appreciation for not only this and previous help, but for a life-long friendship, that I affectionately dedicate this book to him. Last, the reader who may be familiar with my prior books will not be surprised to see the name of Adolph Lowe, of the Graduate Faculty of the New School for Social Research, who has read the manuscript in several stages with painstaking care and his usual acumen. I am fortunate to have such a friend in a teacher and such a teacher in a friend. Needless to say, none of the above are to be held responsible for the errors of omission and commission which, despite their efforts, may yet remain.

I wish also to acknowledge gratefully permission to quote from works copyrighted by Harper & Brothers, Harcourt, Brace & World, Inc., Alfred A. Knopf, Inc., The Macmillan Company, and Charles Scribner's Sons.

ROBERT L. HEILBRONER